Caomhánach
People
Places & Papers

Caomhánach

People
Places & Papers

ISBN 978-0-9556926-0-4

A directory of notable Clann members,
place names, books and archives.
2nd Edition

Copyright © 2008 James M. Kavanagh

For Elizabeth, Thomas, Katia & Dmitry

Acknowledgements

A number of people have helped to create this book: Alena Sleptsova Kavanagh (Dublin), Judi King (Arkansas), James F. Cavanaugh (Belize), James J. Kavanagh (Michigan), Sinéad Coleman (Dublin), Patrick Cavanagh (Australia). The celtic font used on the front cover was created by Sean Cavanaugh.

Contents

Caomhánach Surname	1
Clann Arms	3
Time Line 1171 - 1735	13
Notable Family Members	35
Place Names - America	97
Place Names - Canada	115
Place Names - Australia	119
Place Names - Elsewhere	121
Awards	131
Books	135
Manuscripts & Papers - America	149
Manuscripts & Papers - Australia	157
Manuscripts & Papers - Canada	159
Manuscripts & Papers - Ireland	163
Manuscripts & Papers - UK	171
Manuscripts & Papers – Elsewhere	173
Articles, Periodicals & Journals	175
Bernard Cavanagh	181
Thomas Henry Kavanagh VC (1820 – 1882)	189
Hobart Cavanaugh (1886 – 1950)	210
James Kavanaugh (1826 - 1885)	213
Lawrence Kavanagh II (1764 – 1830)	220
Hubbard Hinde Kavanaugh (1802 - 1884)	225
Williams Marmaduke Kavanaugh (1866 – 1915)	243
Frank William Cavanaugh (1876 – 1938) The "Iron Major"	247
Clann Gathering Journal 2002	259
Notable People Index	273
Place Index	279

Caomhánach Surname

The names Kavanagh, Cavanaugh, Cavanah and other similar surnames derive from a single 12th century Irish family name – Caomhánach. This Gaelic word means comely or handsome and was first used as a sobriquet by Domhnall "Caomhánach" MacMurchada. A number of theories have been proposed to explain why Domhnall may have used this name but we may never know the true reason. One theory suggests that the name reflected Domhnalls physical appearance as he has been described as a handsome man in some historical texts. Another theory is that Domhnall took the name in honour of St. Caomhán (St. Kevin). Yet another possibility is that the name reflected his royal status.

Whatever the original reason, Caomhánach has since mutated into a bewildering array of modern variations. A number of factors have contributed to this including illiteracy, local accents and pronunciation, laziness in record keeping, transcription errors and in certain cases deliberate alteration. It is important to remember that all modern variations are equally valid and "correct". If there is one "true" way to spell the family name then it is in its original Gaelic form - Caomhánach.

Clann Arms

In strict heraldic terms a coat of arms is granted to an individual for their own exclusive use. The arms may not be transferred to a sibling or inherited by children. As a result many coats of arms may be associated with a particular family or clann down through the centuries. The "Family Coat of Arms" is a modern invention; it is nothing more than an informal badge to indicate an individual's connection, or association with a particular surname or family branch.

In countries that still maintain a heraldic system of registered arms such as Britain, Ireland and Canada anyone may apply for a coat of arms. Nobility is not a requirement but an applicant will need to meet some elementary conditions and must submit a detailed design to the registry office. The submission process can often take many months to complete and delays can occur if the registry finds conflicts with existing arms or inconsistencies in the design. It is important to bear in mind that a successful grant of arms does not convey any particular rank, title or privilege on the recipient.

The royal families of Ireland employed a variety of designs on their great seals as a means of recognition and also to officially authorise or sign legally binding documents. The Irish system had been in use long before the arrival of the Normans in the 12th century, though the Norman system was more highly developed and was also regulated by a central authority. Gaelic families quickly appropriated many of the colours and symbols used by the Normans and incorporated them into their own designs.

One of the oldest surviving Gaelic seals (Fig. 1a) once belonged to Donough Caomhánach. The seal was captured in 1419 when Donough was imprisoned in the Tower of London, where he remained until ransomed in 1428. Donough probably inherited the seal from his father the legendary king of Leinster Art Óg Kavanagh.

Fig. 1a

The layout of arms is a largely a matter of individual choice; the symbols and their placement within a design all have a particular significance for the bearer. Today we can only speculate on what the images in Donough's arms represent. One source[1] has offered the following suggestion: The angel above the shield recognises that the sovereign ultimately yields power only to God while the second angel supporting the shield indicates that the sovereign rules only with the support of God. A lion stands on either side of the shield in cowed submission. The lions may reflect the Kings primary responsibility to protect the church. Many churches across Europe were built with two lions guarding the main

---

[1] James J. Kavanagh, Clann Chaomhánach Genealogist, in conversation. 2002

entrance. Alternatively, the lions might be a reference to King Milesius of Spain, who bore three lions on his own design, and from whom Donough's family claimed descent. Around the outer edge of the seal lies the following Latin inscription: "SIGILLUM • DONATI • MACMUIARCHA • DA • REGIS LAGEIE" – Seal of Donough, The MacMurrough, King of Leinster.

Fig. 1b

The centre of the seal (Fig. 1b) features a shield containing a lion and two crescents. The two crescents are widely believed to represent sickles and indicate the hope for a bountiful harvest. This design has proved a remarkably popular one with members of Clann Chaomhánach; it is repeated in whole, or in part on many subsequent designs. Clann Chaomhánach's arms bear this very same design today.

The following pages show some of the arms granted to individuals from the Caomhánach family.

Cavanagh

Az. a lion pass. Betw. three crescents ar. Crest : Out of a crescent ar. A garb or. Source: The General Armory, Page 178

Cavanagh

Fermanagh, Ireland 15th Century. Argent a lion passant vert charged gules, in chief two humet sable. Source: International Coat Of Arms Register, Ireland.

Cavanagh, Nathaniel

of Co. Wexford + Bath. Ar. Lion pass gules, in base fleur de lys az, between two crescents of the second. Crest: Crescent gules, wheat sheaf or. Source: NLI MSS 8049/3

Cavanagh, Murtaghe

of Garkhill. Granted 12th October 1582. 1st Qtr. gules, a lion rampant argent, armed and langued azure. 2nd Qtr. Vert, a cross molines, with six cross crosslets, three on either side of the furst all Or. 3rd Qtr. Argent, 3 worms (or lizards) embowed (or curled) vert. 4th Qtr. Azure 3 garbs Or for McMurrough. from the Carew MS 635, fol 41. Source: MS 8049.

Kavanagh

Vert a cross crosslet or, within an orle of cross crosslets of the last. Source: The General Armory, P.552

Kavanagh, Baron of Bellian

Az a lion ramp. Arg. Armed and langued gu. Within a bordure of the second. Source: General Armory Two. Alfred Morants additions and corrections to Burkes General Armory

Kavanagh, Donel Spagniagh

Ar. a lion pass. gu. In base two crescents of the last.

Kavanagh, John

(Baron of Elinton; Fun.Ent. of John Kavanagh, d. 8 Oct. 1682). Ar. six annulets, three, two and one, sa. on a chief gu. three mullets of the field. Source: The General Armory, P.552

Kavanagh, John Baptist

of Ballyleigh, Templeudigan & Bohemia. Allowed by Hawkins, Ulster 1774. Ar. a lion pass. Gu. in base 2 crescents of the last. crest: issuant from horns of a crescent gu. a garb ormotto: mea Gloria fides. - Faith is my glory

Kavanagh, Nicholas

of Nantes, France. Allowed by Hawkins, Ulster 1768. Ar. a lion pass. gu. In base two crescents of the last. Crest: issuant from horns of a crescent gu. a garb of the last. Motto: Virtus sola nobilitat - Virtue alone ennobles

Kavanagh, Thomas

of Coolgreany, County Wexford. Registered by Hawkins, Ulster, 1717. Ar. In dexter chief a lion pass. Guard. Gu., in sinister chief a lizard pass. Vert, and in base a dexter hand apaumée couped at the wrist of the second. Crest: A Dexter arm embowed, vested purp. Holding in the ppr. a sword ar. Pommel and hilt. Or.

MacMurrough

(cos. Carlow and Wexford; reg.Ulster's office, brances of the Sept of Kavanagh) Ar. A lion ramp. Holding betw. The paws a battle axe gu. Crest – Out of the horns of a crescent or, a garb issuant gu. Source: Burkes General Armory

von Kavanagh

Seal of von Kavanagh of the Brandenberg Anspach Regt. In the Saxon service. In the state archives at Dresden. No colour information is available. Based on the arms of other Kavanaghs who received a grant of arms in Germany it is likely that the shield was argent/azure. Source: NLI MSS 8049/3

Ansbach-Kavanagh Infantrie Regiment
Flag & Uniform

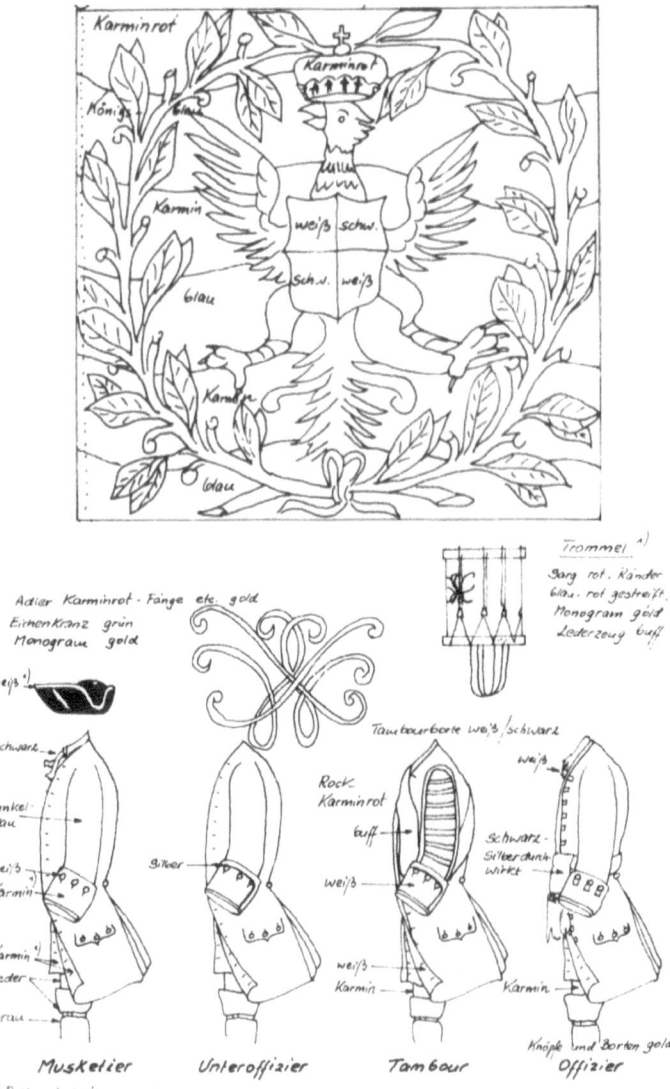

The regiment was commanded by Felix von Kavanagh. Image is courtesy of Dan Schorr. Source: Bemalungsangaben für die zeit des Spanishen Erbfolgkrieges 1701-1714

Arms of Sir Orfeur Cavenagh

Arms appear on Cavenagh Bridge, Singapore. Image courtesy of Peter Dunlop - www.recordsingapore.com.

Arms from the grave of Brian na Stroaké kavanagh

Time Line 1171 - 1735

1171

Domhnall "Caomhánach" MacMurchada is proclaimed King of Leinster following the death of his father Diarmuid macMurchada.

1175

Domhnall "Caomhánach" MacMurchada is treacherously slain by O'Foirtchern and O'Nolan (AFM M1175.7)

Domhnall Óg Caomhánach, son of Domhnall Caomhánach MacMurchada, succeeds as King of Leinster.

1193

Murtough, the son of Murrough Mac Murrough, Lord of Hy-Kinsellagh, dies (AFM M1193.7)

c 1260

Murtough Mac Murrough Cavanagh is proclaimed King of Leinster

1282

Murtough Mac Murrough, King of Leinster, and Art, his brother, are slain by the English at Arklow. Murtough is murdered at the instigation of the Lord Justice Stephen de Fulbourn. (TKV p.435) (AFM M1282.1)

1292

Maurice Cavanagh is proclaimed King of Leinster.

1295

Maurice provides hostages to the English as a condition of good behaviour, and a payment of 600 cows for damage done. He also swears to make war on any of his men who break the truce. (HOMI p.212)

1302

Walter Wogan commands a small force in Wexford to 'repress the rebellion of the MacMurroughs and O'Byrnes' (HOMI p.218)

1327

Domhnall, son of Art, is proclaimed king of Leinster. (OX [3]) He boldly displays his banner near Dublin but is soon captured and imprisoned in Dublin Castle.

1330

In January Domhnall escapes from Dublin Castle with the aid of Adam Nangle (HOMI p.246) Nangle is later captured, hung and drawn for his part in the break out.

1339

Domhnall, king of Leinster dies. His son Domhnall is proclaimed king of Leinster.

1347

Domhnall, king of Leinster dies. Art Mór, son of Murtough is proclaimed king of Leinster.

1354

Muircheartach (Murtough) MacMurrogh joins forces with John O'Byrne to fight the English. Murtough is captured and imprisoned in Dublin. John O'Byrne besieges Rokeby in Wicklow castle and requests the release of Murtough. During peace negotiations, Rokeby summons Murtough by sea to Wicklow but instead of releasing him, Rokeby executes Murtough as a warning to the O'Byrnes, MacMurroughs and other Gaelic chiefs. The execution results in widespread outrage and anger throughout Ireland.

1358

Art Mór and Domnhall Reagh are proclaimed rebels at a parliament in Castledermot.

1359

In January a parliament meeting at Kilkenny grants a subsidy for the war on "Art Kavenagh, who, lately preferred by the king as McMurgh, has now become a traitor." (HOMI p.283)

1361

Art Mór MacMurrough, King of Leinster, and Donnell Reagh, heir apparent to the throne of Leinster, were treacherously made prisoners by the son of the King of England. They afterwards died in prison. (AFM M1361.2)

Diarmait Láimhdearg (Red Hand) Caomhánach is proclaimed King of Leinster. (OX [6])

1367

Lionel, Duke of Clarence instigates the creation of the Statutes of Kilkenny which attempts to curtail the increasing absorption of English settlers into the Gaelic way of life. The response of Art MacMurrough Kavanagh is to march his army to Kilkenny, but the Duke of Clarence retreats. Their armies eventually meet near Dublin where both sides suffer heavy losses before the Irish eventually retreat.

1369

Diarmait Láimhdearg is captured and executed by Sir William de Windsor. (AFM M1369.7) (OX) (TKV p.436) (HOMI p.297)

Donnchadh Caomhánach is proclaimed King of Leinster (OX [7])

1373

Art Óg MacMurrough Kavanagh, son of Art Mór, is at war and takes the constable of Carlow castle prisoner. As a result a permanent guard is ordered for Carlow. (HOMI p.302)

1375

Donough Kavanagh, King of Leinster, was treacherously slain by the English, among whom he had often before spread desolation. (AFM M1375.1)

Art Óg MacMurrough Kavanagh, son of Art Mór, is King of Leinster (OX [8])

1377

Art MacMurrough Kavanagh, 'claiming to be captain of the Irish of Leinster', had made war on Leinster counties and could only be pacified by payment of the fee of 80 marks which he alleged to be owed to him by the king." (HOMI p.310)

Art son of "Dermot McMorgh of Kenseley" appears before the Justiciar of Ireland and promises that he and his countrymen will be faithful to the English King. He further promises to go to war with the King against any insurgents of Leinster and to make faithful stay with the king for a year from 2 February, receiving a fee of 40 marks (HOMI p.310)

1378

Although nominally at peace Art Óg is threatening to burn Carlow. He soon joins with O'Carroll, O'Brien and others in open war. (HOMI p.311)

1385

Lieutenant Courtenay, is preoccupied fighting Art MacMurrough, O'Nolan, O'Byrne and O'Toole. (HOMI p.318)

1386

Numbers of the English of Ossory felled by MacMurrough, King of Leinster. (AFM M1386.8)

On November 1st, Art MacMurrough signs a truce.

c 1390

Art MacMurrough marries Elizabeth Calf. The Statues of Kilkenny outlaw marriage between colonists and natives so Elizabeth's inheritance of land in Kildare passes to the English crown. Art swears to make continuous war until his wife's rightful inheritance is restored to her.

1392

Art MacMurrough burns the town of Carlow. Castledermot pays him 84 marks to turn his attention elsewhere. (HOMI p.324)

1394

On October 2nd, Richard II of England arrives in Ireland to subdue Art Mac Murrough and other rebel chiefs. He brings with him an army numbering almost 10,000 men. As a demonstration of his own power Art attacks the fortified city of New Ross. He ransacks the city and "carried away from it gold, silver, and hostages" (AFM M1394.8)

Mac Murrough, i.e. Art, the son of Art, waged war with the King of England and his people, and numbers of them were slain by him. He went at last to the King's house, at the solicitation of the English and Irish of Leinster; but he was detained a prisoner, on account of the complaint of the Lord Justice, i.e. the Earl of Ormond. He was afterwards liberated; but O'Brien, O'More and John O'Nolan, were kept in custody after him. (AFM M1394.11)

1395

The King of England departed from Ireland in May, after a great number of the English and Irish chiefs of Ireland had gone into his house; and Mortimer was left by the King in Ireland as his representative. Although Mac Murrough had gone into the King's house, he did not afterwards keep faith with him. (AFM M1395.13)

The English of Leinster attempted to make MacMurrough (Art) prisoner, by treachery; but this was of no avail to them, for he escaped from them by the strength of his arm, and by his valour, so that they were not able to do him any injury. (AFM M1395.20)

1396

On February 16th, Art MacMurrough submits and pays homage to Richard II at Ballygorey in Co. Carlow. Richard is not present so his place is taken by Sir Thomas Mowbray. Apart from Art, two other Kavanaghs are present at the ceremony – E. MacGarret Kavanagh of Hy Kinsella, who also pays homage, and Thomas 'Caragh' Kavanagh. (CAV)

1399

Richard II returns to Ireland in May, swearing "he would take no rest until he had avenged himself upon MacMore" (AMK p.62)

1400

On the instruction of King Henry IV, the new lieutenant, John de Stanley confirms the letters patent granted to Art MacMurrough by Richard II. (HOMI p.340)

1402

Thomás Carrach, brother of Art Óg, is drowned at Kineagh (TKV p.435)

1405

MacMurrough waged war with the English; during which the Contae Reagh, together with Carlow and Disert-Diarmada, were plundered and burned. (AFM M1405.5)

1408

MacMurrough waged war with the English, in which he was victorious. (AFM M1408.14)

1413

A victory was gained by Mac Murrough (Art, the son of Art Kavanagh), Lord of Leinster, over the English of Contae

Reagh; and great numbers of them were slain, and others taken prisoners. (AFM M1413.10)

1414

Art Kavanagh, son of Diarmaid Láimhdearg, heir to the kingdom of Leinster, dies. (AFM M1414.13)

1416

A victory was gained by Mac Murrough over the English of Contae Reagh the county of Wexford, of whom he killed or took prisoners three hundred and forty; and on the following day a peace was made with him, and hostages were given him. (AFM M1416.26)

1417

Diarmaid Láimhdhearg, son of Art Óg MacMurrough Kavanagh dies (TKV p.436) (AFM M1417.3) (OX)

Art Óg MacMurrough Kavanagh, King of Leinster dies at Ros-Mic-Briuin from poisoning. His kingdom is divided into two – everything east of the Blackstairs Mountains goes to Donough Mór Kavanagh (Lord of Garryhill), everything west of the Blackstairs goes to Gerald Cavanagh (Lord of Ferns)

Donough Mór Kavanagh (Lord of Garryhill) is proclaimed King of Leinster. His descendants will form the Garyhill, Ballyloughan, Ballyloo and Park septs.

1419

Donough Mór Kavanagh, King of Leinster is captured by John Talbot, the Lord Furnival.

Gerald Cavanagh (Lord of Ferns) becomes the de facto chief of the MacMurroughs Kavanaghs in his brothers' absence. The sons of Gerald will eventually form the Enniscorthy, St. Mullins and Leverock septs of the Clann.

1423

Gerald Cavanagh burns and plunders Wexford and the surrounding county (HOMI p.362) He later promises to serve the King faithfully (HOMI 363)

1427

After eight years in England, Donough Mór Kavanagh is released from prison and returns to Ireland. (HOMI p.365) According to the AFM the Irish had managed to pay the ransom required for his release. Alternatively the English Crown may have planted Donough among his countrymen in the hope that he would be more favourable to their cause than his brother Gerald. Whatever the reason for his release, Gerald did not return control of Leinster to his brother. When the newly appointed Lieutenant of Ireland, John de Grey arrived shortly after Donough, he found that Gerald was in control of a large number of kernes (a lightly armed foot soldier) and others with whom he could destroy the countryside. Before Grey had time to establish himself, Leinster rose with three thousand men under the MacMurrough banner alone. They laid waste to the town of Connell in County Kildare and while Grey was occupied elsewhere the MacMurrough army cut a trail of destruction from one end of Wexford to the other. The Irish only relented after being paid 213 marks to do so. They then took Castledermot before Grey finally managed to negotiate a peace.

1431

Gerald Cavanagh (Lord of Ferns) dies. (AFM M1431.7) (TKV p.436)

Donough Mór is no longer a King in name only; he is once more "The MacMurrough" and in control of Leinster:

Mac Murrough, Lord of Leinster, i.e. Donough [Mór], the son of Art Kavanagh, made an incursion into the county of Dublin, and the English rose up to oppose him. In the early part of the day Mac Murrough routed the English, killed numbers of them, and deprived them of much booty; but the English re-assembled on the same day, and having overtaken Mac Murrough's people in the evening, when they were possessed of great spoils, defeated them, and killed many of their soldiers, who were under the conduct of Mac-an-Mhidhigh, the son of Teige, one of the O'Briens, and the two sons of O'Conor Kerry. O'Toole was taken prisoner. (AFM M1431.24)

1432

MacMurrough, Lord of Leinster, greatly ravaged the territory of the English; and the English made an attack upon Mac Murrough, but they were routed, and Walter Tobin was taken prisoner in the conflict; and many others were wounded, killed, or taken prisoners. (AFM M1432.21)

1442

Donough Mór's son Murtough is killed by the English in County Wexford. In revenge Donough Mór extracts a blood price of 800 marks. (AFM M1442.16) (TKV p.189)

1449

Donough Mór MacMurrough submits to Richard duke of York. Domhnall Reagh may have been Donough's representative at the ceremony. (HOMI p.380)

1455

Donough Mór abdicates, possibly due to blindess. (OX [9]) (TKV p.436)

Domnhall Reagh Kavanagh, son of Gerald Kavanagh (Lord of ferns) is proclaimed King of Leinster. (OX [10])

1460

Domhnall Reagh Kavanagh founds a Franciscan Friary at Enniscorthy. (MSS 8052/1)

1465

Gormlaith Kavanagh, the daughter of Donough Mór, and wife of Henry O'Neill of Tyrone, dies. (AFM M1465.2) (TKV p.190)

1475

Domnhall Reagh Kavanagh, King of Leinster is injured in an accident and suffers a broken leg. (TKV p.437). On April 3rd, he makes a grant to the convent of Duiske. (Mss D.1816)

1476

Domnhall Reagh Kavanagh, King of Leinster, dies. (M1476.14) (OX) (TKV p.437)

Murrough Ballach (the Freckled) Kavanagh, son of Donough Mór, is proclaimed King of Leinster. The sons of Murrough will eventually form the Garyhill and Ballyloughan septs of the Clann. (OX [11])

1478

Donough Mór, former King of Leinster, dies. (TKVV p.36)

1480

The Earl of Kildare seizes Leighlinbridge from Murrough Ballach.

1496

The Earl of Kildare wrests control of Carlow from Murrough Ballach. In October Murrough Ballach and other Gaelic chiefs send envoys to Dublin to convey their submission.

1501

Cahir, son of Murrough Ballach is appointed abbot of Duisk. (TKV p.190)

1511

Murrough Ballach dies. (TKV p.190)

Art Buí (the Yellow) of the Enniscorthy sept, son of Domhnall Reagh, is proclaimed King of Leinster. (OX [12])

1517

Art Buí dies in Enniscorthy on November 25th. (TKV p.437)

His brother, Gerald whose, descendants will form the Ferns sept, is proclaimed King of Leinster. (TKV p.438)

1519

Donough Kavanagh, a prosperous and wealthy man, and one of the chief nobles of Leinster, dies. (AFM M1519.9)

1523

Gerald, King of Leinster dies in January and is buried in Leighlin (TKV p.439) (OX)

Gerald's brother, Maurice, son of Domhnall Reagh, is proclaimed King of Leinster. (OX [14]) (FallOfClan)

1525

Maurice, King of Leinster, surrenders to Piers Butler at Arklow. (TKV)

1526

Cahir MacArt disposes of Cahir, son of Murtough Óg, son of Murrough Ballach by burning him at Dromroe. (TKV p.193)

1531

Maurice, King of Leinster, dies. (TKV p.438)

1532

Cahir McInnycross, son of Morrough Ballach, is proclaimed King of Leinster (OX [15]) (FallOfClan) Cahirs name in Gaelic is Cathaoir Mac na hInghine Crosda, meaning 'son of the ugly girl' According to Kenneth Nicholls he is the last of his Clann to be clearly recognised by the English authorities in Dublin as "The MacMurrough" (TKV p.192)

1536

In May, Cahir McInnycross "Captain of his nation" signs a peace treaty with Lord Deputy Grey. Under the terms of the treaty Cahir promises (a) to be a failtful subject (b) not to assist or keep company with Irish rebels (c) to assist the Lord Deputy where necessary (d) to repair all damages made by him against the king (e) To allow the kings subjects to pass through his lands unmolested (f) to provide John Juvenis O'Bryn and the son of John Baulagh, commonly called "Shane Ballagh's son," as hostages. On each occasion that Cahir breaks the terms of the treaty he must forfeit 200 cows to the Lord Deputy. In return the Lord Deputy will provide Cahir with "such annual stipend as other Deputies have been accustomed to give him and his ancestors" (CCM p.93)

On July 14th an indenture is signed between Cahir and Lord Depurt Grey. It is agreed that (a) MacMurrough shall be keeper and constable of the castle and dominion of Ferns (b) Gerald Kavenagh, commonly called Gerald Sutton will be sub-constable (c) Macmurrough and Gerald must surrender the castle when required by the Lord Deputy (d) Two hostages must be provided by MacMurrough – his son Maurus, currently held in Dubin Castle and Geralds son, Arthur currently in the custody of the Earl of Ossory. The Earl of Ossory and his son James Butler, Lord O'More, and Moriertaghe Mc Arte Boy and his son Charles Kavenaghe are their sureties for the performance of their promises (CCM p.96)

1537

A grand jury of Wexford complains that John Purcell, Bishop of Ferns, has allied himself with Cahir MacArt Kavanagh, whom he has assisted to burn the town of Fethard. (BOMI p.135)

In March William Sayntloo (St. Loe) writes to Cromwell - "These pensioners of Kavenaghes, when I had power, did bear yearly rents to the King's Majesty and now by tribute of other powers destroy the King's obedient subjects." (CCM p.116)

In August the Lord Deputy writes to Henry VIII – "Since our other letters concerning our proceedings against O'Conner, upon the willful proceedings of the Kavenaghes ("Of whom we have made so oft mention to be exiled, and that place to be inhabited by your Grace"), I your Deputy marched towards them with 14 days' victuals, and took two piles of the O'Nolans their adherents, which we prostrated. Thus the Kavenaghes were constrained to put in their pledges." (CCM p.125)

Towards the end of the year arrangements for the ordering of the Cavenaghes, Byrnes and Tooles are summarised – (a) They are granted land which they hold for the King of England by knights service (b) They shall be obedient to no one but the King (c) They must heed any call from the Lord Deputy in times of war (d) The orders of English courts are to be valid in Carlow (e) The Irish are to abandon their Irish style of dress except for "their harness and habiliments of war in time of need" (CCM p.133)

1538

Cahir MacArt Kavanagh, son of Art, escapes from Dublin castle having been captured previously by William St. Loe (BOMI p.212)

Cahir Carrach, son of Murtough, son of Art Buí, dies. (TKV p.731)

1540

In January an indenture is signed between the Lord Deputy and Cahir McIncrosse Cavenagh, otherwise called McMurgho, who was to pay yearly tributes and sums of money with "refections and sustentions" of all the galloglasses, as his ancestors had done and to go with the Deputy to every hosting with 12 horsemen and 30 kerne (CCM p.157)

In May the Lord Chancellor and Master Treasurer of Ireland are in Kildare to contain the Kavanaghs, O'Tooles and O'Connnors. (CCM p.162)

Anthony St. Ledger, the newly appointed Lord Deputy of Ireland engages the Kavanaghs on Monday, July 22nd. Having entered their territory he spends the next ten days destroying it with fire. The Kavanaghs have already been fighting the Earl of Ormonde for some weeks and are forced to surrender from exhaustion. The MacMurrough renounces his name and promises "never more to elect nor choose among them none to bear the same name, ne yet to be their governor" (BOMI p.234)

1543

In September Cahir McInnycross enters into indenture with the Lord Deputy St. Ledger and "in effect surrendered the greater part of his authority" (TKV p.192)

Cahir McInnycross dies. (TKV p.192)

Murtough, son of Art Buí, is proclaimed King of Leinster. (OX [16]) (TKV p.730)

1547

Murtough, son of Art Buí, King of Leinster dies. (TKV p.731) (OX)

Cahir MacArt, son of Art, son of Diarmaid Láimhdhearg, is proclaimed King of Leinster. (OX [17]) (TKV p.442)

Sir William Brabazon leads a campaign against Cahir MacArt and other chiefs Leinster (HCOT p.273)

1549

Cahir MacArt, son of Art receives a pardon. (TKV p.442)

1550

Cahir MacArt, son of Art receives a pardon. (TKV p.442)

In July King Edward VI instructs the Lord Deputy to "endeavour especially to reduce to order that part of the land called Leinster, wherein dwell the Cavernaughes, Tooles and Byrnes." (CCM p.230)

Domhnall "Spáinneach" Caomhánach is born.

1551

King Edward VI appoints Sir James Croft as Lord Deputy of Ireland and instructs him to "reduce Leinster to order, wherein the Kavanaghs, Tooles, and Byrnes do inhabit." (HCOT p.277)

1554

Cahir MacArt travels to Dublin and publicly renounces his title and rights as King of Leinster. In return he is created Baron of Ballyanne on November 4th, 1554. He is entitled to sit in the "House of Peers" and acknowledged as "Captain of his Country" (FCK) The agreement also states that the Clann Tánist - Murrough, son of Maurice, son of Domhnall Reagh is to be created Baron of Coolnaleen on his accession. (TKV p.439)

Cahir MacArt dies. (AFM M1554.1)

Murrough, son of Maurice, son of Domhnall Reagh is declared "The MacMurrough". (OX [18])

In agreement with the terms of 1554 Murrough should also be created Baron of Coolnaleen but no public record has been found. (TKV p.439)

1555

Dermot MacCahir, son of Cahir MacArt is appointed Tánist by the English crown on May 17th. (TKV) This appointment of Dermot is a watershed for the Clann, for it marks the first time that the Tánist was not elected from within its own ranks.

1556

The Kavanaghs rise up and range freely through large parts of Leinster, progressing to the walls of Dublin. They are so powerful that St. Ledger is forced to negotiate the peace on Kavanagh terms. (BOMI p.386)

In May the Kavanaghs are attacking the south county Dublin. The citizens of Dublin give chase, killing many and surround the rest at Powerscourt. On May 5th, the English under Sir George Stanley lay siege but are required to send for reinforcements. Outnumbered and with no hope of escape the Irish surrender and are taken to Dublin. On May 15th sixty prisoners are hanged and their heads spiked on the gates of Dublin Castle. The following day fourteen more are hanged. Others are forced to ride half dressed through Dublin on ponies in order to ridicule the "rebel army" (Check the year for this - History of the Clan O'Toole claims 1551)

1557

Murrough, King of Leinster is hung, drawn and quartered for high treason at Leighlin. (TKV p.439) (AFM M1557.2)

Although Dermot MacCahir, son of Cahir MacArt, is Tánist he yields to his brother Brian MacCahir. (TKV 443) Although chief of his name i.e. "The MacMurrough", Brian MacCahir is not acknowledged as "Captain of his Nation"

Criomhtann [Criffin], son of Murrough, son of Domhnall Reagh also stakes a claim to be "The MacMurrough" (OX [19])

1558

Art Buí, son of Murtough, son of Art Buí dies. (TKV p.731)

1560

Queen Elizabeth appoints Domhnall, son of Dermot, from the line of Murrough Ballach as chancellor of Leighlin. (TKV p.191)

1565

The Kavanaghs, O'Byrnes, and O'Tooles harass the county of Kildare (RBTK p.25)

In July, Art Boye Cavenaghe is invited to the home of the English Captain Hearne and is treacherously slain by the captain after dinner (CCM p. 369)

1567

Queen Elizabeth appoints Domhnall, son of Dermot, from the line of Murrough Ballach as Bishop of Leighlin on May 7th. (TKV p.191)

1570

Domhnall "Spáinneach" Caomhánach is brought to Spain by Thomas Stukeley. (MSS 8052/3). Domhnalls nickname "Spáinneach" is derived from the time he spends in Spain.

1572

In September one hundren bowmen are placed under the control of Wexford "for the repressing of Bryen McCahir Keveneaghe's rebellion" (CCM p.99)

1574

In correspondance with the Lord Deputy the Privy Council orders "At Laughlen (Leighlin) under Sir Peter Carowe and for the order of the Cavenaghes; horsemen, 20; footmen 10." (CCM p.460)

1578

Brian MacCahir dies. (TKV p.444)

1580

In May, a number of Kavanaghs return home to Clonmullen after serving loyally under the Earl of Ormond, whose protection they enjoy. They are attacked by Thomas Mastserson the Seneschal of Wexford and hanged. (CCM p.262)

1581

In April the Lord Deputy considers a conference with the Cavanaghes of Carlow to recruit them into the service of the crown. Also, a "promise of life to any that are now out in rebellion, if by service they shall first deserve their pardon." (CCM p.322)

On July 6th, Walpole writes to Burgley "The Kavanaghs, O'Byrnes, O'Tooles. O'Connors, and O'Moores keep a third of the Pale waste." (HCOT p.312)

In Wexford Patrick Cavanagh, a sailor is one of a number charged with assisting Viscount Baltinglass in his attempt to escape from Ireland. He is found guilty of treason and hung, drawn and quartered.

Criomhthann [Criffin] MacMurrough is also taken prisoner for assisting Baltinglass. For his part Criomhthann is sent to Dublin where, on October 4th, he is found guilty of high treason and subsequently hung, drawn and quartered. [TKA p.441]

1583

Donnogh, son of Cahir Carragh, who claims to be "The MacMurrough" is executed. (CCA) (FallOfClan)

Domhnall "Spáinneach" Caomhánach, son of Donnogh, claims the title "The MacMurrough" and reasserts his family claim to the throne of Leinster. (OX [20])

1581

The Lord Deputy FizWilliam writes to Sir. G. Carew stating that he has killed Derby Cavenagh and that ke keeps his head safe on the walls of Dublin Castle. (CCM p.51)

1595

Domhnall "Spáinneach" Caomhánach joins forces with the O'Byrnes of Wicklow and ravages the countryside from Dublin to Wicklow (RBTK p.36)

1597

In March Caroe McDonnell Cavanagh, uncle to one of Feagh's [McHugh O'Byrne] sons, is taken prisoner. (CCM p.256)

In March a prisoner named Morris McHugh Cavanagh is brought in [to Dublin] by Captain Kellie (CCM p.257)

1600

Domhnall "Spáinneach" Caomhánach makes peace with the Lord Justice in autumn (AFM M1600.39)

1601

March 28th - pardons are granted for the following: Cahir MacEdmund macArt of Borris. (MSS 8052/7)

May 15th – pardons are granted for the following: Donal Spaniah Kavanagh of Clonmullen, Murtagh Mac Gerald Kavanagh of Clonmullen, Cahir Carragh Mac Donogh Kavanagh of Ryland, Criffen Mac Cahir Kavanagh of Annagh, Criffen Mac Gerald Mac Cahir (Kavanagh) of Clonmullen, Donal Mac Criffen Kavanagh of Tomagaddy, Edmund Mor bryan Mac Cahir Kavanagh of Kiltealy, Turlogh ban Kavanagh of Borris, Criffen Mac Art Kavanagh of Ballybane. (MSS 8052/7)

1603

Domhnall "Spáinneach" Caomhánach renounces his titles and claims. (OX)

1631

Domhnall "Spáinneach" dies.

1643

Sir Morgan Kavanagh, son and heir to Domhnall "Spáinneach" dies at the Battle of Polmonty on March 18th.

1650

On July 29th Donal Kavanagh, grandson of Domhnall "Spáinneach" leads an ambush on Cromwell's forces that are under the control of Hewson and Reynolds. The Irish launch their attack in the town of Clonegal but despite their bravery they are decimated. An English soldier later recorded that "By nightfall we could cross the river dry-footed over the bodies of the Irish."

1661

Brian "na Stroaké" Kavanagh is born.

1690

Brian "na Stroaké" Kavanagh takes part on the Battle of the Boyne. He is involved in a duel with an officer of King Williams's army which leaves him with a large facial scar from which he earns his nickname.

1691

Brian "na Stroaké" Kavanagh takes part in the Battle of Aughrim.

1735

Brian "na Stroaké" Kavanagh dies.

In December Colonel Felix von Kavanagh of Clonmullen is killed following a pistol duel and buried at Unterreichenbach, Bavaria.

Sources

AFM	Annals of the Four Masters.
AMK	The life and conquests of Art Mac Murrogh. Magee, T. D.
BOMI	The Beginnings of Modern Ireland. Wilson, Philip. Maunsel and Company Ltd. 1914
CAV	Carloviana. Art MacMurrough and Richard II. O'Toole, Edward. 1971
CCA	Clann Chaomhánach Annual 2002 p.39.
CCM	Calendar of Carew Manuscripts.
HOMI	A History of Medieval Ireland. Otway-Ruthven, A.J. Ernest Benn Ltd, 2nd Edition 1980.
HCOT	History of the Clan O'Toole and other Leinster septs.
OX	A New History of Ireland Vol. II. Oxford University Press (the number in [] indicates succession)
RBTK	Historical Reminiscences of O'Byrnes, O'Tooles, O'Kavanaghs, and other Irish Chieftains. O'Byrne, Clarinda Mary
TKV	The Kavanaghs. Nicholls, Kenneth. The Irish Genealogist Vol.5 No.5 (1977)

Portrait, reputed to be Domhnall "Spáinneach" Caomhánach
(c1550 – 1631)

Notable Family Members

Caomhánach, Domhnall "Spáinneach" (c 1550 – 1631)

Generally recognised as the last king of Leinster. Earned the sobriquet "Spáinneach" from time spent in Spain. Married Eleanor Kavanagh, daughter of Brian McCahir Kavanagh of Borris. Died 12th, March, 1631.

Cavaignac, Eléonore Louis Godefroy (1801 - 1845)

French republican activist. Son of Jean Baptiste Cavaiagnac (q.v.) Took part in the July revolution of 1830 and the uprisings in Paris of 1830, 1832 and 1834. Captured and imprisoned in the last uprising but managed to escape and flee to England the following year. Returning to France in 1841 he joined the staff of the publication La Reforme and began to publicise the republican cause. Died on 5th, May, 1845. Buried in Montmatre, Paris where he is commemorated by a statue by the sculptor Francois Rude.

Cavaignac, Jacques-Marie (1773 – 1855)

Born 11th, February, 1773. Brother to Jean-Baptiste Cavaignac (q.v.) A general in the French army. Commanded the cavalry of the XI. Corps during the French retreat from Moscow. Awarded the title Vicomte Cavaignac. At one point Jacques-Marie was the inspector-general of the cavalry and Commander of the Legion d'Honneur. Died 23rd, January, 1855.

Cavaignac, Jean Baptiste (1762 – 1829)

A Republican diplomat and General in France. Born at Gourdon. Died on the 24th, March, 1829 in Brussels. Father of Louis Eugene and Eléonore Louis Godefroy

Cavaignac, Louis Eugene (1802 - 1857)

Republican politician. Born in Paris on the 5th of October to Jean Baptiste Cavaignac (q.v.). Served with distinction during the French conquest of Algeria and was promoted to the rank of General in 1844. Elected Governor General of Algeria in 1848. During the turmoil of the February revolution Cavaignac was elected to the French National Assembly and returned to Paris were the newly formed Government of the Second Republic appointed him Minister for War. Towards the end of June 1848 thousands of Parisian workers took to the streets in open revolt when their state wages were withdrawn. Fearing the consequences of inaction the National Assembly granted dictatorial powers to Cavaignac on June 24th. He employed the full strength of the army to crush the revolt and was later named President of the Council of Ministers. In 1848 Cavaignac contested the presidential election opposing Louis-Napoléon Bonaparte but was unsuccessful after garnering one and a half million votes against Bonaparte's five and a half million. Following a coup d'etat by Bonaparte in December 1851 Cavaignac, along with other members of the opposition was arrested and imprisoned but was released soon after. Cavaignac was twice elected to the National Assembly but, refusing to swear allegiance to Emperor Napoléon was forced to surrender his seat (1852 and 1857). He retired from active political life and died on October 28th 1857 at Sarthe.

Cavanagh, Aileen (1929 – 1992)

Born 26th, December, 1929 in New York City. Family moved to Boston when Aileen was still young. As a child Aileen took a keen interest in nature and joined the junior explorer club of the New England Museum of Natural History. At the age of twelve she gave her fist public speech and live demonstration on "How to Skin a Snake" Graduated from Boston Girls' Latin School in 1947 and then entered Boston University where she studied physics. Graduated in 1951 with an A. B. degree in physics and a minor in chemistry. First full time employment was with Tracelab where she developed a device to measure radiation. In 1955 she joined Bell Labs, working on the first computerised air defence system known as SAGE, as well as communications systems based on aircraft relayed microwaves. Served as President of the Society of Women's Engineers in 1963, a vital role in a male dominated profession. Left Bell Labs in 1967 to join the New Jersey Department of Community Affairs as Chief of the Bureau of Research and Analysis. There she developed and operated a computer system that formed the basis of a state-wide planning and analysis tool. The system verified centralised many of the state and local government social and financial statistics and also verified local government audits. Aileen became a recognised expert in the use of new technologies in government and lectured widely on its uses. In 1972 she moved to Massachusetts where she served as a consultant and college instructor at a number of colleges and universities. In 1982 she joined the staff of MITRE where she was involved in the AWACS program for Saudi Arabia and in 1988 she moved on to Horizons Technology to work on the acquisition management and source selection for the C-130 and C-141 aircraft. In 1990 Aileen served as president of the IEEE Engineering Management society. Died on 27th, September, 1992 in Atlanta.

Cavanagh, Archdeacon Bartholomew Aloysius (1821 – 1897)

Born in Annaghdown, Co. Galway in 1821. One of thirteen children born to John Cavanagh and his wife Kate. Ordained in 1846 and assigned as curate to Westport, becoming senior curate two years later. Transferred to Knock-Aghamore in 1867. In both parishes he tended to the poor, hungry and helpless as the potato famine ravaged Ireland and many were evicted from their homes. In 1879 following the first accounts of religious visions at Knock, Bartholomew began to record and document the visions and reports of miracles and cures. The following year his records were published in the Weekly News, winning widespread fame for the town of Knock as a place of pilgrimage. Died on 8th, December, 1897 and is buried in Knock parish church.

Cavanagh, Bernard (c1813 - 1845)

Gained notoriety in throughout Ireland and England as "The Fasting Man" Bernard claimed that he could live without food or water for years at a time. During a tour of England in 1841 he was discovered buying food, was arrested and subsequently imprisoned on dubious grounds. Died April, 1845.

Cavanagh, Christian "Kit" AKA 'Mother Ross' (1667 – 1739)

Born in Dublin to a brewer, Kit married a servant by the name of Richard Welsh. Welsh was conscripted into army service in 1692 and in an effort to locate him Kit disguised herself as a man and enlisted. She fought under Marlborough in Holland against the French and later transferred to the cavalry in the Scots Greys. Though she eventually found her husband she elected to remain in service and was wounded at Ramillies. During treatment her disguise was uncovered but, due to her undoubted bravery, she was allowed to remain in the army serving as an officer's cook. When Welsh was killed in battle Kit married Hugh Jones who also died in battle in 1710. Two years later she left the army and moved to England married a man called Davies and became an innkeeper. She died in Chelsea Hospital and was buried with full military honours. See: The Life and Adventures of Mrs Christian Davies, commonly called Mother Ross, Defoe, 1740

Cavanagh, Dan J. (1883 - ?)

Born in 20th, March, 1883 in St. Charles, St. Charles County. Democratic member of the Idaho state House of Representatives from 1933 to 1937.

Cavanagh, Edward / Eduardo (1834 – 1915)

Born 24th, August, 1834 in Long Linn, Mullingar, Co. Westmeath. Son of John Cavanagh and Anne Byrne. At seventeen years of age Edward immigrated to Argentina, arriving aboard the "William Peele" on 9th, January, 1851.

There he founded a famous cattle dynasty. His family have represented Argentina in the sport of Polo at international and Olympic level. Edward died at the aged eighty one on 16th, December, 1915. There is a town Cordoba, Argentina name in his honour.

Cavanagh, Donald J.

Served as chief of Clann Chaomhánach 2000 to 2002.

Cavanagh, Edward F. (? - ?)

Fire Commissioner for the city of New York circa 1954.

Cavanagh, George (1808 – 1869)

Born in India, the son of a major in the army of the East India Company. Moved to Sydney, Australia in 1825 where he married Jemima Smith. Joined the staff of the Sydney Gazette in 1833 and rose to the position of editor. Moved to Melbourne and created The Port Phillip Herald newspaper, publishing the first edition on January 3rd, 1840. The initial run was given away free but later editions sold for sixpence and within one year it is the leading newspaper. Both he and the paper seemed to court controversy and were often involved in litigation. He advocated separation of the colony from New South Wales. George was President of the Melbourne Cricket Club on nine occasions.

Cavanagh, Ernest William (1880 – 1969)

Born Mulligans Flat, Ginninderra, Canberra. Son of Patrick and Mary Cavanagh. His father was born in 1830 and arrived in Australia on the "Panorama" on 13th, September, 1849. Ernest was a prominent member of the social and agricultural circles in the Australian Capital Territory. His family had first settled at Mulligans Flat in the Ginninderra district around 1832. Ernest was chairman of the ACT Bush Fire Council and was awarded a national medal for fifty five years of service to the board. He played an active role in many of the areas societies and institutions such as the ACT Pastoral and Agricultural Association, the National Sheep Dog Trial Association and the ACT

Technical College. In 1968 Ernest was awarded an MBE for service to his community. Ernest Cavanagh Street in Gungahlin Town Centre is named after him. Died on July 6th, 1993, unmarried.

Cavanagh, Major James (1831 - 1901)

Born in Co. Tipperary, Ireland. Emigrated to New York at the age of fourteen and enlisted in the Sixty-Ninth regiment in 1852. Captained company C during the American civil war and fought with distinction on many occasions. Rose to the rank of Major and became known as "The Little Major." During the battle of Fredericksburg on 13th, December, 1862 he was shot in the hip and severely wounded. When the regiment was absorbed into the National Guard he rejoined to become its Lieutenant Colonel and later it's Colonel. In 1893 he was made a Brigadier-General. Retired in 1894 but later served with the New York Custom House as an inspector.

Cavanagh, James Luke (1913 - 1990)

Born on 21st, June, 1913 in Adelaide, Australia. Labor Party Senator for South Australia 1962–81. Minister for Police and Customs (6 June 1975 – 11 November 1975), Minister for Works (19 December 1972 – 9 October 1973), Minister for Aboriginal Affairs (9 October 1973 – 6 June 1975) in the Whitlam government. Died on 19th, August, 1990 and received a state funeral on 23rd of August at Port Adelaide.

Cavanagh, James P. (1922 - 1971)

Born 17th, March, 1922. Screen writer. Wrote the first draft of the screen adaptation for "Psycho" but it was never used. In 1957 he won an Emmy award for "Fog Closes In". Died on 25th, September, 1971.

Cavanagh, Jerome Patrick (1928-1979)

Born in Wayne County, Michigan on 16th, June, 1928. Mayor of Detroit from 1962 to 1970. Elected at the first attempt he was, at the time the youngest ever mayor in the United States. Died 27th, November, 1979 in Louisville.

Cavanagh, John (1796 - 1883)

Born in Tipperary, Ireland. Son of Richard and Mary Cavanagh, the fourth of nine children. Left Ireland for Canada circa 1819 and together with a companion named William Mooney moved to Huntley, Ontario. The settled on LOT 11 CON 12 and divided it equally between themselves. Mooney did not have enough provisions to last though the winter and was forced to leave for Hull, Quebec. This left John as the first permanent settler in Huntley. John married Jane Rivington (1798 – 1880) and together they had six children – Dennis (1822), Catherine (1825), Eliza (1828), John (1832), Michael (1835) and William (1836). John donated some of his land for use by the local church, school and cemetery. Today the Cavanagh family still sit at pew number 1 on the south side of the church. John died 11th, May, 1883, in Huntley Township, Carleton County, Ontario.

Cavanagh, John Albert (? - ?)

Font designer and author of "A Handbook on Lettering" (1931) and "Lettering and Alphabets" (1946)

Cavanagh, John Bryan (1914 - 2003)

Born on 28th, September, 1914 in London, England. Son of Cyril Cavanagh and Anne Murphy. Couturier to the stars of 1950's and 1960's Britain. Started his career in the early 1930's as a junior assistant to Edward Molyneux in London. Remained with Molyneux until 1940, when he joined the army to serve in WWII. Following the end of the war travelled between the US and England looking for work and was eventually invited by Pierre Balmain to join him in Paris, where John remained for four years. In January 1952 John opened his own salon at 26 Curzon St. in London. His first collection made an immediate impact with one review claiming that "A new star shines in the London Couture sky. Seldom has a more beautiful and discreet collection been seen that than of John Cavanagh." In March the same year John was adopted as a member of the Incorporated Society of London Fashion Designers. His creations proved to be extremely popular and Vogue magazine described his clientele as moving "with the times in an establishment world: their kind of life ranges from the country weekend to jet propelled globetrotting" Perhaps his most famous client was Princess Marina, the Duchess of Kent and her family. When the young Duke of Kent was married in 1961 John was commissioned to design the wedding dress. The 1960's heralded a new era in fashion with the emphasis on youth and daring designs. The Couture houses suffered as a result of the new direction and in 1974 John closed his salon. John died on 24th, March, 2003.

Cavanagh, John Joseph (1863 - 1957)

Born in Norwalk, Connecticut. Son of Thomas Cavanagh. Employed in a small hat making business before joining the staff of the Crofut & Knapp Hat Company of South Norwalk. Quickly rose to the position of president and successfully guided the company through a series of mergers and acquisitions. The company changed its name to Cavanagh and Dobbs and in 1931 changed again to the Hat Corporation of America. In 1958 the company overtook the John B. Stetson Co. of Philadelphia to become the largest hat manufacturer in America. John also ran a famous hat shop on Park Avenue in New York for many years. A prominent member of the Norwalk community and in 1893, helped to create Norwalk Hospital, serving as its president for many years. Served as Mayor of South Norwalk from 1902 to 1903 and later of Norwalk from 1908 to 1909. Married Agnes Garvan of Hartford, Connecticut in 1902. A Knight of The Military Order of Malta. The Norwalk museum contains a permanent display of corporate records relating to the hat company, sponsored by the Cavanagh family.

Cavanagh, Joseph A. (1883 - ?)

Born on 27th, April, 1883 in Missaukee County, Michigan. Republican Member of the Michigan State House of Representatives for Midland County. His house at 415W

Main, Midland is on the National Register of Historic Places – Ref. #89001434.

Cavanagh, Maeve (? - ?)

Poet, author and cartoonist. Played a prominent role in urging the Irish nation to rise against the rule of England. Described as the "poetess of the revolution" by James Connolly her poem "Ireland to Germany" was quoted in the British House of Commons as evidence of a conspiracy. Her works include Sheaves of Revolt (1914) A Voice of Insurgency (1916) A Ballad for Rebels (1916)

Cavanagh, Michael (1822 -1900)

Born in Cappoquin, County Waterford. Son of Andrew Cavanagh and Mary Cullinane. A member of the "Young Ireland" movement Michael tried to forcefully overthrow the British Government in 1848 and again in 1849, before escaping to America. There he was a prominent member of the Fenian movement, serving as secretary to John O'Mahony. In 1892 wrote a biography of Thomas Francis Meagher, leader of the Irish Brigade during the American civil war. Michael died on 21st, June, 1900 and is buried in Mount Olivet Cemetery, New York. In June 2001 a monument to Michael was erected in the square of his hometown, Cappoquin. In May 2002 a historical group called the Michael Cavanagh Society was also founded in Cappoquin.

Cavanagh, Michael (1890 - 1917)

Born 18th, Dec, 1890 in Lawrence, MA. Fought under the name "Mike Glover". First professional fight occurred on March 17th, 1908 against Red Shaw. Defeated Matt Wells on 1st, Jun, 1915 in Boston, MA to win the Welterweight Championship of the World. Lost the title on 22nd, Jun, 1915 to Jack Britton. Last fight occurred on 13th, Jun, 1916. Managed by Dave Daugherty (1908-1910 and Al Lippe (1910-1916). Died 11th, Jul, 1917 in Middleboro, MA

Cavanagh, Michael F. (1940 -)

Born in Detroit, Michigan on 21st, October, 1940. Chief Justice of the Michigan Supreme Court from 1991 to 1995.

Cavanagh, Moyra (? - ?)

Born in Doneraile, County Cork, Ireland. Joined the No. 2 Voluntary Aid Detachment in October 1915 and served in several hospitals in France. Though not fully qualified in nursing, four wards were placed under her control and in august 1918 she was promoted to assistant nurse. Awarded the Military Medal for "gallantry and devotion to duty during an enemy raid" on 30th, July, 1918. During a raid Moyra had fought her way through two wrecked wards to find patients and remove them to safety. Also awarded the Bronze Star and three blue Service Chevrons.

Cavanagh, Patrick (? – 1571)

One of the "Wexford Martyrs". In 1581 Viscount Baltinglass was attempting to flee Ireland having failed to encourage a revolt of Irish Catholics. He planned to leave via the port of Wexford and came to rely on the assistance of Mathew Lambert (a baker) and Patrick Kavanagh, Robert Meyler and Edward Cheevers (sailors) among others. They were discovered, arrested and tried for treason. Subsequently found guilty they were then hung, drawn and quartered in July 1581. The group was beatified on 27th, September, 1992 by Pope John Paul II.

Cavanagh, Paul (1888 - 1964)

Born 8th, December, 1888 in Chislehurst, England. Popular actor in Hollywood in the 1930's to 1940's. Played leading roles in many movies such as "Tarzan and His Mate" (1934), Champagne Charlie (1936) Co-starred with Mae West in the 1935 production of "Goin To Town". Appeared alongside Vincent Price in "House of Wax" (1953) and Basil Rathbone in three of the Sherlock Holmes movies of 1945. First appearance was in the 1928 production "Two Little Drummer Boys" and his last film was the low budget horror "Four Skulls of Jonathan Drake" (1959) He made more than one hundred and ten appearances on the silver screen and towards the end of his career also made a number of guest appearances on television shows such as "Perry Mason" and "Adventures of Superman." Died on 15th, March, 1964.

Cavanagh, Peter (1915 - 1981)

Impressionist and entertainer. Peter stared in a BBC radio show called "The Voice of Them All" (1955) mimicking popular stars and politicians of the day. For his radio show he would invite on a guest and then challenge the audience to spot the real celebrity. He also appeared in a number of Royal Command performances.

Cavanagh, Roberto (1914 - ?)

Born 12th, November, 1914 in Argentina. Roberto was perhaps, one of the greatest Polo players ever produced by South America. He represented Argentina at the 1936 Berlin Olympics, winning a gold medal. Part of the America Cup winning team of 1936. Gold Medal winner at the 1949 World Championship. Rated as the World's Greatest Polo player for the year 1954

Cavanagh, Sarah (? - ?)

Member of the first all-female crew to take part in sailings Americas Cup in 1994.

Cavanagh, Terence James (1926 -)

Born July, 1926 in Edmonton. Alberta, Canada. Educated at Grandin and St. Joseph's High School. Elected to city council of Edmonton, Canada in 1971. In 1975 became the first native of Edmonton to serve as City mayor, when he served a two-year term. Later served a one-year term as Mayor in 1988.

Cavanagh, Thomas "Tommy" (1928 -)

Born on 29th, June, 1928 in Liverpool, England. Appeared as a guest player for Preston football club during WWII, before signing as a professional in 1949. Joined 3rd division

Stockport in 1950 and 2nd division Huddersfield in 1952. Helped Huddersfield win promotion to the 1st division in 1953. Transferred to Doncaster in 1956, then Bristol City in 1960, before ending his playing career with Carlisle United in 1961. Moved into football management beginning as a player / manager at Cheltenham Town. Joined Brentford first as a trainer and later, in 1965 served as manager. The following year he joined the staff of Nottingham Forest serving as trainer/coach before moving on to coach at Hull. Joined Manchester United as a trainer in 1972, and in 1979 was appointed assistant manager by Tommy Docherty. Remained with United until 1980. In 1985 he joined the training staff at Burnley. Just three months into the season the manager, Martin Buchan resigned and Cavanagh took over. Resigned on health grounds on 30th, June, 1986

Cavanagh, Thomas J. Jr. (1914 - 1996)

New York City police detective. Solved the infamous 1963 Wylie-Hoffert double murder case. Thomas was the inspiration for the 1973 movie "The Marcus-Nelson Murders" starring Telly Savalas. The movie was then transformed into the television series "Kojak." Retired from the force in 1975 at the rank of detective lieutenant. Died 2nd, August, 1996 aged 82.

Cavanagh, Tony (1949 - 2003)

Played on the wing for Dundalk Football Club after leaving Glentoran in August 1972. Voted Player of the year in 1974. Won league championship in the 1975/76 season and FAI Cup in 1976/77. Played eighteen times on the left wing for the US based Philadelphia Atoms. In 1977 he joined Sligo Rovers where he remained for three seasons before retiring.

Cavanagh, Victor George Jnr. (1909 – 1980)

Born 19th, June, 1909 in Caversham, Dunedin, New Zealand. Son of Victor George Cavanagh Snr. (q.v.) and Alice Foster. Early career was in newspapers. Held a variety of positions such as compositor at the Otago Daily

Times and director of the Evening Star. With a robust attitude to what he regarded as the antiquated and eccentric habits of journalists, Victor soon earned a formidable reputation in the print industry. Made his cricket debut for Otago in 1927 and went on to score over 1,000 runs in 27 first-class matches and was, on one occasion named as 12th man for his country. Appointed coach to the Southern Rugby Football Club in 1934, a position his father earlier held. The following year his team won the Dunedin Championship. In 1936 both Victor and his father were appointed as coaches to the Otago Rugby Football Union. After World War II Victor coached Otago to three unbeaten seasons between 1947 and 1949, the later accomplished in the absence of eleven players who were on tour with the national side. Elected ten years later to the Otago management committee and began to institute rule changes to encourage a more fluid game. Served, in 1966, as president of the Otago union and the following year was appointed a life member. Died on 20th, July, 1980 at his home in Dunedin.

Cavanagh, Victor George Snr. (? - ?)

Significant domestic rugby union coach in New Zealand. Coached both the Southern Rugby Football Club and University A premier sides. Took Southern to the Dunedin premier championship in 1912. Retired before returning to coach University A for 15 years from 1922 to 1936. During his fifteen years in charge the students won the championship 11 times. The V. G. Cavanagh Trophy is played annually between University A. and Southern in memory of Victor and his son Victor Jnr. (q.v.)

Cavanagh, Walter Frederick (1943 -)

Born 10th, June, 1943 in New York City to Walter Frederick and Helen Theresa. In January 2000, Walter entered the Guinness Book of Records for holding the largest number of credit cards issued to an individual (1,397). In April 2005 Walter held 1499 cards.

Cavanagh, William J. (1886 – 1959)

Born on 7th, July, 1886 in Lawrence, Massachusetts. William developed an interest in the sport of boxing early in his childhood. At 14 he took part in his first fight at the Lennox Athletic Club in Boston when one of the scheduled fighters failed to show up. That first fight was against "Kid Hope" and he won it by default when the other boxer walked out. Apparently he had overhead Williams' friends encouraging him and boasting that he would murder his opponent. After his second bout boxing was declared illegal in his home town and he had to wait over a year for the next one in Cambridge. At seventeen William travelled to New York to turn professional and there he spent several years fighting as a welterweight. In 1906 William married and two years later he began to coach boxing, eventually opening a sym on 100th Street and Broadway. To earn extra money for the upkeep of his family he co-starred in a vaudeville act which ended in a fight. He was also an accredited boxing referee with the New York State athletic Commission. After moving up to middleweight William went to Canada and won the national championship. In 1918 he sold his gym and joined West Point Academy as a boxing instructor to the Corps of Cadets and the Army Intercollegiate ring team. He is credited with having developed twenty-three intercollegiate champions and under his guidance the Cadets won four intercollegiate team titles. William remained at West Point until his retirement in 1948. Following his retirement he purchased a golf club in Central valley, New York and travelled the world coaching troops in the art of boxing and as a physical education adviser. In 1928 William wrote an instruction manual "Instructions in Boxing. Mass boxing as it should be taught to classes of boys or men." William died on August 7th 1959.

Cavanah, Charles Cheatham (1871 - 1953)

Born 26th, September, 1871 in Greensboro, North Carolina. Son of Frank and Ruth Cavanah. Practiced law in Boise,

Idaho and was also the Idaho State Supreme Court Crier between 1892 and 1895. Served as a District Court judge for Idaho. Nominated by Calvin Coolidge on 22nd, December, 1926, confirmed by the Senate on 3rd, January, 1927, and received his commission on 3rd, January, 1927. Assumed senior status on 3rd, January, 1942. Died 30th, June, 1953 and is buried in Boise, Idaho. His home is on the National Register of Historic Places (Building Ref. #82000185)

Cavanah, Frances (1189 – 1992)

Born in Indiana. A prolific writer of children's education books related to significant events and figures in American history. She also edited a series of books on world culture. Attended DePauw University. Her works include "Boyhood Adventures of Our Presidents", "Abe Lincoln Got His Chance", "Our Country's Freedom" and "Famous Paintings - A Guide to the Masters".

Cavanaugh, Bartley W. (1904 - 1981)

Born in Sacramento, California, Served as the city manager for eighteen years. After leaving college employed as a real estate salesman and later as a district manager for a cement company. Following election to the local housing authority he was selected by the city council to serve as the sixth city manager. Died in 1981 aged 77. A golf course in Sacramento has been named in his honour.

Cavanaugh, Carey Edward (1955 -)

Born on 7th, January, 1955 in Jacksonville, Florida. Son of Edward James Cavanaugh and Sylvia Lee Koontz. Carey's ancestor Michael left Ireland for Boston in 1849. Received a Bachelors degree from the University of Florida; Masters from the University of Notre Dame. Teaching Soviet and East European politics at a university in Ohio when he joined the State Department in June, 1984. In 1992 established a US Embassy in the newly created Republic of Georgia and served as Charge' d'Affaires. Later worked on conflict resolution in Tajikistan, Abkhazia, South Ossetia and also played a significant role in the negotiations over Cyprus between Greece and Turkey. In 1999 appointed as Special Negotiator and Co-Chairman of OSCE's Minsk Group and was confirmed as an Ambassador in that capacity by President Clinton on 31st, May, 2000. Currently a Senior Inspector in the Office of the Inspector General at the State Department.

Cavanaugh, Christopher (? - ?)

Won gold at the Los Angeles Olympics swimming the 4x100m freestyle relay with Michael Heath, Matt Biondi and Ambrose "Rowdy" Gaines. Also won a 4x100 gold at the World championships in 1982.

Cavanaugh, Christine (? -)

Provided the voice for a talking pig in the 1995 film "Babe" Has also provided voices for a number of popular children's cartoon characters such as Chuckie in Rug Rats and Dexter in Deters Laboratory. She has also made onscreen appearances in a number of television programs such as ER, The X Files and Cheers.

Cavanagh, Daniel J. (? - ?)

Deputy Chief of the New York Fire Department circa 1910

Cavanaugh, Frank William AKA "The Iron Major" (1876 - 1938)

Born 28th, April, 1876 in Worcester, MA. Graduated from Dartmouth, Hanover, NH. Coached the Dartmouth football team from 1911 to 1916 with a 42-9-3 record. Fought in WWI and was severely wounded by shrapnel, which also resulted in temporary blindness. His exploits and bravery earned him the nickname "The Iron Major". Joined Boston College as football coach in 1919, and the following season his team won all eight of their games. Left Boston College for Fordham in 1926. The foundation for all of Frank's teams was a strong defence and his Fordham back line was so effective that they became known as the "Seven Blocks of Granite" By 1937 Frank was almost completely blind, and his coaching was done through his assistants. In 1943 a movie "The Iron Major" was made chronicling his career. Inducted into the National Football Foundation & College Hall of Fame in 1954. Died on 29th, August, 1938.

Cavanaugh, G. J. (? -?)

Ran the war postal department for the Chicago Daily News.

Cavanaugh, Dr. Gary (1940 -)

Born 10th, April, 1940 in Blockton, Iowa. Son of Col. Michael A. Cavanaugh and Jean Yvonne Audas-Menelaus. Educated at various schools in Vienna, Austria, New York, California and Iowa. Attended Drake University and the University of Iowa. Served in the US Air Force as a Flight Surgeon with the rank of Captain from 1969 to 1971. Married Sylvia Elaine Williams in 1967. A Board Certified Psychiatrist, practicing in Stockton, California since 1973. Member of the Clinical Faculty at the University of California, Davis School of Medicine. Chief of Clann Chaomhánach 2004 – 2006.

Cavanaugh, Hobart (1886 – 1950)

Born John Hobart Cavanaugh on 22nd, September, 1866 in Virginia City, Nevada. Son of Jack A. Cavanaugh and Alice May Galloway. A popular actor of stage and screen, who performed alongside many of Hollywood's leading stars such as Al Jolson, Clark Gable, Ronald Reagan and Claudette Colbert. Died on 27th, April, 1950.

Cavanaugh, Inez Maude (1909 - 1980)

Born 29th, January, 1909 in Chicago. Jazz singer and journalist. In 1937 Inez met a Danish aristocrat named Baron Timme Rosenkrantz, whose companion she became until his death in 1969. During their time together they recorded a number of tracks including "'Is This To Be My Souvenir?" (1938) and "An Evening at Timme's Club" with Teddy Wilson in 1968. Inez contributed artist profiles to Metronome magazine and also wrote sleeve notes for a number of albums such as the original edition of Duke

Ellington's "Black Brown & Beige" (1944), "A Night In Tunisia" for Don Byas (1963) and Billie Holiday's "Greatest Hits". Following WWII Inez ran a Parisian bistro / jazz club called "Chez Cavanaugh". According to US Social Security records Inez died in California, November 1980. Additional info courtesy of Donald Clarke - Musicweb Encyclopedia of Popular Music.

Cavanaugh, James (1892 – 1967)

American songwriter. Composed the words for a number of popular songs such as "Gaucho Serenade" and "Mississippi Mud" (with Harry Barris). Co-wrote, with Milt Coleman the lyrics of the Walt Disney tune "The Wedding Party Of Mickey Mouse" (1931) which tells the story of how Mickey and Minnie were wed.

Cavanaugh, James Francis (1910 – 1973)

Born 6th, June, 1910 in Watervliet, New York to Joseph Thomas Cavanaugh and Johanna Clancy. Attended St. Patrick's school and the LaSalle Institute in Troy. Trained as a draftsman with General Electric and later became a drafting manager. Retired from General Electric in 1973. Married Margaret Hayes on 11th, October, 1932. Served as mayor of Watervliet from 1967 until his death in 1973. Chaired the Albany County Charter commission. During his administration much progress was made in the city through urban renewal, housing projects, the opening of a youth centre, the establishment of a senior citizens centre, and the opening of the northern section of the Hudson River Arterial Highway. The Troy-Watervliet Bridge and a firehouse were also constructed during his period in office. The James F. Cavanaugh Memorial Park located below the bridge on the Watervliet side is named in his honour. James died on 15th, November, 1973 in Watervliet and is buried in St. Patrick's Cemetery Watervliet, New York.

Cavanaugh, James Francis (1930 -)

Born on 29th, July, 1930 in California. Son of James Henry Cavanaugh and Frances Lucille Luckenbach. Served with the US Navy from 1947 to 1952. Studied nuclear chemistry at Chicago University and the University of North Carolina and later worked at Los Alamos. Edited the Bowhunting Manual (1962) and helped to re-establish archery as an official sport of the Olympic Games. Studied geology at Boise, Montana, Louisiana and Colorado School of Mines. Employed as Independent oil/gas producer and retired in 1988. Founder and Chairman of the Society of Irish Re-enactors. Director, Vice Chairman and Chairman of Clans of Ireland. Served as chief of Clann Chaomhánach from 1995 to 1996. Appointed Chief Herald of Clann Chaomhánach for life.

Cavanaugh, James H. (1973 -)

Born 1937, Orange, New Jersey. Educated at Fairleigh Dickinson University (B.S., 1959), University of Iowa (M.A. 1962) (Ph.D. 1964) Joined the Presidents Domestic Council staff in 1971 to assist in the development of health policy and programs. Appointed in 1973 as Associate Director for Human Resources, helping to develop and coordinate the President's domestic policy in the areas of health, education, welfare, labor and veterans affairs. Appointed Deputy Assistant to the President for Domestic Affairs in January 1976. Appointed Deputy Assistant to the President in August, 1976.

Cavanaugh, James Michael (1823 – 1879)

Born in Springfield, Hampden County, Massachusetts on 4th, July, 1823. Studied law and was admitted to the bar in 1854. Opened a law practice in Davenport, Iowa. Later that year moved to Chatfield, Fillmore County, Minnesota where he continued to practice law. Elected to the House of Representatives, serving from 11th, May, 1858 to 3rd, March, 1859. Moved to Colorado in 1861 where he returned to law and also tried his luck at mining. In 1866 his travels took him to Montana and he served that state in the House of Representatives for two consecutive terms from March 1867 to March 1871. After failing to secure nomination for a third term James moved to New York

City before returning to Leadville, Colorado in 1879. Died on 30th, October, 1879 and is interred in Green-Wood Cemetery in New York.

Cavanaugh, John B. (? - ?)
of Manchester, Hillsborough County, N.H. Member of New Hampshire state senate 16th District, 1905-06.

Cavanaugh, Rev. John Joseph. (1899 - 1979)
Born in Bennington, Michigan on 23rd, January, 1899. Third son of Michael Cavanaugh and Mary Keegan. After graduating from Notre Dame John sold cars for the Studebaker Corporation before returning to Notre Dame to study and was ordained in 1931. Served as the fifteenth president of Notre Dame University between 1946 and 1952. Served as Prefect of religion (1933-1938) and vice-president (1940- 1946). John was also a close family friend of US president John F. Kennedy.

Cavanaugh, Rev. John William (1870 - 1935)
Born on 21st, May, 1870 in Leetonia, Ohio. Son of Patrick Cavanaugh and Elizabeth O'Connor. Graduated from Notre Dame in 1890. Gained his Doctor of Divinity from Ottawa University. Ordained a priest on 21st, April, 1894. Professor of rhetoric, 1892-1905 at Notre Dame. President of Notre Dame from 1905 to 1919. Appointed by the government as chairman of the State Commission on Liquor Control.

Cavanaugh, Lawrence "Larry" James (c 1939 - 1999)
A movie special effects master Larry learned his trade under the guidance of Joe Lombardi and worked with many of the great directors on many of the greatest films made. His body of work includes Catch-22 (1970), Apocalypse Now (1979), The Godfather Part III (1990), A View To A Kill (1985) and Face/Off (1997). His last film was the John Woo/Tom Cruise action film, Mission: Impossible 2. Died on 29th, November, 1999.

Cavanaugh, Martin J. (1866 -)

Born 23rd, July, 1866 in Manchester, Washtenaw County, Michigan. Democrat candidate for circuit judge 22nd Circuit, 1899; delegate to Michigan state constitutional convention 10th District, 1907-08; candidate for justice of Michigan state supreme court, 1909.

Cavanaugh, Matt (1956 -)

Born 27th, October, 1956, in Youngstown, Ohio. Named MVP of the 1976 Sugar Bowl in which the Pittsburgh Panthers won the National Championship. Selected in the second round of the 1978 draft by the New England Patriots. Stayed five seasons with the Patriots before being traded to San Francisco in 1983, where he backed up Joe Montana. Traded in 1986 to the Philadelphia Eagles, where he played for four seasons. Played for the Giants in 1990 and '91, where he earned his second Super Bowl ring. In 112 career games, he completed 305 of 579 passes for 4,332 yards, 28 TDs and 30 INTs. Joined the Baltimore Ravens as Offensive Coach in 1999. Returned to the Pittsburgh Panthers as offensive coordinator in January 2005.

Cavanaugh, Matthew P. (1892 – 1989)

Born on 17th, March, 1897. Matthew founded the Holy Cross Alumni Fund in 1947 and served as its director for the next twenty years. In its first year the fund raised $42,500 and by the time Matthew stepped down as director over two million dollars had been collected. In recognition of his outstanding contribution to Holy Cross the college established the Matthew P. Cavanaugh Award. It was first presented in 1970, and Matthew was the first recipient. In 1979 he was awarded the Eleanor Collier Award for the Advancement and Support of Education. Married Ethel Kelleher on 17th, January, 1923 and they had one daughter named Ann. Died on 31st, May, 1989.

Cavanaugh, Peter (1820 - 1883)

Born 1820, in Sligo, Ireland. Travelled to America, age of nineteen, arriving in New York. Within a few years Peter had established a prosperous bakery business and later created a construction company, building houses in Williamsburg and New York. Following a financial crash in 1856 Peter tried his hand at farming in Sullivan County but soon gave up, and moved to California in 1858. From there he headed north to try his luck in the gold rush at Fraser River before moving to Nevada in 1859. He settled in Carson City and established a bakery and a construction business by the name of Peter Cavanaugh & Son. In 1870 the State Capitol Commissioners requested tenders for the construction of a new Capitol building. Peter's submission was one of six bids and, being the lowest at $84,000 was accepted on 14th, April. The contract required him to submit a bond for fifty percent of the bid the following day. On the 21st of April ground was broken; the foundation stone was laid on the 9th of June. Peter agreed that the building would be ready for occupancy by December but the work was not finished until May 1st, 1871. At completion the cost of the project had almost doubled from the original estimate and Peter lost several thousand dollars. Recognising his integrity and honesty throughout, the State Legislature compensated him for the losses he incurred. In 1872 Peter suffered a stroke which left him paralysed. He had two sons- Peter and Charles and one daughter Maggie. Died on 22nd, June, 1883.

Cavanaugh, Peter C. (1941 -)

Born on 8th, September, 1941 in Syracuse, New York. Son of Donald Joseph Cavanaugh and Isabelle Marion McClasky. Received a B.S. in Social Sciences from LeMoyne College, Syracuse. A DJ and radio executive, Peter got his first break in 1957 when he joined WNDR in Syracuse. He quickly established himself as an influential evangelist for the new sound of Rock & Roll. He later moved on to WFBL, WJMK, WTLB and finally WTAC in Flint, Michigan. He helped to popularise international bands such as The Beatles, The Who and AC/DC and he also helped artists like Bob Seger to break onto the national stage. In 1964 Peter married Eileen Elizabeth

Brimley. The 'C' in Peters name originally stood for Cavanaugh but became a permanent adornment. His second name is in fact Lawrence. His great grandfather, Peter Kavanagh had originated in Ballyloughter, Co. Wexford but left for America in 1848 to escape the famine.

Cavanaugh, Thomas (1869 - ?)

Born 10th, May, 1869, Ireland. Thomas was awarded the US Navy Medal of Honor during the Spanish - American war. He served as a Fireman First Class, accredited to: New York. G.O. No.: 503, 12 December 1898. Medal Citation: On board the U.S.S. Potomac during the passage of that vessel from Cat Island to Nassau, 14 November 1898. Volunteering to enter the fire room, which was filled with steam, Cavanaugh, after repeated attempts, succeeded in reaching the auxiliary valve and opening it, thereby relieving the vessel from further danger. Note: Date of birth is given as 15th, August, 1866, New York in a publication entitled "Military order, Congress medal of honor legion of the United States" - Medal of Honor Legion. 1905

Cavanaugh, Thomas Horne (? – 1909)

A Republican from Salina, Thomas served as Secretary of State for Kansas from 11th, January, 1875 to 13th, January, 1879. Edited and published "The Weekly Partisan" in Olympia, Washington Territory. Died 31st, August, 1909 in Tacoma, Washington.

Cavanaugh, Thos (? - ?)

Mayor-Alderman of Des Moines in 1862.

Cavanaugh, Walter Page (1922 -)

Born on 26th, January, 1922 in Cherokee, Kansas. Son of Charles Clover Cavanaugh and Mary Ellen Page. Page learned to play the piano at nine years of age and won his school piano competition on four consecutive occasions. During WWII Page joined Al Viola and Lloyd Pratt in what would eventually become the "Three Sergeants". At the end of the war became the group changed their name to the Page Cavanaugh Trio and had a huge hit with "The Three Bears" in 1946. Frank Sinatra asked them to accompany him for his sessions at the Waldorf-Astoria hotel. The group appeared in a number of films most notably with Doris Day on her debut in the 1947 film "Romance on the High Seas". Still in love with Jazz music and performing in front of an audience, Page continues to play around the clubs of California.

Cavanaugh, William H. (1876 - ?)

Born in New York. Stage and screen actor and film director. Acting credits include For His Mother's Sake (1912), Stranger (1913), The Sign Invisible (1918), Big Timber (1922), Floodgates (1924) as William Kavanaugh and Red Love (1925). In 1914 William directed and played Rene LeBlanc in Evangeline, a film based on the poem by Longfellow.

Cavanaugh Crum, Bartley (1900 - 1959)

Lawyer, diplomat and an adviser to President Truman. While practicing law in California Bartley defended Rita Hayworth and was associated with public figures such as Orson Welles and John F. Kennedy. He helped defend the "Hollywood Ten", a group of writers and directors who were blacklisted during the McCarthy drive against communism. As a diplomat he played a part in the creation of the state of Israel.

Cavanna, Elise (1902 - 1963)

Dancer and actress born 30th, January, 1902 in Pennsylvania, USA. Played an unfortunate patient alongside W.C. Fields in The Dentist (1932) Later played Fields' wife overbearing wife in the 1933 production of The Barber Shop. Co-wrote the cookbook "Gourmet Cookery for a Low Fat Diet" with her second husband James Barrett Welton. Died 12th, May, 1963 in Hollywood, California.

Cavanna, Elizabeth Allen "Betty" (1909 - 2001)

Born on 24th, June, 1909 in Camden, New Jersey. Daughter of Victor and Emily. During her childhood Betty suffered with Polio which left her with a limp throughout her life. She majored in journalism at the New Jersey College for Women in New Brunswick from 1925 to 1929 and received the Bachelor of Letters degree. In 1929 she joined the staff of the Bayonne Times in New Jersey as a reporter. The following year she moved to the Westminster Press in Philadelphia, where she remained in various roles for over ten years. In 1941 she married Edward Talman Headley and together hey had one son. Betty and Edward remained married until his death in 1952. In 1941 she decided on a career as a fulltime writer and published her first book in Puppy Stakes in 1943. Over the course of the next fifty years she produced seventy books mostly dealing with the problems faced by adolescent girls as they struggled to make sense of their own identity. Betty also wrote under two pseudonyms; Betsy Allen and Elizabeth Headley. In 1957 she married her second husband George Russell Harrison and together they travelled the globe before his death in 1979. In the 1970's she turned to writing mystery novels claiming that she was no longer in tune with teenagers and their problems. Two of her books were runners up for the Edgar Allan Poe Award: Spice Island Mystery (1970) and the Ghost of Ballyhooly (1972) Betty died 13th, August, 2001 and is buried in Vezelay, France.

Cavanough, Owen (1762 - 1841)

Born in Gosport, England Owen was an able seaman on the ship "Sirius" which sailed to Australia as part of the First Fleet. Traditionally Owen is considered to be the first man from the fleet to set foot on Australian soil at Sydney Cove. He took part in the first expedition to Botany Bay and was stranded on Norfolk Island when the Sirius was shipwrecked in 1790. After his discharge Owen married Margaret Dowling a convict from Ireland. He died as a result of accidental drowning on 27th, November, 1841.

Cavenagh, Prof. Francis Alexander (1884 - 1946)

Born on 8th, March, 1884. son of Frank Cavenagh. Educated at University College, London, graduating in 1904 and gained a distinction in classics at the M.A. examination in 1909. Elected a Fellow in 1910. Professor of Education at Swansea (1921-1933) Head of the Education Department at King's College, London (1933-1934) Professor of Education at Reading University (1934-1937) Appointed Professor of Education, King's College, London in 1937. During the 1914-18 war Cavenagh served in The Artists Rifles and in the R.G.A. Publications include "The Ethical End of Plato's Theory of Ideas" (1909). Married Susie in 1911, daughter of William Evans, of Liverpool. Died 21st, April, 1946.

Cavenagh, General Sir Orfeur (1820 –1891)

Governor of the Straits Settlements, 1859-1867.

Cavenagh, Wentworth (1822-1895)

Mayor of Adelaide in 1874. Minister in the South Australian government. Premier of South Australia for sixteen months from 1876. Commissioner of Crown Lands, under Mr Henry Strangways, from Nov. 1868 to May 1870. Born at Hythe in Kent and arrived in South Australia from Victoria in 1854. Member for Yatala in the Assembly of South Australia from 1863 to 1881. Commissioner of Public Works in the Sir Henry Ayers Government from March 1872 to July 1873. In 1887 he received permission to bear the title "Honourable" after marrying Ellen, daughter of George Mainwaring, who on the death of her brother in 1891, became entitled to the Whitmore hall estate in Staffordshire, England. Wentworth assumed the additional name of Mainwaring. He departed Australia for England in 1892.

Cavenagh, Lt. Col. Wentworth Odiarne (1856 - 1935)

Son of General Sir Orfeur Cavenagh. Head Special Constable for St. Margaret's during WWI. Chairman of St. Margaret's Conservative Association. Founder and first master of the Foreland Lodge of Freemasons. Magistrate for Kent from 1918. Wentworth is responsible for researching and compiling extensive manuscripts of Clann members who served with the Imperial families of Europe - "The Wild Geese". He also published a number of articles on Clan Kavanagh. The results of his research can be found in a number of valuable manuscripts in the National Library of Ireland.

Cavenagh Leveson, Sir Arthur (1868 – 1929)

Admiral in the British navy and Director of the Operations Division from 1914 to 1915. British National Portrait galley contains a painting in which Arthur is a sitter: reference # NPG 1913.

Cavenagh-Mainwaring, Captain Maurice Kildare (1908 – 2003)

Born 13th, April, 1908 in Staffordshire. Son of Major James Gordon Cavenagh-Mainwaring and Evelyn Dutton Green. Educated at Cheltenham College, and entered the Royal Naval College at Dartmouth in 1928. After leaving Dartmouth he entered the submarine service. On February 15th, 1933, Maurice married Iris Mary Denaro and they had one son together - Charles, born in 1944. In 1950 he was awarded the DSO for some daring submarine raids he commanded in HMS Tuna along the coats of France and Norway. Towards the end of WWII Maurice helped to train the next generation of submariners before a posting to the 2nd Submarine Squadron in the Far East where he was second in command. From 1952 to 1954 Maurice commanded the shore establishment HMS St Angelo on Malta. His final tour of duty took him to Paris as naval attaché from 1957 to 1960. He was appointed an ADC to Queen Elizabeth II in 1960 and the same year was made a commander of the French Legion of Honour by President de Gaulle. Died on 9th, January, 2003.

de Boulger Kavanagh, Demetrius Charles (1853 - 1928)

Author of many works of many biographies and books on the subject of Asia. Works include "Central Asian portraits: the celebrities of the khanates and the neighbouring states", "England and Russia in Central Asia", "Belgium" and "China".

Dillon-Kavanagh, Georges A. (1870 - ?)

Born 1870, France. Represented France in Fencing at the 1900 and 1906 Olympic Games. Georges won two gold medals (Foil, individual, Épée, team) and one silver (Épée, individual) at the Athens games in 1906. His three medals earned him a place in the table of the top twenty medal winners at 1906 games. US Foil champion in 1896 and 1899. US Sabre champion in 1899.

Kavanagh, Arthur MacMurrough (1831 – 1889)

Born on 25th, March, 1831 at Borris House, County Carlow. Son of Thomas Kavanagh and Lady Harriet Le Poer Trench. Landowner and justice of the peace. Though born without arms or legs Arthur managed to live a full life and became, among other things, a skilled horseman, fisherman, hunter and traveller. Served as High Sheriff of Kilkenny in 1855 and Carlow in 1857 and also served as a Magistrate for Counties Carlow and Wexford. Represented County Wexford at the Westminster parliament from 1866 to 1868. Represented County Carlow from 1869 to 1880. Married Frances Leathley in 1855. Died December 25th, 1889. Arthur's remarkable life has been chronicled in a number of books.

Kavanagh, Blatchford (? - ?)

Blatchford was a young boy with a remarkable voice who rose to national fame in America toward the end of the 19th century. Trained at the Grace Church choir of Chicago his range extended from a low G to a high C. Blatchford toured the county under the guidance of Henry B. Rooney. His talent was such that Mme. Adelina Patti, at that time the most famous soprano in the world travelled specifically to San Francisco to hear him. In 1983 or 1894 Blatchford was performing in front of a capacity audience at the Central Music Hall in Chicago when his voice broke. Both men and women were moved to tears when they realised that they had witnessed the passing of a singular voice.

Kavanagh, Brian "na Stroaké" (1661 - 1735)

Brian was a soldier with a fearsome reputation. He was reputed to be the tallest man serving in the army of King James. Brian fought with distinction at the battles of the Boyne (1690) and Aughrim (1691). At the Boyne he was involved in a duel with an officer of King Williams's army which left him with a large wound on his cheek. The resulting scar earns him the nickname 'na Stroaké.' Died 6th, February, 1735.

Kavanagh, Colonel Charles Toler McMurrough (1864 - 1950)

Born 25th, March, 1864, third son of Rt. Hon A. McMurrough Kavanagh; C.B. 1909; Entered the army 1884, joining the 3rd Dragoon Guards. Transferred to the 10th Hussars. Captain 1890; Major, 1900; Served South Africa, 1901. Command 10th Hussars, 1904. Commanding 1st Cavalry Brigade, 1909-13; Late 10th Hussars. Awarded D.S.O. 1902; C.V.O. 1909; M.V.O. 1906. Died 11th, October, 1950.

Kavanagh, Corina (1890 - 1984)

Influential businesswoman and socialite in Buenos Aires, Argentina. At 17 years of age Corina married William "Willie" Ham (aged 42) in London, and they spent a number of years living in Paris. When William died Corina married Carlos Maignini and later Augusto Casares. In 1933 Corina commissioned a skyscraper known as "Edificio Kavanagh". The original idea had been her brothers - Diego Garret Kavanagh. When construction was completed, Edificio Kavanagh was the tallest reinforced concrete structure in the world. Corina lived on the top floor of the building until her death in 1984. A street in Buenos Aires is named in Corina's honour.

Kavanagh, Denis (1906 - 1984)

Born 6th, May, 1906 in Carlow, Ireland. Denis' movie career began in the nineteen twenties when he performed flying stunts in films such as the 1927 production "Wings". He later moved into screenwriting and directing and his credits include Starlight Serenade (1944), Flight from Vienna (1956) and Fighting Mad (1957). In 1937 Denis was involved in editing a production of "I, Claudius" which was to star Charles Laughton. The film was abandoned when Laughtons co-star, the actress Merle Oberon was injured in a car crash. During WWII Denis served as an RAF fighter pilot in the North Africa. Denis died on 14th, June, 1984

Kavanagh, Sir Dermot MacMurrough (1890 - 1958)

Born 9th, January, 1890. Son of Walter MacMurrough Kavanagh MP. Crown Equerry to Queen Elizabeth II from 1941 to 1955. Joined the 11th Hussars (Prince Albert's Own) in 1909 and fought in France during WWI. Promoted to Lt. Col in 1932 and commanded the 11th Hussars from 1932-1936. Promoted to Colonel in 1939 and served in France in 1940. Equerry to King George VI from 1937 to 1941. Crown Equerry from 1941 to 1955 and in 1957 was appointed Extra-Equerry to Queen Elizabeth II. Made G.C.V.O in 1953. Married Gaynor Phoebe Claude in 1920. Died 27th, May, 1958.

Kavanagh, Dudley (1838 - 1914)

Born in Ireland in 1838. Won the first the first official American Billiard Championship in 1858. Successfully defended title against Michael Foley in April 1859. Helped create the National American Billiards Association in 1867 and also published the "The Billiard World". Died 12th, March, 1914.

Kavanagh, Edward (1795 - 1844)

Born 27th, April, 1795 in Newcastle, Lincoln County, Maine. Son of James Kavanagh and Sarah Jackson. Edwards father was a prosperous merchant who left Wexford, Ireland for America in 1780. Edward attended Montreal Seminary, Montreal, Canada, and Georgetown College. Graduated from St. Mary's College, Baltimore In 1813 .Elected to the Maine legislature in 1826. Elected as a Jackson Democrat to Congress in March, 1831 and served two terms. Appointed chargé d'affaires to Lisbon, Portugal on 3rd, March, 1835 and remained there until his resignation in June 1841. On returning to America he was elected to the Maine State senate in 1842 and 1843. Following the election of Governor John Fairfield to the United States senate Edward served as acting governor of Maine from 7th, March, 1843 to January 1844. He was the first Roman Catholic to hold such an office anywhere in the United States. Died 22nd, January, 1844 at Newcastle, Maine.

Kavanagh, Fergus (? -)

Born 5th September, 1938 to Gerald Kavanagh and Margaret Kelly. Gerald was born and raised in John Kavanaghs pub (The Gravediggers) in Glasnevin, Dublin. The pub has been run by the family for seven generations. Fergus followed in his fathers footsteps when he took an apprenticeship as a Compositor. Retired in 2003. Married Dorothy Jordan in 1970 and they have three children: Ciarán (1971), Claire (1974) and Felicity (1978) Fergus was elected Tánaiste of Clann Chaomhánach in 2006 and will serve as Chief of the Clann 2008 – 2010.

Kavanagh, Giles (1884 - 1952)

Born 1st, September, 1884 in Bay City, Michigan. Son of John Kavanagh and Katherine Dunn. Employed for many years in the world of newspapers, Giles began at the Bay City Democrat before moving on to the Bay City Times and the Detroit News before finally returning to manage the Democrat where he remained until 1926. For the next four years he served as the executive secretary of the Democratic State Central Committee. In 1929 he rejoined the staff of the Detroit News. Left the newspaper in 1935 when he was appointed a collector of internal revenue. Giles married Mary Adeline Washington on 28th, April, 1908. They had five children together – Pauline, George, Maureen, Thomas Giles and John Phillip. Giles co-wrote the song "My Michigan" with H. O'Reilly Clint. In May 1937 this song was adopted as an official song for the State of Michigan. Giles was also the father of Justice Thomas Giles Kavanagh who served on the Michigan Supreme Court. Died on 9th, December, 1952.

Kavanagh, Graham (1973 -)

Born on 2nd, December, 1973 in Dublin, Ireland. Began a soccer career playing for Home Farm before moving to England to join Middlesbrough. Made his debut for Middlesbrough on 21st, October, 1992 and went on to complete thirty-five appearances over a five year period. Joined Stoke for £250,000 and captained that side in the 2000 Auto-Windscreens Shield Cup competition. After five years at Stoke Graham moved to Wales after signing for Cardiff City. His transfer fee of £1,000,000 was a club record. He captained Cardiff when they defeated the Premier League's Leeds United in the FA Cup on 4th, May, 2002. That same season he was named as Cardiff's Player of The year. Joined Wigan Athletic in March 2005. Has made a number of appearances at international level for the Republic of Ireland including: v Czech Republic (away on 25th, March, 1998), v Sweden (home 28th, April, 1999), v Northern Ireland (home 29th, May, 1999), v Brazil 18th, February, 2004, v Cyprus (home 4th, Sep, 2004). Scored 1 international goal (v. Sweden 28th, April, 1999)

Kavanagh, Henry Edward "Ted" (1892 - 1958)

Born in Auckland, New Zealand where he was educated at the Sacred Heart College, Auckland, and Auckland University. Moved to England in 1916 to study medicine but WWI interrupted his studies and he joined the New

Zealand forces. After the war Ted decided to leave medicine and became a free lance journalist and sketch writer. In 1919 he married Miss Agnes O'Keefe, of Edinburgh and together they had two sons; Kevin and Patrick. Ted quickly realised the opportunities presented by the continuing development of radio as a popular medium. He forged a close personal and working relationship with Tommy Handley and together they formed a formidable comedy partnership in the 1930's. The reached the height of their popularity during the 1940's when Ted created the characters behind the hit radio show ITMA (Its That Man Again) including Colonel Humphrey Chinstrap. At its height ITMA, which starred Tommy Handley, was the most popular show in Britain and sometimes reached an audience of 40% of the population. The last ITMA was broadcast on 6th, January, 1949. Awarded a Knighthood of St Gregory by Pope Pius XII in 1952. Died on 17th, September, 1958 in London.

Kavanagh, Jack (1879- 1964)

Born in Ireland in 1879. Fought for the British during the Boer War. Emigrated to Canada in 1907 where he subsequently became a prominent trade union leader in Vancouver. Joined the Socialist Party of Canada in 1918 but was expelled the following year. Helped to create the Canadian Communist Party in 1921 and served as its first chairperson. Moved to Australia in 1925 where he helped to rejuvenate the Communist Party of Australia, serving as its chairperson between 1925 and 1929.

Kavanagh, James – Baron of Ballyane (? - 1848)

Son of Baron Simon Henry Kavanagh of Ballyane, Baroness Leopoldine Moscon. James served as a Colonel in the Imperial army of Austria and was a chamberlain to the Emperor. He married Baroness Pauline Wernhardt, daughter of General Baron Wernhardt, Governor of Transylvania. Together they had two children - Paula (1847) and Harry (1844). There is confusion over whether Paula is in fact a boy named Paul. James was killed at

Vicenza in 1848, fighting under Radetsky against the Sardinians and Italian revolutionaries.

Kavanagh, James (1756 - 1828)

Born in Wexford, Ireland. Emigrated from Wexford to the United States, travelling first to Boston before settling in Damariscotta Mills, Maine. There he established a general mercantile store with his business partner and lifelong friend Matthew Cottrill. Together they purchased sawmills and founded a shipyard at Damariscotta Mills. Kavanagh and Cottrill proceeded to establish themselves as leading businessmen and citizens and did much to help encourage the growth of the catholic community of Newcastle. Both provided much of the funding to help build Saint Patrick's Church at Damariscotta Mills. In 1803 James built the Kavanagh Mansion which still stands today. On June, 16th, 1794 James married Sarah Jackson, daughter of Andrew Jackson of Boston. One of their children, Edward (1795 - 1844) became the first Catholic Governor of Maine. James died 3rd, June, 1828 at Damariscotta, Newcastle, Maine.

Kavanagh, James (1856 - 1903)

Born 1856, Wicklow, Ireland. Son of Michael. A stonemason by trade, James was the foreman during the construction of the Fastnet lighthouse on the southwest coast of Ireland. Construction began in 1899 and over the course of the next four years he would spend up ten months camped on the craggy outcrop. In June 1903 James set the final stone, number 2,074 in course 89. A remarkable feat of engineering it its day, the Fastnet lighthouse remains as the tallest, widest rock lighthouse in Irish or British waters. James died on 6th, July, 1903 and he is buried in a cemetery at Three Mile Water just outside Wicklow Town.

Kavanagh, Bishop James (1914 – 2000)

Born 3rd, March, 1914. In 1932 James entered the diocesan seminary, Holy Cross College, Clonliffe. Ordained a priest at Maynooth College in 1939. From 1942 to 1945 he served as army chaplain Clancy Barracks, Dublin. Studied at Campion Hall, Oxford from 1945 to 1947 and obtained a Diploma in Economics and Political Science with Distinction. Served as curate for the parish of Crumlin between 1947 and 1949 before moving on to the parish of Westland Row. Joined University College Dublin in 1956 and appointed Professor of Social Science. Appointed Auxiliary Bishop of Dublin on March 12th; 1973. Served as Parish Priest of Larkhill/Whitehall parish between 1976 and 1980. Retired as Auxiliary Bishop in 1991. Throughout his life James was a respected arbiter in many industrial disputes, hunger strikes and hostage situations. Died 8th, August, 2002.

Kavanagh, James (1931 -)

Born 21st, January, 1931 in Dublin, Ireland. Represented Ireland thirty five times in rugby, making his debut against France on 4th, January, 1953. A Flanker, he scored 4 tries during his international test career. Final appearance was against France on 14th, April, 1962.

Kavanagh, James Joseph (1943 -)

Born 19th, March, 1943 in Detroit, Michigan. Retired from US Air Force in 1978 with the rank of Master Sergeant. Employed by Volkswagen in America & Germany as a QA and reliability engineer. BA magna cum Laude in Business, History and Language from the University of Maryland. Associate in Applied Science (AAS) degrees from the Community College of the Air Force in Communications Technology and Technical Interpreting / Translating (German). Elected Tánaiste of Clann Chaomhánach in 2004 and served as Chief of the Clann 2006 – 2008.

Kavanagh, Captain John (1826 - 1862)

Born 1st, January, 1826. Son of Morgan Kavanagh and Margaret Redmond. Member of the Irish Confederation in Dublin. During an attempted revolution in 1848 John rode from Dublin to Ballingarry, Co. Tipperary where he fought alongside William Smith O'Brien. He was severely wounded in the leg and was forced to escape to Dublin via circuitous route. There the British authorities pursued him after issuing a warrant for High Treason. He managed to flee to England, then France and finally to the USA. He was employed by a wholesale business in Boston until the civil war. Enlisted in the Union army joining the 37th regiment, New York Volunteers. Appointed a Captain in the Irish Brigade on 3rd, January, 1862. Killed on 17th, September, 1862 at the battle of Antietam, one of 23,000 bodies to fall in the bloodiest encounter of the war. In his obituary in The New York Times, dated 25th, September, 1862 John was described as "a most energetic and fearless officer. He fell at the head of his company in the heat of battle. He had won for himself the enthusiastic devotion of a numerous circle of friends."

Kavanagh, John Baptist – Baron of Gniditz (? - 1795)

Son of Bryan-na-Stroaké Kavanagh and Mary Murphy. Settled in Bohemia and married Katarine von Kallhammer.

Kavanagh, John Patrick (1913 – 1985)

Born 30th, April, 1913 in Hawera on New Zealand's north island. John was the eldest of ten children born to Laurance Kavanagh and Margaret Harris. His early education took place at nearby St. Josephs School before moving north to a scholarship at the Sacred Heart College in Auckland. In 1932 John moved to Holy Cross College in Mosgiel where he spent the next four years studying to enter the priesthood. On September 6th 19336 he was ordained and soon after he sailed for Rome to take a postgraduate course in doctoral law. John returned home in 1940 and was appointed to serve the parish of St. Peter and Paul and later to St. Josephs in Wellington. Four years later when seven hundred Catholic refugees arrived from Poland, John was entrusted with their care. Liaising national and local government he ensured every aspect of their physical and spiritual welfare was attended to and for his effort John was honoured in both New Zealand and Poland. On November 30th 1949 John was appointed auxiliary bishop of Dunedin and on December 26th 1957 succeeded to become its fourth bishop. During his term of office John made a significant contribution to the private education system of New Zealand lobbying for public funding and taking part in negotiations on the Private School Conditional Integration Act of 1975. In 1979 he accompanied Pope John Paul II to Poland for the pontiffs remarkable trip to his homeland. John died on July 10th 1985 at the Mater Misericordiae Hospital in Dunedin and he is buried in Andersons Bay Cemetery.

Kavanagh, Joseph (? - ?)

One of the leaders of the assault on the Bastille in Paris during the French revolution. Joseph was the subject of a contemporary pamphlet "Les exploits glorieux du célèbre Cavanagh. Cause première de la liberté française."

Kavanagh, Joseph Malachy (1856 - 1918)

Born in Dublin. An artist renowned for his landscapes and religious portraits. Won the Albert scholarship of 1881. Studied at the Académie Royale in Antwerp with two other notable Irish artists, Walter Osborne and Nathaniel Hone. Keeper of the RHA and lost many of his works when the RHA building was destroyed by fire in 1910. The National Gallery of Ireland holds three paintings: "The Old Convent Gate, Dinan" (1883), "Sheep in a Landscape" and "A November Evening" AIB Bank holds another of his works "Cockle Pickers" (c 1890)

Kavanagh, Julia (1824 - 1877)

Born 7th, January, 1824 at Thurles, County Tipperary. Daughter of Morgan Kavanagh and Bridget Fitzpatrick. Popular 19th century novelist and biographer. Received much of her education in France and she returned to that country on a number of occasions throughout her life. Her experiences and observations of life in France found their way into many of her books. Her works include "The Three Paths" (1847), "Madeleine" (1848) and "Women in France during the Eighteenth Century" (1850). Aside from her writing, most of Julia's adult life was spent caring for her mother Bridget. A portrait of Julia, painted by Henri Chanet hangs in the National Gallery of Ireland. Died 28th, October, 1877 at Nice, France.

Kavanagh, Lawrence II (1764 - 1830)

Born in 1764 to Lawrence Kavanagh I. There is confusion of the identity of Lawrence's mother – some sources state Felicité le Jeune, others Margaret Farrell. Lawrence was a prominent businessman in St. Peters, Nova Scotia. In 1822 he became the first Catholic to take his seat in the Nova Scotia assembly. Died on 20th, August, 1830 at St. Peter's, Cape Breton Island. Note: Lawrence also appears under the name Laurance in a number of publications.

Kavanagh, Lawrence III (1790-1862)

Born in St. Peters, Nova Scotia. Son of Lawrence Kavanagh II (1764 – 1830). Peter was the Lighthouse keeper at Louisbourg from 1840 to 1860/1862.

Kavanagh, Lawrence IV (c 1823-1898)

Born in St. Peters, Nova Scotia. Son of Lawrence Kavanagh III (1790-1862) and Catherine Murphy. Inherited his fathers duties as lighthouse keeper at Louisbourg from 1860/1862 to 1898 for which he was paid an annual salary of $460.00. He was also a Justice of the Peace and a Customs Collector.

Kavanagh, Lawrence (c 1805 - 1856)

A stonemason and quarryman by trade Lawrence was convicted of burglary on 24th, August, 1828. Sentenced to transportation and sailed on the "Ferguson", arriving in Sydney, Australia in 1829. There he soon engaged in a life of crime including robbery under arms and bushranging. In 1831 he was sentenced to 14 years on Norfolk Island, an institution reserved for the colonies most hardened and unrepentant criminals. In prison he clashed with authority frequently; on 13 February 1833 he received forty lashes for insolence. In 1834 he failed in an attempted escape. In

1842 he managed to escape but was quickly caught. He was then sentenced to life imprisonment in the high security facility at Port Arthur, Tasmania. There he met and made friends with two other inmates named Martin Cash and George Jones. The three of them managed to escape in December and set up a wooden fort on Mount Dromedary. From there they raided into Derwent, Bagdad, Pittwater and New Norfolk spreading fear across the territory of Tasmania. In August 1843 Cash and Kavanagh were in Hobart disguised as sailors. They were recognised and in the shootout that followed Cash escaped but Kavanagh was wounded and captured. Cash was captured later and in September 1843 both he and Kavanagh were found guilty of a number of offences and sentenced to hanging. One hour before the execution was due to take place the sentence was commuted and they were taken to Norfolk Island. At Norfolk Cash became a reformed character but Lawrence continued down the path of crime. In October 1846 he joined another bushranger named William Westwood in mutiny. Four men were killed in the desperate and unsuccessful bid for freedom. For his part in the attempt Lawrence Kavanagh was hanged on 12th, October, 1856. He is buried in Murderer's Mound, outside the Cemetery on Norfolk Island.

Kavanagh, Liam (1935 -)

Born on 9th, February, 1935. Member of the Irish Labour party who dominated the Wicklow constituency in the 1970's and 1980's. First elected to the 19th Dáil in 1969 he went on to retain his seat at every election until narrowly defeated in 1979. He was elected to the European parliament in 1973, 1977 and 1979. Served as a government minister in three departments; Minister for Labour and Public Service (1981-1982), Minister for the Environment (1983–1986), Minister for Tourism, Fisheries and Forestry (1986-1987). Served on Wicklow County Council from 1974 to 1981 and continues to serve since his re-election in 1987.

Kavanagh, Leneen (? -)

Born in Ottawa, Canada. Emigrated to Australia in 1954. Married Francis Gerard Forde in 1955 and Angus McDonald in 1983. Appointed a Companion of the Order of Australia in 1993. Queenslander of the Year in 1991. Served as the 22nd Governor for the state of Queensland from July 29th, 1992 to July 29th, 1997.

Kavanagh, Lionel B. (1889 – 1991)

Born in Providence, RI. Lionel was a pioneer in the fledgling plastics industry and made many important contributions in the area of injection moulding. He founded the Standard Tool Company in 1911, which became one of the largest companies of its type in the world. St. Anselm's college in Manchester, NH has a Kavanagh Hall and Kavanagh field named in his honour. More information can be found in the book "Mold Of Fortune: Lionel B. Kavanagh & The First Half Century Of Plastics", Kean, Sumner, Standard Tool Co., Leominster, Mass., 1959.

Kavanagh, Judge Marcus A. (1859 – 1937)

Served on the Superior Court of Cook County, Illinois and on the Superior Court in Chicago. Marcus wrote a number of books related to crime such as "The criminal and his allies", "You be the Judge" and "The Man They Couldn't Hang". Marcus married Herminie McGibney in 1905 and she released the second edition of her book "Darby O'Gill & the Good People" under the name Herminie Templeton Kavanagh in 1932.

Kavanagh, Martin "Marty" Joseph (1891 - 1960)

Born on 13th, June, 1891 in Harrison, New Jersey. Martin played baseball and made his debut on 18th, April, 1914 for the Detroit Tigers. A versatile player Martin played playing every position except pitcher and catcher. In 1916 he moved to the Cleveland Indians before joining the St. Louis Cardinals in 1918. After a short stint with the Cardinals he returned to the Detroit Tigers in the same year. Died 28th, July, 1960 in Eloise, Michigan.

Kavanagh, Michael (? - ?)
Getaway driver following the Phoenix Park Murders. On 6th, May, 1882 Lord Frederick Cavendish, British Secretary for Ireland, and Thomas Henry Burke his undersecretary were assassinated in the Phoenix Park, Dublin. "The Invincibles," a splinter group of the Fenian movement, carried out the assassinations.

Kavanagh, Michael (1950 - 1998)
Writer, researcher and local historian. Founder of the Medal Society of Ireland and a member of various medal societies around the world including South Africa and America. Founder member of Patrick Kennedy Appreciation Society. Served as first chief of Clann Chaomhánach 1993 to 1994. Married Rita, with whom he had two daughters; Kate and Sarah. Died 17th, may, 1998

Kavanagh, Morgan Peter (c1800 – 1874)
The time and location of Morgan's birth are unsure but he is generally thought to have been in 1800 in either Tipperary or Dublin. Morgan was a language teacher who penned some unusual and eccentric works on language. Married Bridget Fitzpatrick in 1823. A daughter Julia Kavanagh was born in Thurles in 1824. Morgan moved his family from Ireland to England and then onto France before returning to settle in London in 1844. Resided at 28 Dean St., Soho and in December 1850 rented rooms to Karl Marx. Separated from Bridget and took a common law wife by the name of Marie Rose with whom he had two sons; Alfred and Alexander and a daughter, Mathilda. Hoping to cash in on his daughter, Julia's literary success he published "The Hobbies" in 1857 citing her as editor. Critics ridiculed the book; one reviewer in The Athenaeum stating it was "the most foolish novel we have ever read". Julia was forced to publicly repudiate any connection with the work. Morgan died in February 1884 having suffered a

fractured skull in a street accident. At the resulting coroners inquest a Luisa Kavanagh claimed to be his wife.

Kavanagh, Muiris "Kruger" (1894 – 1971)

Born 1894 in Dún Chaoin, Co. Kerry. Emigrated to US in 1913 where he became publicity manager for MGM studios. Served as bodyguard to Eamon De Valera during the latter's tour of America to raise money for the Irish cause. Returned to Ireland in 1920 and established a guesthouse in his hometown. Brendan Behon wrote a song to celebrate the granting of the public license. The guesthouse became famous as a popular destination for artists, poets, painters and actors. Muiris died 15th, April, 1971.

Kavanagh, Niamh (1968 -)

Born 13th, February, 1968. In 1993 while working for Allied Irish Bank in Dublin, Niamh was selected to represent Ireland in the Eurovision song contest. Niamh had agreed to perform the Jimmy Walsh song "In Your Eyes" just two weeks before the Irish regional competition. At the final on May 15th she performed the song in front on a worldwide television audience of 350 million to win the Eurovision for Ireland. Also sang lead vocals for a number of songs on the soundtrack to the popular Alan Parker film "The Commitments". Released her debut album "Flying Blind" in 1994

Kavanagh, Patrick (1904 – 1967)

Born 21st, October, 1904 in Iniskeen, Co. Mongahan. Eldest son of James and Bridget Kavanagh. Although trained as a cobbler like his father, Patrick soon gave up that profession and settled down to farming on the harsh land of Iniskeen. Released his first poetry compilation "The Ploughman And Other Poems" in 1936. Encouraged by his brother Peter, who did much to support him throughout his life, Patrick moved to Dublin in 1939. There he worked as a journalist and film critic on "The Irish Press" In 1942 he published the first poem to receive widespread acclaim; "The Great Hunger" although the work also earned him a black reputation in certain circles. The Gardai were ordered to seize all copies of the poem because of allegations that it contained obscenities. In the 1950's Patrick produced a newspaper entitled "Kavanaghs Weekly" with his brother Peter but a poor sales forced its closure after sixteen editions. His works revealed the brutal realities of life endured by many in rural Ireland but he also found ways to express the beauty and wonder in the everyday places and things that others overlooked. Died 30th, November, 1967 and he is buried in his hometown of Inniskeen.

Kavanagh, Patrick (1929 -)

Born on 2nd, September, 1929 in Dublin, Ireland. Represented Ireland in rugby as a flanker, making his international debut against England on 29th, March, 1952. Capped twice, final appearance v Wales on 12th, March, 1955.

Kavanagh, Patrick Alexander (1951 -)

Born March 13th, 1951 in Liverpool, England to Augustine Kavanagh and Margurite Brown. Elected Tanaiste of Clann Chaomhánach in 1993 and served as chief of Clann Chaomhánach 1994 to 1995. Married to Grace.

Kavanagh, Patrick Bernard (1923 - ?)

Born 18th, March, 1923. Son of Michael and Violet (nee Duncan) Kavanagh Deputy Commissioner, Metropolitan Police, 1977-83; Served with Manchester City Police (1946-64), Cardiff City Police (1964-69) S. Wales Constabulary (1969-73) Joined Metropolitan Police in 1974. CBE in 1977; QPM in 1974.

Kavanagh, Patrick J. (1931 -)

Born 6th, January, 1935 at Worthing, Sussex, England to Henry Edward Kavanagh and Agnes O'Keefe. Lecturer, actor broadcaster, author and poet. Awarded the Richard Hillary Prize in 1966 for his memoir "The Perfect Stranger". His first novel "A Song and Dance" was awarded the Guardian Fiction Prize in 1968. Received the

Cholmondeley Award for poetry in 1992. Columnist on The Spectator (1983–1996) and for The Times Literary Supplement (1996–2002). Appeared in the popular TV comedy show Father Ted. Author of "Finding Connections" which traces his ancestors' journey from Ireland to the new world.

Kavanagh, Peter (1910 - ?)

Born in Dublin in 1910, Peter played for Glasgow Celtic FC in the late 1920's and early 1930's. After signing from Dublin club Bohemians in April 1929, he made his debut for Celtic playing against Hearts on August 10th. Went on to make 35 appearances and score 5 goals before leaving for Northampton in August, 1932. There he made one appearance v Brentford on 27th, December. Represented Ireland at international level on two occasions; 26th, April, 1931 in Barcelona v Spain (1-1) and 13th, December, 1931 at Dalymount Park v Spain (0-5). Died in Leverndale Hospital, Glasgow.

Kavanagh, Rose AKA 'Uncle Remus' (1860 - 1891)

Born 23rd, June, at Killadroy, Co. Tyrone. Poet and writer who counted W. B. Yeats and Charles Kickham among her friends. Contributed to the Dublin University Review, The Nation, Shamrock Young Ireland. Under the penname 'Uncle Remus' she compiled a very popular childrens column. Suffering from tuberculosis she died after contracting a cold while visiting her mother on 26th, February 1891. Yeats wrote an obituary in the Boston Pilot which included the following tribute "a young inspiration whose great promise was robbed of fulfilment first by ill-health and then by an early death'. In 1909 the Reverend Matthew Russell, an admirer of Roses work, edited a collection of her poems entitled 'Rose Kavanagh and her verses'.

Kavanagh, Simon Henry - Baron of Ballyane (? - 1830)

Son of John Baptist Kavanagh, Baron of Gniditz and Katarine von Kallhammer. Married Baroness Leopoldine Moscon and through that union inherited a castle and estate at Mali Tabor, in what is now Croatia. Together they had two sons – James and Emil. James served in the Austrian Imperial Army. Emil served in the army for a time and died unmarried in Gratz in 1888. Simon died in Vienna in 1830.

Kavanagh, Stan (? - ?)

Born in Australia? A popular actor and accomplished comical juggler Stan performed with the Ziegfeld Follies of 1936. The following year he appeared in The Big Broadcast of 1937 with Jack Benny and George Burns.

Kavanagh, Terrence (1912 - ?)

Born in Dublin 1913. Football player with Everton, Notts County and Exeter. Joined Everton in 1935 but did not make any first team appearances. Joined Notts County in 1936 and made three appearances wearing the number 6 shirt. In 1937 he signed with Exeter, making six appearances.

Kavanagh, Terry (1863 - 1908)

An Irish jump jockey who competed in the English Grand National on a number of occasions and won the race on Manifesto in 1897. His other wins also include the Lancashire Chase (1895) on Gentle Ida, the Grand Sefton (1890) on Choufleur, the Jubilee Handicap (1892) on Niblick and the Sandown Grand Prize (1893) on Gillstown. It is rumoured that in order to make the necessary riding weight he was willing to carry sacks of potatoes by day and sleeping in a manure heap at night.

Kavanagh, Justice Thomas Giles (1917 – 1997)

Born August 14th, 1917 in Bay City, Michigan. Son of Giles Kavanagh and Mary Adeline Washington. Received AB degree from University of Notre Dame in 1938 and LLB from Detroit College of Law in 1943. Served in the Court Of Appeals from1964 and elected to the Supreme Court in 1968. Re-elected in 1976. Credited with bringing calm to the court and unifying a divided judiciary. Thomas was fond of saying that "the members of the Court through sheer happenstance and the vicissitudes of politics, ambition, age, health, and geography had been thrown together like survivors sharing a single life raft, and it was our task and our duty to work together for the common benefit." In his opinion it was the supreme courts duty to "protect the individual from the government" Thomas was known as "Thomas the Good" to distinguish him from Justice Thomas M. Kavanagh who also served on the Michigan Supreme Court bench.

Kavanagh, Thomas Henry VC (1821 – 1882)

Born 15th, July, 1821 in Mullingar, County Westmeath (see note) Thomas was a civil servant in India at the time of the Indian Mutiny of 1857. Along with other British residents, Thomas and his family were trapped inside the British Residency during the siege of Lucknow. When the situation grew desperate Thomas volunteered to make his way through the city streets and meet with a relief force so that they could be guided quickly and safely to the residency. Thomas disguised himself as a native, no easy task as he was six feet tall, had blue eyes and a shock of red hair. With the aid of a native guide named Kanoujee Lal he managed to rendezvous with the relief force and liberate the Residency. The mission was accomplished against overwhelming odds and for his bravery Thomas was awarded the Victoria Cross. Thomas died on 13th, November, 1882 at Gibraltar. He is buried in North Front Cemetery of Gibraltar, Government of Gibraltar ID # 4567. A picture of Thomas can be found in the National Portrait Gallery in London – "The Relief of Lucknow" (1859) #NPG 5851. As of 2008 his medal is held by a private collector in Ontario. The disguise worn during his escape from

Lucknow is housed at the National Army Museum, Chelsea.

Note: Although generally regarded as having been born in Mullingar, no documentary evidence has been found. An American newspaper, The Daily Miner of Butte, Montana, reported the following on January 8th, 1883: "was born in the county of Cork. He doubtless had relatives in this country, as his grandfather was compelled to fly to America after Emmet's rebellion, in which he had taken an active part."

Kavanagh, Thomas Kenrick "Ken" (1923 -)

Born 12th, December, 1923 to John Joseph Kavanagh and Dorothy Miller. Australian motorcycle champion; rode for Norton, a British motorcycle manufacturer. Also drove for the Maserati formula one team in 1958. Titles include: Isle of Man T.T. (1956), Imola (1955) Hockenheim (1954) Silverstone (1953) Ulster GP (1953) British Championship (1952) Hedemora (1952) Ballarat (1951)

Kavanagh, Thomas MacMurrough MP (1798 - 1837)

Conservative representative for Carlow in the parliament at Westminster. Once regarded as one of the wealthiest commoners in Ireland. Father of Arthur MacMurrough Kavanagh (1831 – 1889)

Kavanagh, Justice Thomas Moore (1909 – 1975)

Born 4th, August, 1917 near Carson City, Michigan. Justice of the Michigan Supreme Court. Graduated from the University of Detroit. Practiced in Detroit for three years before returning to Carson City where he served as both City Attorney and City Clerk. Elected Attorney General in 1954 and 1956. Elected to the Supreme Court in 1958 and re-elected in 1966. Served as Chief Justice on three occasions. In his private life Thomas was a strong support of his local church and loved sports. He played on the office Bowling team while serving on the Supreme Court. Thomas was known as "Thomas the Great" to distinguish him from Justice Thomas G. Kavanagh who also served on the Michigan Supreme Court at the same time.

Kavanagh, Thomas Christian (1912 - 1978)

Born 17th, August, 1912 in New York City. Son of Patrick F. Kavanagh and Anna C. Unger. Civil Engineer. After finishing high school Thomas decided to build a career in engineering. A scholarship allowed him to travel to the Technological University of Berlin Germany where he became a fluent German speaker. On his return voyage to America he met Kerstin E. Berglund and would marry her five years later. Thomas earned a B.S. and M.C.E. degrees from the City College of New York. At New York University he earned a M.B.A. in finance and a science doctorate. Thomas was employed as structural designer by a number of engineering firms in New York where he worked on bridges, highways, power plants floating docks and refineries. During World War II he served as an aircraft engineer. After the war he served as an assistant professor of civil engineering before moving Pennsylvania State University in 1948. In 1952 he rejoined NYU as the Chairman of the Civil Engineering Department and the following year began to work part time with the consulting firm Praeger & Maguire. Thomas was soon a full time partner and the firm became Praeger-Kavanagh and eventually Praeger-Kavanagh-Waterbury. During his time with the company Thomas played a leading role in many prestigious projects such as the world's largest telescope at Arecibo in Puerto Rico, the Hawkins Point floating bridge on the St. Lawrence River, Canada and he was also involved in the planning of the subway system for Caracas, Venezuela. In 1964 Thomas was one of the original founders of the National Academy of Engineering and served on its council. He was the author of over one hundred technical books related to engineering and its role in society. Thomas died on 23rd, May, 1978 in Florida.

Kavanagh, Captain Thomas S. J. (? -?)

Served with the Boston Police Department. Author of a number of books related to law enforcement, punishment and police procedures. Works include "Minute Police Talks - A Complete Police Manual with Civil Service Questions and Answers"

Kavanagh, Trevor (1943 -)

Born 19th, January, 1943 in Middlesex, England. Son of Bernard George Valentine Kavanagh and Alice Rose Thompson. British political commentator and columnist. Worked on regional newspapers in England beginning with The Surrey Mirror, before eventually moving to Australia and joining the staff of Rupert Murdoch's News Corp. Returned to England in the seventies eventually joining The Sun newspaper as its political editor. Awarded Journalist Of The Year in 1977. Trevor was once described by the Wall Street Journal as "the most powerful journalist in Britain".

Kavanagh Abdullah, Dr. Mikaail MBE (1945 -)

Born Michael Kavanagh on 20th, December, 1945 in Surrey, England to Stephen and Dorothy. Travelled the world as an academic biologist before finally settling in Malaysia. In 1983 he joined the World Wildlife Fund (WWF) where he worked with the Sarawak Forest to create national wildlife reserves. Worked with Malaysian state agencies and governments to develop strategies for the use of natural resources. Appointed CEO of WWF Malaysia in 1991. Awarded Malaysian knighthood in 1996 and MBE in 2000.

Kavanagh Boylan, Celia (1948 -)

Born 4th, January, 1948 in Lancashire, England. Daughter of Edmund Kavanagh and Cecilia Turner. Originally trained as dispensing optician but returned to college to study systems analysis and computer programming. Served as Chief of Clann Chaomhánach from 2002 to 2004.

Kavanagh Dalton, Bridget (1948 -)

Born 1948 near Kildavin Co. Carlow. Read pharmacy at University College Dublin, Graduated with honours in 1969 B.Sc. (Pharm). Married in 1975, raised three children. Founder member of Clann Chaomhánach. Served as chief of Clann Chaomhánach 1998 to 2000.

Kavanagh Wachtel, Marion (1876 - 1954)

Born 10th, June, 1876 in Milwaukee, Wisconsin. Artist noted for her landscapes. Studied at the Art Institute of Chicago and later under William Merritt Chase in New York. Married fellow artist Elmer Wachtel in 1904 and changed the spelling of her surname from Kavanaugh to Kavanagh. Marion was most famous for her watercolour renditions of the Californian countryside although she also captured images of Arizona, the High Sierras, and Mexico. Died in Pasadena on 22nd, May, 1954.

Kavanaugh, Benjamin Taylor (1805 – 1888)

Born 23rd, April, 1805 in Jefferson County, Kentucky. Son of Williams and Hannah Kavanaugh and a brother of Bishop Hubbard Hinde Kavanaugh. An itinerant preacher in the Methodist Church, he was assigned to the Indian mission on the Mississippi River in 1839. Studied medicine and later held a chair in the medical department at the University of St. Louis. Served as an Army chaplain in the Confederate Army during the American Civil War. Professor of intellectual and moral science in Soule University, Chappell Hill. In 1865 Benjamin was in Texas where he remained for three years, spending much of his spare time exploring the minerals and geology of the area. Based on his observations he became convinced that oil would be found in Texas. Helped to form the San Augustine Petroleum Company. Married 1st: Margaret Lingenfeller on 3rd, April, 1827; 2nd: Sue Stith Barre. Died in Boonsborough, Kentucky 3rd, July, 1888.

Kavanaugh, Daniel (1948 -)

Born 28th, October, 1948 in Seattle, Washington to Owen P. Kavanaugh and Delia Brady. Served as chief of Clann Chaomhánach 1996 to 1998.

Kavanaugh, Major Delaney C. (1836 – 1903)

Born October, 1836 in Jefferson, Indiana. Son of Philemon Kavanaugh and Margaret Palmer. Served in the union army during the civil war with the 6th Indianna Infantry Regiment. Promoted to rank of Major on 17th, May, 1862. Married Kate Hartly Spam. Died 26th, February, 1903 in Stuttgart, Arkansas. Buried in "Officers Circle of Soldiers," National Cemetery, Little Rock, Arkansas.

Kavanaugh, Ethel (1901 - ?)

Ethel wrote a book about her adventures creating a homestead in Alaska entitled "Wilderness Homesteaders". Also contributed to "The Alaskan Sportsman" magazine.

Kavanaugh, Frances (? -)

A screen writer whose career spanned the 1940's and 1950's with credits on over fifty movies. She received her first credit in 1941 and her work includes Cattle Queen (1951), The Arizona Ranger (1948), Arizona Roundup (1942) and Lone Star Men (1941).

Kavanaugh, Frank Kimbrough (1869 – 1957)

Born 23rd, September, 1869 at Oddville, Harrison County, Kentucky. Attended the Kentucky Military Institute from 1886 to 1889. Though his family was steeped in politics and Methodist preaching, Frank entered the sedate world of books when he became the assistant State librarian for Kentucky in 1890. He remained at the State library for over fifty years and became well versed in every aspect of Kentucky Law. Studied law under Judge T. L. Edelen and was admitted to the bar in 1897, though he never practiced. Wrote many books relating to operation of the law in Kentucky such as the "Kentucky Directory" and "Official Manual for the Use of the Courts, State and County

Officials and General Assembly of the State of Kentucky ". Died 9th, June, 1957. At the time he was described as the Patriarch of State employees.

Kavanaugh, James (1826 - 1885)

Born 19th, March, 1826 - Deer Park Parish, Co. Wexford Ireland. Emigrated to America and settled in Skagit County, Washington. First US Marshal in the North West and was also the first Sheriff of Whatcom County. Kept a diary of his life & times which provides an important insight into lives of early pioneers in Skagit. Died 19th, June, 1885. Buried in Pioneer Cemetery, Lot 5 - Block 8, Pleasant Ridge, LaConner, Skagit Co., Washington.

Kavanaugh, James (?-)

James was born in Kalamazoo, Michigan. Fourth of seven sons born to Frank and Hazel Kavanaugh. Popular poet and writer focusing on spiritual matters and the place of the individual in modern society.

Kavanaugh, Harry C. (? – 1924)

Chief of Police in Anchorage from 2nd, May, 1923 to 3rd, January, 1924. Recruited from Cordova on a salary of $250. On 2nd, January, 1924, Harry was shot while attempting to arrest a drunk and died the following day. Died 3rd, January, 1924.

Kavanaugh, Bishop Hubbard Hinde (1802 - 1884)

Born on 14th, February, 1802 in Clarke county, Kentucky. Son of Williams Kavanaugh and Hannah Hubbard Hinde. An influential preacher for the Methodist Church in the Southern states and the east coast. Appointed bishop in May 1854 at the general conference held in Columbus, Georgia. Helped to guide the Methodist church through the troubling times of the civil war. His advice was sought my many Kentucky state officials including Governor Clarke and Governor Wickliffe. Died 19th, March, 1884 in Columbus, Mississippi.

Kavanaugh, Kenneth William (1916 -)

Born 23rd, November, 1916 in Little Rock, Arkansas. Son of Charles B. and Lillian Kavanaugh. The youngest of three children. Graduated from Little Rock Senior High School in 1936, entered Louisiana State University and joined the football team. While at LSU Ken also starred in baseball and later played minor league baseball for the St. Louis Cardinals. Ken joined the Chicago Bears as a second round draft in 1940. The Bears won the NF Championship in 1940 and 1941. His career was interrupted when he signed on as Air Force Pilot during World War II. He flew on anti-submarine duty in the Caribbean before being posted to England in1944 where he flew B-24 and B-17 bombers. By the end of the war he had reached the rank of Captain and been awarded the Distinguished Flying Cross for "Extraordinary achievement while serving as commander in the air squadron formations on heavy bombardment missions against the enemy". After his return to America Ken rejoined the Chicago Bears in 1946 and his team went on to win the championship. It is worth mentioning that Ken scored a touchdown in each of the three championship winning games he played in. Nicknamed "The Home Run Hitter", he earned NFL All-Pro honours and created a record for most touchdowns per catch, a record that still stands today. At the end of his playing career Ken joined the coaching staff of the New York Giants from 1955 to 1970, becoming a scout for that team the following year. He is one of the NFL's 300 All-Time Greatest Players, is on the NFL Hall of Fame Team of the '40s, and the Chicago Bears All-Time Team. He has been elected into the National Collegiate Football Hall of Fame, the LSU Hall of Fame, Louisiana Sports Hall of Fame, and the Arkansas Hall of Fame. Ken married Ann Porter on 24th, October, 1942 and together they had two children: Kristy and Ken Jr.

Kavanaugh, Margaret "Mags" (1954 -)

Born Margaret Mary Anne McMahon MacMurrough Kavanaugh, on 10th, March, 1954 in Baltimore, Maryland.

Attended Notre Dame Prep School for 13 years before leaving for Hollywood, California. Attended the Lee Strasberg Theatrical Institute for 5 years. While working on the movie "Repo- Zero to Sixty" (1978) Burt Reynolds noticed her practicing stunts and enquired who the driver was. Discovering it was a woman, he declared that "the Mags is driving the mags*," and the nickname stuck. Her works include Carrie (1976), Star Wars (1977) and Escape from New York (1981). * a type of car wheel.

Kavanaugh, Rhoda (? - ?)

In 1903 created a private school in Lawrenceburg, Kentucky in order to educate her daughters, a niece and other children. Later expanded the school and changed its focus to preparing students for a life in the military. Rhoda helped send fifteen students to West Point and a further one hundred and fifty to the Annapolis naval academy. The house, now known as Kavanagh House, still survives and is on National & State Historical Register. Retired in 1946.

Kavanaugh, Walter J. (1933 -)

Born 30th, June, 1933. Son of Joseph Francis Kavanaugh and Mary Agnes Rafferty. Republican Senator for New Jersey. Attended the University of Notre Dame and achieved a BSC in Domestic Marketing. Served as a jet and helicopter pilot in the U.S. Air Force from 1955 to 1976 reaching the rank of Lieutenant. Elected to the New Jersey Senate in 1998. General Assembly 1976-98, Majority Budget Officer 1996-98, Deputy Speaker 1994-95, Assistant Majority Leader 1986-89, Assistant Minority Leader 1985, Deputy Assistant Minority Leader 1980-81, Assistant Minority Whip 1977, Minority Whip 1978-79.

Kavanaugh, Williams Marmaduke (1866 – 1915)

Born 3rd, March, 1866 in Eutaw, Greene County, Alabama. Son of Rev. Hubbard Hinde Kavanagh and Anna Kimbrough. Graduated from the Kentucky Military Institute in 1885 as the ranking cadet officer. Employed by the Arkansas Gazette in Little Rock, Williams rose to become its managing editor. Appointed county sheriff of Pulaski in 1896 before election as county judge in 1900. Represented Arkansas in the Senate from 29th, January to 3rd, March, 1913. Died on 21st, February, 1915.

Kavanaugh Hocker, Miss Willie (1862-1944)

Born on 21st, July, 1862, in Madison County, Kentucky. Daughter of Captain William Kavanaugh Hocker and Virginia Frances Brown Hocker. A public school teacher in Pine Bluff and Jefferson County for 34 years, she loved to promote Arkansas history. On 26th, February, 1913 a design submitted by her was accepted by the General Committee of the Daughters of the American Revolution as a prototype for the Arkansas state flag. Her original design appeared essentially as the flag does today, except that the central white diamond contained only three blue stars, lying in a straight line from left to right. The committee requested that she alter the design to incorporate the word "Arkansas" in the centre of the diamond. Willie submitted a new flag, adding "Arkansas" and placing two blue stars below and one above the name. Her design remained unchanged until 1923, when the Legislature added a fourth star to the diamond to represent the Confederacy. At first there were two stars above the name and two below, but legislation in 1924 positioned a Confederate star above the state's name and the original three below it. When shre retried from teaching Willie moved to a cottage in Wabbaseka, Arkansas, where she died on 6th, February, 1944. She is buried in the Hocker family plot at Bellwood Cemetery.

Kavanaugh Oldham, William (1865 – 1938)

Born 20th, May, 1865 in Richmond, Kentucky. Son of William Kavanaugh Oldham and Catherine Brown. Attended Central University Richmond. In 1885 he settled in Pettus, Lonoke County, Arkansas where he was a cotton planter. Entered politics as a Democrat in the lower house of the Arkansas General Assembly of 1907. Served as a member of the upper house from 1911 to 1913 and as president of the Senate in 1913. Following the resignation of Governor Robinson in 1913, William served as acting Governor for Arkansas for six days. Died 6th, May, 1938 at his home in Pettus and is buried in Oaklawn cemetry, Little Rock.

Mac Murchada, Diarmuid (1110 – 1171)

Appointed King of Leinster at the age of sixteen. From the beginning of his reign he faced a number of military and political setbacks as he opposed the High King, Turlough O'Connor and the King of Breifne, Tiernan O'Rourke. He survived the setbacks and slowly began to build a power base in Leinster. A combination of political defeats and personal troubles saw him flee Ireland in 1166. In an effort to regain his thrown he travelled to England to seek the aid of King Henry II. Though unable to aid Diarmuid directly, Henry gave him permission to recruit an army from the men of his own Kingdom. Diamruid eventually persuaded a band of Norman Knights to travel to Ireland and assist him in his campaign. After winning the back the crown of Leinster, Diarmuid turned his attentions to the crown of Ard Rí or High King. Unfortunately he died before he could achieve victory. Diarmuid was the father of Domhnall "Caomhánach" mac Murchada, patriarch of Clann Chaomhánach. Died in May 1171.

Moling, Saint (614 – 696)

Born in Sliabh Luachra in County Kerry. Moling is the patron saint of Clann Chaomhánach. He holds close ties to the village of St. Mullins in County Carlow where he constructed a church. His feast day is June 17th.

Rev. Hubbard H. Kavanaugh
(1802 - 1884)

Influential Bishop in the Southern Methodist Church.

Thomas H. Kavanagh VC
(1821- 1882)

Awarded the Victoria Cross for his part in the relief of the siege at Lucknow, India.

Hobart Cavanaugh
(1886 - 1950)

Popular star of stage and screen. Roles include Rose of Washington Square (1939) and Up In Central Part (1949)

Arthur MacMurrough Kavanagh
(1831 – 1889)

Represented counties Carlow and Wexford at Westminster.

Paul Cavanagh
(1884 – 1964)

Actor, performed in a number of the Sherlock Holmes movies, starring Basil Rathbone.

Edward Kavanagh
(1795 – 1844)

Served as acting Governor of Maine in 1843, the first catholic to hold such office in the US.

Walter Page Cavanaugh
(1922 -)

Popularly known as Page Cavanaugh, a Jazz musician who also enjoyed a brief film career, alongside Doris Day.

Wentworth Cavenagh
(1822 – 1895)

Mayor of Adelaide in 1874. A number of Australian landmarks are name in his honour.

Dudley Kavanagh
(1834 - 1914)

American Billiard Champion in 1858, 1859.

Stan Kavanagh
(? - ?)

Juggler and actor. Featured in Ziegfeld Follies.

Ken Kavanagh
(1923 -)

Isle of Man T.T. Champion.

Sir Orfeur Cavenagh
(1820 –1891)

Governor of the Straits.

James Michael Cavanaugh (1823—1879)

Representative from Minnesota and a Delegate from the Territory of Montana.

Possible portrait of Lawrence Kavanagh (c 1805 - 1856)

A bush ranger in Australia and member of the infamous Cash, Kavanagh & Jones gang.

Grave of Diarmuid macMurchada. Ferns, Co. Wexford.

Place Names - America

Alaska

Cavanaugh Creek
Nome (CA)
Prospectors' name reported on the 1908 "Map of Seward Peninsula" by Arthur Gibson.

Alabama

Kavanaugh Drive
Huntsville
Origin: Unknown. Huntsville have no records relating to the origin of the name.

Arkansas

Cavanaugh
Forth Smith, Sebastian County
Possible connection to a Thomas S. Grover Cavanaugh.
Source: Arkansas State Library

Kavanaugh Boulevard
Little Rock
Named in 1936 by the City Council of Little Rock in honour of Williams Marmaduke Kavanaugh.
Source: Arkansas State Library.

Kavanaugh House
1854 S. Arch Street, Little Rock
The home of William Marmaduke Kavanaugh. Purchased in 1899 the house remained in the family until 1976.
Source: The Quapaw Quarter Associations "The Chronicle", Vol. 28, No. 2

Arizona

Kavanagh Ln.
Flagstaff
Named by and after John Kavanagh. John's family moved from Ireland to Canada and then to Arizona. John moved

to Flagstaff in 1971 and purchased 80 acres. Johns father was Maurice and his mother was a Byrne.
Source: City of Flagstaff, AZ

Kavanagh Way
See Kavanagh Ln., AZ.

California

Barney Cavanah Ridge
Placer
Origin: Unknown.

Bartley W. Cavanaugh Golf Course
Sacramento.
Named after Bartley W. Cavanaugh who was appointed city manager in 1946.

Cavanagh Inn
10 Keller St., Petaluma.
A two-storey house constructed in 1902 for John Edward Cavanagh. John was the son of John W. Cavanagh and a prominent businessman in Petaluma. Now run as a B&B.
Source: Petaluma Museum.

Cavanagh Park
Petaluma
Name in honour of John W. Cavanagh Snr.
Son of John Cavanagh (1824 –) from Dublin, Ireland who arrived in Petaluma in 1857 and established a waterworks and lumber company. John left Ireland in 1850 and travelled to San Francisco first. Commemorates the locations of the Cavanagh Warehouse where potatoes and other local products were stored for shipping to San Francisco and the Cavanagh Lumber Yard loading dock. Both no longer exist. John's son John W. Jnr. "Jack" (1919 – 1995) served seven terms on the city council and also served as mayor and deputy mayor.
Source: Petaluma Museum

Cavanagh Road
Glendale
Origin: Unknown.

Cavanaugh Grade
Mendocino
Origin: Unknown.

Cavanaugh Gulch
Mendocino
Also known as Sartori Gulch.
Origin: Unknown.

Cavanaugh Canyon
Shasta
Origin: Unknown.

Kavanaugh Ridge
Mono County
Named after Stephen "Steve" Kavanaugh circa 1900. Stephen was hired by a M. P. Hayes to drive a tunnel along a gold vein high on the ridge from the East Fork of Green Creek. Steve named the Chemung mine after his hometown in Illinois. Although the mine produced the more than a millions dollars of ore Steve never became rich.
Sources: "Mono Diggings" by Wedterz, Frank S. & "Naming the Eastern Sierra" by Sowaal, Marguerite.

Kavanaugh Creek
San Luis Obispo County
Name after John Patrick Kavanagh who settled near the creek in the 1880's. John was born in New York State and moved to California at the age of 27. He mined in Placer County and then settled at the creek in 1887. John's parents were originally from County Cork in Ireland. His wife, Johanna McDonnell was born in Kinsale, County Cork.
Source: California History Room, California State Library

Colorado

Kavanagh Park
Woodland Park

Named in honour of Father Michael F. Kavanagh the first Pastor of Our Lady of the Woods Church in Woodland Park from 1954-1955

Connecticut

Cavanaugh Brook
New Haven
After Thomas Cavanaugh who owned land on Hanover Dist. boundary, 1878.
Source: Connecticut Place Names p. 389

Cavanaugh Pond
New Haven
Origin: Unknown. Possible connection with Cavanaugh Brook, CT

Cavanaugh St.
Norwalk
Origin: Unknown. Possible connection to John J. Cavanaugh of the Norwalk Hat Company. John purchased 2 acres of land in Norwalk in 1900.

Kavanaugh Hill
Woodbury, Weekeepeemee River
Origin: Unknown. Possibly after Charles Kavanaugh who arrived around 1913/1914. Had one daughter, Clare. She married a Charles Stockwell. Charles died around 1960.
Source: Woodbury Public Library.

Georgia

Kavanaugh Park
Savannah.
Located on Abercorn Street, between 46th and 47th Streets. Possible named in honour of Alderman Michael J. Kavanaugh, who served from January 12th, 1907 until his death on December 18th, 1910. First listed by name in annual municipal report for 1910.
Source: Glenda E.A. Anderson, Directory, Municipal Research Library, Savannah.

Iowa

Cavanagh House
Reno St., Iowa City
James Cavanagh (1806-1879). James was born in Ohio and lived in Cass County, Michigan before moving to Iowa and Johnson County around 1840. For a number of years he farmed in the Solon area, northeast of Iowa City, then established residence in the house on Reno Street, probably in the late 1860's. James was active in local politics, serving at various times as county auditor, county commissioner, Justice of the Peace, and a member of the 7th General Assembly. One of his eight sons, Mathew (b.1832), carried on his father's political and civic activism in Iowa City, as a local attorney, county sheriff, city council member (1862) and mayor (1878). Also known as Cavanaugh-Zetek House.
Source: City of Iowa City

Cavanaugh Bottom
Jackson County
Origin: Unknown. Possible connection with Morgan Cavanagh one of the earliest settlers in Jackson county.
Source: Iowa State Library

Idaho

Cavanah House
107 E. Idaho St., Boise.
Home of Charles Cheatham Cavanah (1871 - 1953) Charles practiced law in Boise, Idaho and he was also the Idaho State Supreme Court Crier for a time between 1892 and 1895
Source: National Register of Historic Places (Building Ref. #82000185)

Cavanaugh Siding
Bear Lake
Origin: Unknown.

Cavanaugh Bay
Bonner

Origin: Unknown.

Kavanaugh Creek
Bonner
Origin: Unknown.

Illinois

Cavanagh Cemetery
Kewanee, Wetherfield Township, Henry County.
Origin: Unknown
Possible connection with the family of James Cavanagh (1844 - 1920) a native of Weathersfield township. James had a farm at Kewanee.

Cavanah Lake
Monroe
Origin: Unknown

Cavanaugh Bluff
Morgan
Origin: Unknown

Kavanaugh Cemetery
West Township, Effingham
Origin: Unknown

Thomas Kavanagh Stadium
5556 W 77th Street, Burbank
Origin: In honour of Thomas P. Kavanagh, head coach for St. Laurence College football team from 1970 to 1977. Thomas holds the majority of Laurence's football coaching records. His teams never experienced a losing season and his overall record stands at 67-14-4. Tom passed away in November 1984. The football stadium was dedicated in his memory on Friday, August 24, 2001.
Source: St. Laurence High School.

Indiana

Cavanaugh Hall
Notre Dame University.

Constructed as a male, freshman residence hall in 1936 and dedicated in honour of Rev. John W. Cavanaugh, Notre Dame's fifth president.

Cavanaugh Hall
Indiana University / Purdue University.
Origin: Named in honour of Robert E. Cavanaugh (1881-1960). Robert was Professor of Education, Indiana University (1946-1951) and Director of the University Extension Service (1921-1946)
Source: National Council on Public History,

Kentucky

Cavanaugh Creek
Jackson
Origin: Unknown.

Kavanaugh Camp
Crestwood, Oldham County.
After Bishop H. H. Kavanaugh

Kavanaugh Road
Crestwood, Oldham County.
After Bishop H. H. Kavanaugh

Kavanagh House
241 East Woodford Street, Lawrenceburg.
The home of Rhoda Kavanaugh who ran a Naval preparatory school in her house that helped send candidates to West Point.

Kavanaugh Cemetery
Boyd County
Possible link to Bishop H.H. Kavanaugh

Kavanaugh Road
Boyd County
Possible link to Bishop H.H. Kavanaugh

Louisiana

Charles J. Cavanaugh Hall
Louisiana College, Pineville

Named after Charles J. Cavanaugh, professor of biology from 1945 to 1977. Charles was born in 1911 in Vernon Parish, Louisiana. He graduated from Louisiana College in 1932 and received his Master of Science degree from the University of Tennessee in 1934. He did graduate studies at University of Virginia, New York University and University of Missouri. He began teaching at Louisiana College in the summer of 1932 and also taught at New York University, Union University, and Hofstra College. Charles returned to Louisiana College in 1945 where he served as a professor of biology and chairman of the department.
Source: Louisiana College

Kavanaugh Road
Ruston
Origin: Unknown. Possible connection to Bishop H.H. Kavanaugh

Maryland

Kavanagh Road
Baltimore
Runs along a tidal inlet called Chink Chrek, which enters Bear Creek, a tidal arm of the Patapsco River.. Appears on the maps in 1952 in laying out the spacious Lynch property into a residential subdivision called West Inverness. The name appears on a plat for laying out the streets made in October 1952 by the Loch Raven Construction Company. The name was selected by developers. There is no property owner named Kavanagh on the same property in the 1915 Atlas of Baltimore County
Source: John McGrain, Baltimore County Historian

Kavanaugh Street
Baltimore
Origin: unknown. The street runs for one block on the west side of the city near U.S. 1 and Monroe Street.
Source: John McGrain, Baltimore County Historian

Maine

Kavanagh Mansion
Damariscotta
Built circa 1803 by James Kavanagh a local businessman and later occupied by his son Edward (1795 - 1844) who was the first Catholic governor of Maine.

Kavanagh School (site of)
301 Congress Street, Portland, Maine
In 1877, Winifred Kavanagh, sister of Edward Kavanagh, first Catholic governor in all of New England, gave $25,000 to build the Kavanagh School for girls, kindergarten to grade 9. It opened in 1879 to 450 pupils with a teaching staff of eight Sisters of Mercy. In 1910, Cathedral High School for girls occupied the building until it was tom down in 1969. More than 2,500 young women graduated from Cathedral during its era. It was replaced by Catherine McAuley High School which opened in 1972 on Stevens Avenue.

Kavanagh Street
Lewiston, ME 04240
Street name was accepted by the City Council on November 29, 1951. The Lewiston Evening Journal of the next day reports, "The board approved the street committee's recommendation for acceptance of Kavanagh Street. The proposed way extends from Russell St. to Fairlawn Ave." Probably in honour of Edward Kavanagh (1795 – 1844) a former governor of Maine.

Massachusetts

Cavanagh Stadium
Birch Street, North Quincy.
Named for Staff Sergeant Charles Cavanagh, who was killed while serving his country on March 6, 1945 in Germany. Cavanagh served with Company C, 28th Infantry Regt, 8th Division. He was born in Quincy on June 21, 1904 and a plaque was dedicated at the park on June 22, 1947. The current plaque was rededicated on June 14, 2000.

Source: City of Quincy Massachusetts.

Michigan

Cavanagh House
415 W. Main, Midland
The residence of Joseph A. Cavanagh, a Republican Member of the Michigan State House of Representatives for Midland County. The house was registered with the National Register of Historic Places in 1989.

Cavanaugh Lake
Washtenaw County
Origin: Unknown. Possibly after Martin J. Cavanaugh (1866 - ?) Martin was born on July 23, 1866 in Manchester, Washtenaw County. He was a delegate to the state constitutional convention of 1907-08. In 1909 he was a candidate for a justice of the Michigan State Supreme Court.

Cavanaugh Road
Lansing
Origin: Unknown. Possible candidates: Jerome P. Cavanagh, Mayor of Detroit, Howard W. Cavanagh, Democrat candidate for U.S. Representative from Michigan 3rd District, 1918 and Joseph A. Cavanagh, Republican. Member of Michigan state house of representatives from Midland County

Minnesota

Cavanagh Early Childhood Center
5400 Corvallis Avenue North, Crystal
Built in 1958 and formerly named Cavanagh Elementary School after William H. Cavanagh, about whom nothing is known. The building ceased operating as an elementary school in 1976; when it was renamed Cavanagh Early Childhood Center.
Source: John Sutter, Planner & Redevelopment Coordinator, City of Crystal.

Cavanagh Oaks
Crystal
Possibly named after William H. Cavanagh. See Cavanagh Early Childhood Center, Crystal, MN.

Cavanagh Park
Crystal
Possibly named after William H. Cavanagh. See Cavanagh Early Childhood Center, Crystal, MN.

Cavanaugh Ct
Inver Grove Heights
Origin: Unknown

Cavanaugh Dr
Shakopee
Origin: Unknown

Cavanaugh Lake
Itasca
See also Cavanaugh Road, Cohasset, MN
Origin: Unknown.

Cavanaugh Road
Cohasset
Named by the postal service after Cavanaugh Lake, Itasca.
Source: Deb Sakrison, City of Cohasset.

Cavanaugh Street
Becker
Origin: Unknown.

Kavanaugh Dr
Pillager
Origin: Unknown.

Missouri

Cavanaugh Cemetery
Dent County.
Origin: Unknown.

Montana

Kavanaugh Creek
Park
Origin: Unknown.

Kavanaugh Hills
Park
Origin: Unknown.

North Dakota

Cavanaugh Lake
Ramsey
Origin: Unknown.

New Hampshire

Kavanagh Field
St. Anselm College, Anselm Drive, Manchester
Named after Lionel B. Kavanagh, trustee and benefactor, constructed in 1974

Nevada

Cavanaugh Spring
Pershing
Origin: Unknown.

Cavanaugh Wash
Pershing
Origin: Unknown.

New York

Cavanaugh Drive
Colonie
Origin: Unknown. Dedicated on June 27th, 1991.

Cavanaugh Road
Keene, Essex County
Origin: Unknown.

Cavanaugh Road
Lima, Livingston County

Origin: Unknown. On the 1872 Livingston County Atlas there is a C. Cavanaugh living in the vicinity of the road. On the 1902 atlas there is an M. Cavanaugh living on the road. A Michael Cavanaugh who served with the 27th NY Regiment during the civil war was resident in Lima.

Cavanaugh Road
Marcy, NY 13403
Origin: Unknown.

E. J. Cavanagh Park
Named after Emile J. Cavanagh in October 1974. Emile organized the Eastchester Home Civic Association in 1925. In 1941 he was awarded a plaque designating him as "Protector of the North Bronx."
Source: "History in Asphalt: The Origin of Bronx Street and Place Names" by John McNamara

James Cavanaugh Memorial Park
Watervliet
Named in honour of James F. Cavanaugh (1910-1973) who served as mayor of Watervliet (1968 – 1973)
Source: http://www.watervliet.com/ and his son Michael.

Kavanaugh Ave.
Mechanicville, Saratoga County, NY, 12118
Origin: Unknown.

Kavanaugh Cemetery
Bombay, Franklin County
Located approximately half a mile from junction of Route 37 and Route 95, east of Hogansburg. Contains grave of Patrick Kavanaugh (1812 – 1896)
Origin: Unknown

Kavanaugh Road
Honeoye Falls, Monroe County, NY 14472
Origin: Unknown.

McCavanaugh Pond
Franklin County.
Origin: Unknown.

North Carolina

Cavanaughtown Rd.
Richlands, 28574
Origin: Unknown

Jacob Cavanaugh Cemetery
Wallace
Origin: Unknown

Oklahoma

Kavanaugh and Shea Building
403 College Ave., Alva
A Kavanagh Shea hardware store was situated on this site. Registered on the National Register of Historic Places in 1984.

Ohio

Cavanaugh Park
Elm Ave., Brook Park
Named after Jim Cavanaugh, a councilman and safety director for the city of Brook Park.
Source: Gregory M. Cingle, Finance Directory, City of Brook Park

Oregon

Cavanaugh Creek
Baker County
Origin: Unknown.
Source: Baker County have no water rights records on file.

Pennsylvania

Kavanagh Hollow
Potter County
Names after James Cavanaugh who owned the surrounding land around 1860. On a map of the area compiled in 1869 the location is clearly identified as J. Cavanaugh. James was born in 1884 and was married to

Ann Brine. They had 5 children: Mary, Edmond, Timothy, William and John. The land now lies in an area owned the Commonwealth of Pennsylvania.
Source: Potter County Historical Society

Kavanaugh Branch
McKean
Origin: Unknown.

South Dakota

Sally Cavanaugh Mine
Pennington County
Also "Sally Cavenaugh Mine" Situated six miles southwest of Hill City, was originally located as a gold mine in the spring of 1879, but the names of the original locators and of the mine itself are not known. In 1883 Jeff McDermott relocated it and eventually developed it into a tin property. It was named for a young woman living in the town of Custer at that time.
Source: South Dakota Geographic Names book and South Dakota State Library.

Texas

Cavanaugh Street
Houston
Origin: Unknown. Named sometime between 1951 and 1960.
Source: Houston Public Library

Kavanaugh United Methodist Church
Greenville
Named in honour of Bishop Hubbard Hinde Kavanaugh. Founded as a Methodist Sunday school in 1892. Chartered on 8th, November, 1896. Recorded Texas Historic Landmark (1995)

Vermont

Cavanaugh Cemetery
Clarendon, Rutland County

Family cemetery established in 1792. Last burial in 1928. Contains 24 graves.
Origin: Unknown.
Source: USGS National Mapping Service. Office of the Governor, Vermont.

Washington

Cavanaugh Lake
Skagit County
First known as Minnie Lake, named so for a daughter of the Allen family, who was one of the prime settlers on the lake. There are three possibilities for the current designation. A man with the name Cavanaugh surveyed the Skagit area for the government. He may have been an employee of the English Logging Company, which ceased trading in 1945. The Washington State Historical Society suggests that the name derives from either Cecil Cavanaugh, a Tacoma area lumberman or James Kavanagh a pioneer and logger in Skagit County. Nothing is currently known of either gentleman. The name Cavanaugh Lake first appears in Geographic Dictionary of Washington in 1917.
Source: United States State Board on Geographic Names.

Cavanaugh Pond
King County
The pond was the result of gravel extraction over a number of years by the family of Ronald and Phyllis Cavanaugh. The surrounding area, designated as non-development, was purchased by King County as part of a reclamation project. At the time it had no official name and it was at Phyllis' suggestion that it was designated Cavanaugh Pond. Ronald was a descendant of Martin L. Cavanaugh an early pioneer who arrived in Duwamish in 1862.

Mount Cavanaugh
Skagit County
Name approved by the Washington State Board on Geographic Names in 1997 and the United States Board

on Geographic Names in 1998. The naming of the mountain originated due to a local "Name the Mountain" competition and the community chose Cavanaugh due to the proximity of Lake Cavanaugh.
Source: State Board on Geographic Names, WA

Cavanaugh Creek
Whatcom
Named after an engineer who surveyed the area for the government. See Cavanaugh Lake.

Wisconsin

Kavanagh Bay
Sawyer County
Origin: After John Kavanagh an Irish immigrant. John was a surveyor before settling in Sawyer County and creating a "stopping place" for passing lumber jacks.
Source: Sawyer County Historical Society.

Kavanaugh Place
Milwaukee
Origin: Unknown.

Wyoming

Cavanaugh Peak
Lincoln County
A high spot just out side of Kemmerer. Named after John Cavanaugh who was a business associate of the founders of Kemmerer, P. J. Quealy, and M. S. Kemmerer. John was a resident of NY. The peak was probably named sometime between 1897 and the early 1900's
Source: Lincoln County Library

Place Names - Canada

Alberta

Kavanagh
Leduc County.
Named after Charles Edmund Kavanagh who was the superintendent of Railway Mail Service, Winnipeg (1911). Declared a Hamlet for Alberta Hamlet Street Assistance Improvement Program - M.O. #10/80 - Jan. 5, 1980.
Source: Over 2000 Place Names of Alberta, Holmgren, Eric J. & Holmgren, Patricia M.
Source: Alberta Municipal Affairs

British Columbia

Cavanagh Creek
Lillooet
Origin: Unknown.

Manitoba

Kavanagh Street
Winnipeg
Father Francois Kavanagh (1829 - 1922), from St. Boniface, assigned to St. Francois-Xavier parish, est. 1824; second oldest mission in Manitoba.
Source: Mosaic of Winnipeg Street Names (1974)
Francois-Xavier Kavanagh was born October 1, 1829 at Saint Scolastique P. Quebec. He attended school and entered the Seminary at Montreal at the age of 28 and was ordained Priest in 1866. He came to St. Boniface where he was assigned to the parish of St. Francois Xavier as assistant to Father J.B. Thibault and continued the great work with the parishioners. Father Francois-Xavier Kavanagh was named Parish Priest of St. Francois Xavier in 1869. In 1873 three schools were established which were attended by 186 children and later after the railway was established two more schools were formed. Father Kavanagh owned 3 patended lots in St. Francois Xavier.

They were 129 – 179 – 182. In 1908 Father Francois Xavier Kavanagh was 75 years old, he had served the Parish of St. Francois Xavier forty-two years, that he was given an assistant. In 1909 he left St. Francois Xavier, went back to Montreal for a much needed rest. He came back later, sold his 3 lots and rented a room at the Grey Nuns convent where he said Mass every day. As the years were going by his health slowly failing, he passed away at the age of 93, on April 6, 1922. Buried in the local cemetery, St. Francois Xavier, Manitoba.
Source: St. Francois Xavier Historical Society

Kavanagh Park
Winnipeg
Father Francois Kavanagh (1833 - 1922),
See Kavanagh St., MB

Newfoundland and Labrador

Kavanagh's Lane
Wabana, Bell Island.
Origin: Unknown.

Nova Scotia

Cavanagh Brook
Colchester.
Origin: Unknown.

Cavanaghs Lake
Cape Breton.
Origin: Unknown.

Cavanaghs Run
Yarmouth.
Origin: Unknown.

Kavanagh Creek
Richmond.
Origin: Unknown. Possible link to family of Lawrence Kavanagh (1764-1830)

Kavanagh Point
Richmond.

Origin: Unknown. Possible link to family of Lawrence Kavanagh (1764-1830)

Kavanagh Homestead Ruins
Battery Provincial Park, St. Peters.
The remains of the Lawrence Kavanagh (1764-1830) family home.

Kavanagh Street
St. Peters.
After Lawrence Kavanagh (1764-1830) the first Catholic elected to the Nova Scotia assembly.

Kavanaugh Mills
Colchester County
Origin: Named after J. Cavanaugh who operated a grist mill in the late 19th century.
Source: Place-Names and Places of Nova Scotia (1967) C. Bruce Fergusson (Ed.)

Kavanaugh Mill Road
Colchester County
See Kavanaugh Mill, NS

Kavanaugh Mill Bridge
Colchester County
See Kavanaugh Mill, NS

Lawrence Kavanagh Monument
Battery Park, St. Peters.
In honour of Lawrence Kavanagh (1764-1830) the first Catholic elected to the Nova Scotia assembly. Erected 1st, July, 1968.

Ontario

John Cavanagh Road
Carp.
Origin: Possible after John Cavanagh (1796-1883) the first permanent settler in Huntley Township.

Kavanagh Lake
Kenora.
Origin: Unknown.

Saskatchewan
Kavanagh Lake
In honour of J.P. Kavanagh D.F.C. 166 Squadron. Wellington III BK368 AS-P. J.P. was shot down over Denmark after laying mines in the Kiel Canal on the night of 9/10 March 1943 as part of operation Gardening.
Source: Geographic Names Board, SK
Source: RAF Museum Hendon.

Place Names - Australia

Australian Capitol Territory

Cavanough Street
Woden Town
Origin: In honour of Owen Cavanough (1762 – 1841) a sailor on the first fleet ship the "Sirius". Owen was reportedly the first man ashore at Sydney Cove.
Source: Lorraine Bayliss, ACT Place Names Officer

Ernest Cavanagh Street
Gungahlin Town Centre
Named after Ernest Cavanagh, chairman of the ACT Bush Fire Council for over fifty years.

New South Wales

Kavanaghs Creek
Origin: Unknown.

Northern Territory

Cavenagh Street
City of Darwin
Named by Surveyor Goyder in 1869, after Hon Wentworth Cavenagh-Mainwaring. At ninety-nine feet the street is the widest in the city.

Cavenagh (Hundreth of)
Named in honour of Hon. Wentworth Cavenagh.

Mt. Cavenagh
Origin: Unknown.
Probably after Hon. Wentworth Cavenagh-Mainwaring.

Cavenagh Range
Origin: Unknown.
Probably after Hon. Wentworth Cavenagh-Mainwaring.

Queensland

Kavanagh Creek
Origin: Unknown

South Australia

Cavenagh
Town/ Locality
Origin: Unknown.

Cavenagh Dam
Origin: Unknown.

Victoria

Kavanagh Street
South Melbourne
Named after H.J. Kavanagh a South Melbourne City Councillor from 1880 to 1883.
Source: Land Survey, Victoria

Western Australia

Cavanagh Reef
Origin: Unknown

Cavenagh Range
Named by explorer William Christie Goss on 4th September 1873, after the Hon. W. Cavenagh. Aboriginal name -"Kornanna".Referred to as "Nellie Heath Range" by Frank Hann in 1903-04
Source: Department of Land Administration of Western Australia

Place Names - Elsewhere

Anguilla

Cavanagh Cave
Origin: Unknown

Argentina

Cavanagh
Cordoba
Name after Edward Cavanagh. Edward left Ireland for Argentina in 1851 aboard the "William Peele". He founded a powerful cattle ranching dynasty that also played a prominent role in making the sport of Polo popular in Argentina

Corina Kavanagh Passage
Buenos Aires
Corina Kavanagh (See Edificio Kavanagh)

Edificio Kavanagh (The Kavanagh Building)
Plaza San Martin, Buenos Aires
Corina Kavanagh
Commissioned in 1934 by Corina Kavanagh. On completion in 1936 the building was the tallest reinforced concrete building in the world and the tallest of any kind in Latin America. The building is now a listed historical monument.

Croatia

Mali Tabor Castle
Manor 3 km from Hum na Sutli. This manor, first mentioned in 1490, was destroyed in the 16th century; in its place a four-nave church with internal courtyard was built at the end of the 17th century. Of this structure, only two wings with three cylindrical towers at the corners remain. The castle was owned by the Ratkaj family (1524-1793), and later by Baron Simon Henry Kavanagh.

England

Whitemore Hall,
Whitmore, Newcastle under Lyme, Staffordshire.
Historic home of the Cavenagh-Mainwaring family. The house is open to the public at certain times of the year.

Cavanagh Road
St. Margaret's Bay, Dover, Kent
Origin: Unknown. Possible link to Wentworth Odiarne Cavenagh, a resident of Red House, St. Margaret's-at-Cliffe, and chairman of St. Margaret's Conservative Association.

Kavanagh Street
Warley, Essex.
Origin: Unknown. Named between 1920 and 1939. Originally part of Crescent Road.
Source: Essex record office, Essex County Council.

France

Rue Godefroy Cavaignac
Paris
After Eléonore Louis Godefroy Cavaignac (1801-1845) a republican politician.

Ireland

Kavanagh Avenue
Park West Industrial Estate, Dublin.
The streets/roads in the estate are all named after Irish literary or artistic figures and its proximity to the Grand Canal suggest it is named after the poet Patrick Kavanagh.
Source: Padraic O'Brien, Library Assistant, Dublin City Archives.

Italy

Palacia de Cavenaghi
Milan

Baron Henry Kavanagh, Governor of Milan and Chamberlain to the empress of Austria.
Source: MSS#8049/11 p.23, National Library of Ireland

New Zealand

Kavanagh College
Dunedin
Named in honour of Most Rev. Dr John Kavanagh JCD DD who was Bishop of Dunedin from 1957 until his death in 1985.

Kavanagh Road
Napier
Probably after Thomas Henry Kavanagh VC as other street names in the area are Lucknow Terrace and Havelock Road.

Singapore

Cavenagh Bridge
Named in honour of Sir Orfeur Cavanagh

Cavenagh Street
Named in honour of Sir Orfeur Cavanagh

Cavenagh Gardens
Named in honour of Sir Orfeur Cavanagh

Kavanaugh's Cabins, Alexandria Bay, NY

Kavanagh Mansion, Damariscotta, ME.

Build c1803 by James Kavanagh. Also home to his son Edward Kavanagh (1795 - 1844)

Cavanagh's Restaurant – 260W, 23rd St. NY

Opened in 1876 by John J. Cavanagh of Chicopee, Mass. Originally an oyster bar with 12 tables, the restaurant soon established itself as a landmark in the city. Closed in 1970. Mr. Cavanagh was born c1867.

Kavanaugh Hotel, Harrisonburg, Va.

Cavenagh Bridge, Singapore. Postcard 1901.

Mali Tabor Castle, Croatia

A former Kavanagh castle. Image courtesy of Prof. Dr. Radovan Marjanović Kavanagh.

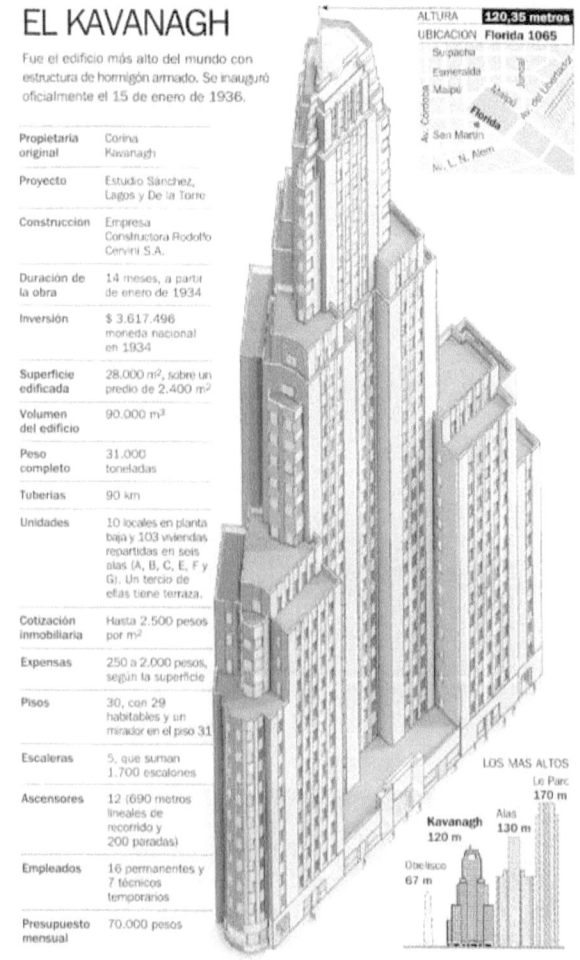

Edificio Kavanagh, Buenos Aires, Argentina

Commissioned in 1934 by Corina Kavanagh and completed in 1936. The building is now a listed historical monument.

Laurance Kavanagh Monument, St. Peter's, Nova Scotia

Dedicated to Laurance / Lawrence Kavanagh (1764 - 1830) a local entrepreneur and the first catholic to take a seat in the Nova Scotia Legislature. Image courtesy of Dan Wall and the Municipality of Richmond County. Inscription reads "THIS MONUMENT STANDS ON THE SITE OF THE HOME OF LAURANCE KAVANAGH, THE FIRST ROMAN CATHOLIC TO SIT AS A MEMBER IN THE HOUSE OF ASSEMBLY OF NOVA SCOTIA. ELECTED IN 1820, HE WAS ADMITTED TO THE HOUSE ON APRIL 3RD 1823, AFTER HIS FELLOW MEMBERS OBTAINED FOR HIM DISPENSATION FROM THE PROVINCIAL OATH. ERECTED BY FATHER WILLIAM B. MACLEOD, GENERAL ASSEMBLY, FOURTH DEGREE KNIGHTS OF COLUMBUS, JULY 1ST 1968. SITE DONATED BY MR. GEORGE COFFEY."

Borris House, Co. Carlow, Ireland.

Awards

Helen M. Cavanagh Award for the Best Master's Student
Presented by Illinois State University. Helen taught American History at Illinois State from 1946 until her retirement in 1971.

Helen M. Cavanagh Award for the Best Master's Theses in American and World History
Presented by Illinois State University. Helen taught American History at Illinois State from 1946 until her retirement in 1971.

Jack Kavanagh Award
Society for American Baseball Research (SABR)
The Jack Kavanagh Memorial Youth Baseball Research Award was established in 1999 by SABR in recognition of Kavanagh's writing and research achievements and his contributions to the society.

Matthew P. Cavanaugh Award
The Cavanaugh Award is presented by Holy Cross, Worcester, Massachusetts. Established in 1970, it is presented each year for outstanding services to the Holy Cross fund. Matthew was founder of the Holy Cross Alumni Fund and during his tenure as Fund Director he helped to raise over two million dollars.

Michael Cavanagh Memorial Merit Award
Awarded annually to a player on the University of New Brunswick Varsity Reds Hockey Team. Award honours Michael Cavanagh (1970-1998) a former member of the Varsity Reds. First awarded by Michaels Mother, Audrey in 1998.

Owen J. Kavanaugh Award
Presented by the International Longshoremen's Association, Great Lakes District. Origin unknown.

Patrick Kavanagh Award
Presented by the Patrick Kavanagh Society, Iniskeen, Co. Monaghan. For poets who have not yet published an individual collection of poems. Open to poets born in Ireland or of Irish nationality.

Rev. John J. Cavanaugh, C.S.C., Award
Presented by Notre Dame University, Indiana, USA
Established in 1985, the Rev. John J. Cavanaugh, CSC Award is conferred on an alumnus/alumna (living or deceased) who is or has performed outstanding service in the field of government, patriotism, public service, local, state and national politics, etc.

The "Iron Major" Award
Fordham University, New York.
In honour of Major Frank "Cav" Cavanaugh. .Awarded to the coach of the year as selected by fellow coaches.

Thomas C. Kavanagh Memorial Structural Engineering Lecture
The Pennsylvania State University.
The Kavanagh Lecture serves as a memorial to Dr. Thomas C. Kavanagh, who distinguished himself as a structural engineer and served as professor of civil engineering at the Pennsylvania State University from 1948 through 1952. During his teaching career at Penn State and other universities, Dr. Kavanagh earned the high regard and admiration of his many students, and his commitment and dedication to the profession of structural engineering serve as a standard for students and practitioners

Victor George Cavanagh Memorial Trophy
Dunedin, New Zealand
In honour of V. G. Cavanagh Jnr. and V.G. Cavanagh Snr. Presented to the winner of an annual match between Southern Rugby Football Club and Otago University

William T. Cavanaugh Memorial Award
Presented by ASTM International

Established in 1987 in memory of the late William T. Cavanaugh, ASTM chief executive officer from 1970 until his death in 1985. The award is given to a person or persons of widely recognized eminence in the voluntary standards system.

Books

The following books are wholly concerned with, or contain significant passages on, members of Clann Chaomhánach over many centuries and across many continents.

A memoir of the life and conquests of Art Mac Murrogh
M'Gee, Thomas D'Arcy
James Duffy. 1847

Airborne to Suez
Cavenagh, Alexander John McMurrough (Sandy)
W. Kimber 1965
Account of a medical officer with a parachute battalion in Cyprus and Suez.

An tAthair Caomhánach agus an Cogoadh Creidimh I gConomara
Ní Shúilleabháin, Máire
Foilseacháin Náisiúnta Teoranta. 1984

Anything Your Little Heart Desires
Boswoth, Patricia
Simon & Schuster. 1997.
A biography of Bartley Cavanaugh Crum, diplomat and lawyer by his daughter.

Art M'Morrough O'Cavanagh – Prince of Leinster
O'Byrne, M. L.
1885
A novel based on the life of King Art MacMurrough Kavanagh

Art MacMurrough Kavanagh. A Sketch of His Life and Times. Epochs of Irish History.
Leahy, E.
The Irish Messenger Office.

Australian Bushranging
White, Charles
Bookstall Co. 1921
Contains an account of the exploits of the Martin Cash, Lawrence Kavanagh and George Jones gang.

Bartholomew Cavanagh family tree
John F. Tourelle
National Library of New Zealand P q929.2 CAV TOU 1999.

Behind The Silken Curtain
Cavanaugh Crum, Bartley
Simon and Schuster. 1947.
A personal account of the Anglo-American Committee of Inquiry on Palestine.

Born Without Limbs
Kavanagh, Kenneth
Family Publications. 1989
Biography of Arthur MacMurrough Kavanagh MP

Caomhánach Pioneers in America
Kavanagh, James M. (Editor)
Private printing 2004. A collection of pioneers and early settlers in America, gathered from a variety of printed sources and the World Wide Web.

Cavanagh: Siothchain Agus Fairsinge
Healey, Mary Emmeline Wilson
1981

Cavanaugh/Kavanaugh - From Ireland to New Brunswick
Cavanaugh, Christine
Private printing, 2005.
Genealogies of all known Cavanaughs to have lived in New Brunswick, Canada, during the 19th and early 20th centuries. Information is taken from census records, provincial archives, Newspapers, church records and other sources

Cavenaugh (Cavnar) lineage book: Ireland, 997-1690, America, 1705-1960
Smith, Othela Boyd (compiled and edited by)
1960
31 leaves, [1] leaf of plates : ill. ; 28 cm. Library of Congress Call Number: CS71.C3669 1960

Climb every mountain. The life of Brother Denis M. C. Cavanagh, S.D.B., Salesian missionary in India and Burma.
Burns, Patrick
Gauhati. Provincial Office. 1980.
An account of the life of Denis Cavanagh, from novitiate in England to a missionary in India and beyond. Denis was born in Enniskillen on September 6th 1917.

Colonel Orfeur Cavenagh, Governor of the Straits Settlements, 1859-1867
Doraisingham Manonmany
Dept. of History, University of Malaya. 1961

Crash Kavanagh
Richardson, Anthony
Max Parrish, 1953.
Biography of Reg Kavanagh, a "crazy Irishman", speedway champion and stunt-driver.

Dermot, King of Leinster and the Foreigners
Furlong, Nicholas
Anvil Books. 1973
Excellent account of the life and times of Diarmuit Mac Murchada. This work goes someway to restoring the reputation of Diarmuit.

Dermot MacMorrogh or the conquest of Ireland
Adams, John Quincy
Carter, Hendee and Co. 1832
A historical tale in four cantos by the former American president.

Diarmait King of Leinster
Furlong, Nicholas
Mercier Press. ISBN 1856355055
Updated and revised edition of Furlongs previous book 'Dermot, King of Leinster and the Foreigners'

Edward Kavanagh: Catholic, Statesman, Diplomat from Maine 1795-1844
Lucey, William Leo
Marshall Jones Company. 1946
Excellent biography of the first Catholic from New England to serve in a state legislature and the federal House of Representatives. Also the first catholic state governor to serve in US.

English action, Irish reaction: the MacMurrough Kavanaghs
Moore, Donal
Dept. of Modern History, St. Patrick's College. 1987

Finding Connections
Kavanagh, Patrick Joseph
Hutchinson. 1990
Travelogue from Carlow to Australia and New Zealand to learn more about ancestors.

Handicaps: six (biographical) studies, of Beethoven, Mary Lamb, R.L. Stevenson, Arthur Kavanagh, Henry Fawcett, W.E. Henley in relation to their infirmities
MacArthy, Mary
Longmans. 1936
Contains a chapter on Arthur MacMurrrough Kavanagh MP

Heath and Begorrey – The Cavanaugh Saga
Smith, H. O.
Private Printing 1997.
Events surrounding the investigation into the murder of Tom Cavanaugh at Brownlee Creek, Idaho in 1917.

Historical Reminiscences of O'Byrnes, O'Tooles, O'Kavanaghs, and other Irish Chieftains
O'Byrne, Clarinda Mary
London. Privately printed, 1843
Contains a handful of references to the Kavanaghs.

History and Genealogies of the Families of Miller, Woods, Harris, Wallace, Maupin, Oldham, Kavanaugh, and Brown
Miller, W. H.
Privately Printed. 1907
The history and genealogies of several families including Miller, Woods, Harris, Wallace, Maupin, Oldham, Kavanaugh and Brown. Part VII contains notes on descendants of Charles & Philemon Kavanaugh of Virginia.

How I Won The Victoria Cross
Kavanagh, Thomas Henry
Ward & Lock. 1860
Personal account of the siege and relief of Lucknow.

In The Shadow Of Mount Leinster
Kavanagh, Art
1993
A History of Ui Cinnsealaigh with notes on Kavanaghs.

Julia Kavanagh in her times. Novelist and biographer, 1824-1877
Forsyth. Michael
Open University, 1999
A PhD thesis on Julia and her works. This item is only available from the British Library Document Supply Centre reference number DXN031282.

Kavanaugh-Bear Lineage Memorial
Kavanaugh Bear, Sophia E.

Laurance Kavanagh
Rankin, D. J.
1941

Reprinted from the Annual Report of the Canadian Catholic Historical Association

Laurance Kavanagh (1764 – 1830) – His Life and Times
Traboulsee, Anthony
Brodie Printing Service. 1962

Le Général Cavaignac. Un dictateur républicain
Ibos, Général.
Hachette.1930

Local DJ. A Rock & Roll History
Cavanaugh, Peter C.
Xlibris. April 2002. ISBN: 1401041639.
An autobiography which captures the spirit, events and people encountered while spreading the gospel of Rock and Roll in America.

Missouri Ordeal, 1862-1864. Diaries of Willard Hall Mendenhall.
Frazier, Margaret Mendenhall
Carl Boyer Newhall 1985,
Mendenhall was a pro Southern non-combatant, living in Lafayette Co., MO. The diaries cover the period from the beginning of 1862, through the year, most of the next year, and a portion of 1864. Includes a Kavanaugh genealogy.

Mold of Fortune: Lionel B. Kavanagh and The First Half-Century Of Plastics
Kean, Sumner
Private printing. Standard Tool Co., Leominster, Mass. 1959

No Hero in the House. Diarmait MacMurchada and the Coming of the Normans to Ireland
Martin, F. X.
National University of Ireland, 1975

One Teacher's Memories
Cavanaugh, William R.

Private printing. 1984.
Recollections of a schoolteacher in St. Thomas, Ontario, Canada.

Portraits in Leadership
O'Brien, Barry
Eigse Na Mainistreach, Fermoy, 1980
Contains a chapter on Art MacMurrough Kavanagh (1357-1417)

Portraits in Leadership Part II
O'Brien, Barry
Eigse Books, 1982
Contains a chapter on Dermot MacMurrough.

Patrick Kavanagh: A Biography
Quinn, Antoinette
Gill & Macmillan. 2003
ISBN: 0717136434
Biography of the poet.

Plain Talk: The Legacy of William E. Cavanaugh at ASTM
Stremba, Henry J. & Wayne P. Ellis
American Society for Testing and Materials. 1990
William was chief executive of the ASTM from 1970-1985 and this book examines his contribution to the organization.

Raíces Celtas – Relato Historico
Ortigűela, Raúl
1997
ISBN 950-43-9832-4
A history and genealogy of Edward Cavanagh and his descendants in Argentina. Founder of the town of Cavanagh in Córdoba.

Reminiscences of an Indian official
Cavenagh, Sir Orfeur
W. H.Allen. 1884

Recollection of his time in India and as Governor of the Straits Settlements

Rose Kavanagh and her Verses
Russell, Matthew
Gill & Son: Dublin and Waterford, 1909.
Some poems from Rose otherwise known as "Uncle Remus"

Sacred Keeper - A Biography of Patrick Kavanagh
Kavanagh, Peter
ISBN: 0915032325
Univ Pr of New England. 1981
Biography of the poet.

Saint Moling Luachra
De Paor, Máire B.
The Columbia Press, 2001
ISBN 1 85607 338 6

Scotland Yard Past and Present: Experiences of Thirty-seven Years
Cavanagh, T.A.
1893
A Chief Inspector's memories of 37 years in the police.

Sharing our story: a genealogy of the Cavanaugh-White family in northwest Iowa
Unknown
1980
Library of Congress Control #:82165352. Call Number CS71.C3669 1980

The Adventures Of Martin Cash.
Burke, James Lester (Editor)
Mercury Steam Press Office. 1870.
The adventures of a group notorious bushrangers including Lawrence Kavanagh as told by Martin Cash to Burke.

The Ancient House of Kavanaugh - as represented in Ireland, England, France, Prussia, and America
   Poynter Kavanaugh, Anna T.
   1908.

The Cavanough Ancestry
   Holdorf, Pat (Complied By)
   1988
   Family tree of the descendants of the first fleeter, Owen Cavanough

The Cruise of the RYS Eva
   Kavanagh, Arthur MacMurrough.
   Hodges Smith and Co. 1865
   Exploits in the Mediterranean aboard his beloved yacht.

The descendands of Micahel and Maggie Kavanagh of Croghan.
   Kavanagh, Shelly
   Private printing. 1997
   Family trees & photographs 32 pages.

The French Republic under Cavaignac, 1848
   de Luna, Frederick A.
   Princeton University Press. 1969

The Humility of Greatness
   Kavanaugh, Ken
   Xlibris Corporation, 2002
   ISBN: 1401064930
   A biography of the authors father, Ken Snr., a decorated WWII pilot and football player who starred in teams for the LSU Tigers and the New York Giants.

The Incredible Mr. Kavanagh
   McCormick, Donald
   Putnam & Co. 1960
   An excellent account of the life of Arthur MacMurrough Kavanagh MP

The Jungle Hunter
Cavanaugh, Joe
Safari Press. 2000
Exploits of a jungle hunter in South America

The Kavanagh Empire: the merchant family of St. Peter's
MacEwen, Harvey A.
Sydney, N.S.: University College of Cape Breton Press. 1996
A monograph on the family of Lawrence Kavanagh and his descendants. According to the UCCB this was never published and Mr. MacEwen passed away in 2000.

The Kavanaghs. Kings of leinster
Kavanagh, Art
Irish Family Names. 2003.
ISBN 0 9538585 1 5
An examination of the Kavanaghs and their history.

The Kavanaghs and The Vaughans
Patricia Kavanagh Wamser
lulu.com
The history of the author's family through several generations. 106 pages.

The Life & Adventures of Mrs. Christian Davies, commonly called Mother Ross
Dafoe, Daniel
Original published in 1740. Republished with an introduction by the Hon. Sir John Fortescue by Peter Davies Ltd. in 1928. There is some dispute over whether Dafoe was the original author. Recounts the adventures of a woman, Christian "Kit" Cavanagh (1667 – 1739) who served in the English army disguised as a man.

The Life and Times of H. H. Kavanaugh, D.D. one of the Bishops of the Methodist Episcopal Church, South
Redford, A. H.
1884

The story of Bishop Hubbard Hinde Kavanaugh with notes on other family members.

The Right Honourable Arthur MacMurrough Kavanagh
Steele, Sarah L. (compiled by)
Macmillan and Co. 1891

The Roman Catholic Church In Cobequid, Acadie 1692-1755 And Colchester County, Nova Scotia 1828-1978, Also Savage Island And The Kavanaghs 1778-1830
Ormond, Douglas S. 1979
Monograph containing an essay on the Savage Island Kavanaghs. National Library of Canada AMICUS No. 5987282

The Song of Dermot and The Earl
Open, Goddard Henry (translator)
Oxford. 1892
An account of Diarmud Mac Murchada and Richard de Clare.

The Very Extraordinary Life and Singular Characteristics of Mr. Cavanagh the celebrated Fasting Man
Cavenagh, Bernard.
C. Lowe, 1841
Available at the British Library.

Transvaal Travels of an American Insurance Agent
Cavanagh, J. A.
Sealy Bryers and Walker. 1900
Recollection of adventures in Africa at the turn of the century.

Venerable Archdeacon Cavanagh, Pastor of Knock 1867 – 1897
Ua Cadhain, Liam
Knock Shrine Society. 1953

Violence in the Model City: The Cavanagh Adminstration, Race Relations and the Detroit Riot of 1967
Fine, Sidney
The University of Michigan Press 1 989.
Describes a turbulent episode for Mayor Jerome P. Cavanagh's administration

We Merry Peasants
Kavanagh, Muriel.
Howard Timmins, 1963.
A Kavanagh family buy a farm in South Africa.

Wilderness Homesteaders
Kavanaugh, Ethel
Caxton Printers. 1950
The adventures of Ethel and her daughter Dorothy. Both headed into the Alaskan wilderness to establish a homestead.

Sir Orfeur Cavenagh (1820 –1891)

Governor of the Straits Settlements 1859-1867. Image courtesy of Doreen Cavenagh Beattie.

Manuscripts & Papers - America

Cavanah, Frances - Papers (1968-1969)

University of Oregon.

Francis was a popular author of children's history books. Contains manuscripts, books, and correspondence with publishers

Cavanagh, Joseph H. - Collection

University of Alaska Fairbanks.

Diary of a journey to Alaska-Yukon, 1898 - 1901. One folder collection containing three small handwritten notebooks, tied with a red ribbon. Extract: "Eagle City, Alaska. May 16th. Seven o'clock breakfast. 8:05 River rising. Not much ice running. We are once more under the Stars and Stripes. "Three cheers for old Glory" was given with a will. Sighted Eagle City at just 11:00 A.M. This is a nice town site, but no town by a damn site. Population 500, four stores, the A.E.A.C., the N.A.T.&T., and the S.Y.T. Ces. Co. of St. S. Infantry 7th, Col Ray in charge. One large saw mill owned by the Gov. Two saloons, two laundries, one private saw mill."

Cavanna, Betty – Papers (1929-1993)

#DG0167. University of Southern Mississippi.

de Grummond Collection. Papers of childrens author Betty Cavanna (1909 - 2001). Autobiographical Material (1929-1946 and undated) Biographical Material (1929-1981) Correspondence (1946-1986 and undated) Photographs and Portraits (1940-1981 and undated) Awards and Honors (1966-1976 and undated) Public Appearances (1948-1985 and undated) Critical Reviews (1945-1987 and undated) Scrapbook (1946-1955 and undated) Financial Records (1944-1986) Promotional Materials (1959-1983 and undated) Miscellaneous Personal Items (1956-1977 and undated) Academic Papers.

Cavanaugh, Unknown. - Oral interview - Delaware in the Depression
Collection Number 179. University Of Delaware.
Interviewed by Myron Blackman.

Cavanaugh, Arthur – Collection (1966-1970)
Howard Gotlieb Archival Research Center
American author and drama critic; b. 1926.

Cavanaugh, Auxilius William – Papers (1924-1964)
Manhattan College. – Archives, Bronx, NY
Photographs, 1924-1964; scrapbook for 50th anniversary celebration of Brother A. William's membership in Brothers of the Christian Schools.

Cavanaugh, Francis P. - Papers (1930s-1968)
IN 46556. University of Notre Dame Archives.
Francis (1900-1982) was Professor of sociology (1928-1932) and (1934-1943), and Dean of the College of Arts and Letters at the University of Notre Dame. Papers contain sermons and speeches by Cavanaugh and a draft of a letter by Cavanaugh to Estes Kefauver on juvenile delinquency.

Cavanaugh, James H. – Papers
Gerald R. Ford Library, Ann Arbor, MI.
A fragmentary subject file on emergency preparedness, social security, option memoranda to the president, and other matters. Also an extensive chronological file of correspondence on all aspects of Cavanaugh's duties. 2 linear feet (ca. 4,000 pages) James served as Associate Director for Human Resources and Deputy Assistant to the President for Domestic Affairs from 1974 to 1976.

Cavanaugh, John Joseph – Papers (1952-1979)
University of Notre Dame Archives.
John was Prefect of religion (1933-1938), vice-president (1940- 1946), and president (1946-1952) at the University

of Notre Dame. Papers include correspondence with members of the Joseph Kennedy family (Rose, Edward, Jacqueline, Joe, and Kathleen), clippings, a plaque given Cavanaugh by the Commerce Council, a scrapbook from the testimonial for Cavanaugh by the Notre Dame Club, Los Angeles, 1952, a copy of the homily delivered by Father Hesburgh at Cavanaugh's funeral, and photographs.

Cavanaugh, John Joseph – Interview

John F. Kennedy Library & Museum.

Kennedy family friend, associate; Roman Catholic priest; vice president (1940-1946), president (1946-1952), University of Notre Dame; director, Notre Dame Foundation (1952-1959). 1966. 21 pp.

Cavanaugh, John W. – Papers (1891-1935)

University of Notre Dame Archives

John was Professor of rhetoric (1892-1905) and president (1905- 1919) of the University of Notre Dame. Contents include personal concerning life at Notre Dame, John's work with the Liquor Control Board of the State of Indiana. A diary (1908); sermons, speeches, class notes, writings, clippings, scrapbook; a draft of Knute Rockne's autobiography.

Cavanaugh, John & Son- papers (1897-1902)

Winterthur Museum, Garden, and Library, Winterthur, DE 19735.

Invoice book of John Cavanagh & Son of Boonville, in Oneida County, New York, covering 1987-1902, evidently a shoe store.

Cavanaugh, Miles J. - Literary papers (1921-1935)

Collection 349. Montana State University.

Literary manuscripts and newspaper clippings created or collected by Miles Cavanaugh by Martha C. Hubbard of Spokane, Washington. Miles Jordan Cavanaugh was a prominent Butte, Montana attorney and businessman.

Born in Denver, Colorado on October 3, 1865, Miles was the son of a miner and prospector of the same name. Included are: autobiographical sketches of himself and his father; correspondence primarily with Grace Stone Coates regarding poetry; speeches on Montana history, politics, and other topics delivered to fraternal orders, political rallies, and social gatherings; poetry written by Cavanaugh and others.

Cavanaugh Family

929.273 C314c. LDS Family History Library

Daniel Cavanaugh (1817-1880), son of Jean Cavanaugh and Anne McKay, was born in Ireland. Married Dora Kerwin (1831-ca. 1872), also born in Ireland, daughter of Jean Kerwin and Juditte Kerevan. Supplement: Update, 1994, xv, 23 p. Compiled by Merritt A. Cavanaugh.

Dumfries settlers--Cavanagh, McLean (MacLean), Pictou County, Nova Scotia

Call no. 1133. LDS Family History Library

James Cavanagh emigrated from County Sligo, Ireland to Pictou, Nova Scotia in 1821, settling in Laggan, Nova Scotia. 1 pedigree chart; 78 x 98 cm. folded to 20 x 25 cm. A supplement is also available: Call no. 929.271 A1 no. 222.

Kavanagh, Edward – Collection

Georgetown University.

Edward Kavanagh was the thirteenth governor of Maine, serving from 1843 to 1844. Contains correspondence, news clippings (1834-1908) including obituaries and articles on his election.

Kavanagh, Michael James P. - Papers

Mss. 2766. Boston Public Library

Collection covers the years 1910-1957. Correspondence dealing with theatrical matters and family matters between Michael James P. Kavanagh (d. 1967), theatre manager, his wife Antoinette (Walker) Stewart Kavanagh

(1874-1970), an actress and playwright, her father Charles Walker (1892-1943), her son Walker Stewart and other family members. 450 items.

Kavanaugh, F. E. – Papers (1860-1887)

MSS 233 BC. The University of New Mexico.

Dr. F.E. Kavanaugh was the owner and operator of a store in Cubero, New Mexico (a small town located sixty miles west of Albuquerque) in the mid- to late- 1800s as well as being a member of the territorial legislature. This collection is comprised of two leather-bound ledgers, the first of which documents the accounts of military personnel by name, rank, and purchases. The second ledger consists of a considerable section entitled "Days Doings of Whiting Ranch." These "doings" are mainly from 1885-1886 and include reports of having seen the first swallow of spring, letters written to his mother, maps of what plants and crops are planted in which parts of the garden, expenses, the weather etc.

Kavanaugh Bros. – Account Books

RLG Union Catalog Record ID: DEWAV000071007-A. Winterthur Museum, Garden, and Library, Winterthur Museum & Country Estate, Winterthur, DE 19735.

The Kavanaugh Brothers ran a saloon in Harrisonburg, Virginia. In 1905, the Kavanaugh Hotel opened, which may have been another family enterprise. Two account books, one covering 1904-1914 and the other 1904-1906, listing sales of alcoholic beverages. The accounts are arranged by customers name. The Kavanaughs sold whiskey, brandy, wine, sherry, beer, and yellow stone by the pint, quart, or gallon.

Kavanaugh Family - Papers

#332. Eastern Kentucky University

A 46 page typed document on the Kavanaugh family beginning with Philemon Cavanaugh who was born in Ireland about 1690. It is very heavily footnoted with wills, letters and deeds transcribed. Photocopy of a court case in Virginia which includes a copy of the will of the above Philemon Cavanaugh in 1743. (11 pages) A brief history of the Kavanaugh family copied from the Miller manuscripts. This history of the family begins with a granddaughter of the above Philemon and follows her children, so except for the first page this document is actually about the Duncan family (4 pages) News clipping of the Cavanaugh family. (1 page)

Kavanaugh, James - Diary.

The Percival R. Jeffcott Collection, Box 8. Centre for Pacific Northwest Studies, Western Washington University.

James (1826 - 1885) was a sheriff for Whatcom and a US Marshal. His diary contains daily entries for the 1860's and is regarded as an important insight into pioneer life in the Pacific Northwest.

Kavanaugh, Hubbard Hinde - Letters (1864-1865)

Collection #1F67M-62. University of Kentucky Libraries - Special Collections and Archives.

Hubbard's correspondence with his wife Annie describing some experiences of the civil war and his opposition to it. Hubbard was at the time a confederate chaplain to the 6th Kentucky Infantry, also known as the "Orphan Brigade"

Kavanaugh, William H. (1844-1926) - Papers (c.1900-1926)

SUNP 1189. University of Missouri.

The papers of Confederate soldier William Kavanaugh of Missouri, consisting primarily of his c.1912 memoir of service with the 2nd Missouri Infantry which he joined at Nevada, Missouri, in 1861, and later with the 2nd and 6th Consolidated Missouri Infantry. Kavanaugh participated in the battles of Lexington, Pea Ridge, Corinth, Vicksburg, and Franklin, Tennessee, November 1864, where he was taken prisoner. Included in the papers are Kavanaugh's pension papers

Kavanough Collection.
Archives & Collections of the University of Mississippi.

Two ledgers- one dated 1854-56, the other 1853-1858. Believed to be from a tavern, as most of the transactions were for drinks or gallons of whiskey. There were a few other things sold such as tobacco and the occasional livestock. Originally believed to be from Aberdeen, MS but there is a late 19th century inscription which reads, "This book came from Houston, Chickasaw County, Mississippi, [F.S.] Kavanough."

Ministerial Orders and Ordination Certificates
Bridwell Library - Southern Methodist University

Contains a number of orders and licenses for, and by Bishop Hubbard Hinde Kavanaugh. e.g. Kavanaugh, Hubbard H., Local Preacher's License, 1823, September 19, Methodist Episcopal Church, Kentucky Conference, Augusta District, signed by Jonathan Stamper, presiding elder, at Shockley's Flemming Circuit. ADS; Kavanaugh, Hubbard H., License to solemnize the rites of matrimony in the State of Kentucky, 1826, March 6, signed by Clifton Hall, Justice, Noah C. Summers, Acting Deputy, George F. Pope, Clerk, Bullitt County, Kentucky. ADS

War of 1812 in the South Collection
MSS 557. Historic New Orleans Collection, 533 Royal Street, New Orleans.

Folder #35.

Provision return for men in the company of the Troop Cavalry of Capt. Charles Kavanaugh, Tennessee Mounted Cavalry. 1813 June 19.

Folder #129.

Request by Maj. Charles Kavanaugh, [Tennessee Volunteer Mounted Gunmen], Washington, [Mississippi Territory], for payment to John Blevins, [Mississippi Territory]. 1815 Apr. 23.

Folder #131.

Request by Maj. Charles Kavanaugh, [TVM] Gunmen, Washington, Mississippi Territory, to Maj. Genl. Andrew Jackson, Nashville, to pay rent to Dr. Cowles Mead for a house used as a hospital.

Manuscripts & Papers - Australia

Cavanagh Papers

Clarence River Historical Society. Grafton, NSW

Family tree for Francis Cavanagh & Ellen Whalen/Wheelen. Marriage cert.: Frank Arthur Cavanaugh & Mary Ann Bauer (1914) Death register: Frank Arthur Cavanaugh (1961). Marriage cert Francis Cavanagh & Ellen Wheelen (1832) Birth cert.: George Arthur Cavanaugh (1860) Death notice for Alice Kavanagh wife of Joseph Kavanagh (1911) Death notice for Hilda Mary Kavanagh wife of Jim (1995)

Cavanough, Thomas (Sergeant)

PR00194. Australian War Memorial Collections.

12 items. Diaries describing service in Australia, Great Britain, North Africa, Syria, Papua New Guinea and Borneo, written 1939-1945; a book of comments on many aspects of service particularly home front, AIF-CMF relations, Americans, Japanese, written 1945. Private papers - permission required to copy.

Cavanough, Mike

MSS1236. Australian War Memorial Collections.

1 item. Autobiographical account titled "What some daddies did in the war", describing his enlistment in the second AIF, posting to Malaya, outbreak of war with Japan, the defence of Malaya and later Java, captivity including work with 'A' Force on the Burma-Thailand railway, transfer to Japan and work in the hospital at Omutu. Copying not permitted.

Kavanagh, Jack – Papers (1899-1982)

Noel Butlin Archives Centre, Australian National University.

Dep. #P12. Political and personal papers, including correspondence, diaries, note books, press cuttings, printed material and photographs. Includes records re the original Old Age & Invalid Pensioners Association of NSW.

Dep. #Z400. Political and personal papers. Diaries, notebooks, correspondence, press cuttings, photographs, and printed material are all included. Includes records relating to the original Old age & Invalid Pensioners Association of NSW.

Manuscripts & Papers - Canada

Cavenagh Family - Collection (1790-1893)
SC023. University of Victoria, BC, Canada.

60 cm of textual records. Members of the Cavenagh family were British Army officers and officers of the East India Company serving primarily in the Straits Settlements, Malaya, Singapore, and Penang. The fonds consists of commissions, certificates, orders, proclamations and other documents of Sir Orfeur Cavenagh, James Gordon Cavenagh, and Gordon Cavenagh; correspondence between Matthew Cavenagh Kinsey (Canada East) and R. Calvert (London), 1864-1867; letterbooks of Henry William Dent, 1881-1893, and Sir Orfeur Cavenagh; private letterbooks and diaries, 1837-1888; and printed material. http://gateway.uvic.ca/

Cavanagh Family - tree, history
F-1019. Goulbourn Museum.

2064 Huntley Road, Stanley's Corners, Ontario. http://www.goulbournmuseum.ca

Cavanagh / Cavanaugh family papers
Region of Peel Archives, Brampton, Ontario, Canada. William Perkins Bull Collection, Box 43, File 846.

Item 1: Joseph Cavanaugh of Centreville, Albion township, Peel County is shown on a list of Stallion Owners in Peel County for the year 1922 with 1 Clyde. Item 2: a transcript of a marriage record from a church (Roman Catholic?) not named which reads: 6 October 1881 – Patrick McCowan, age 27, of Adjala township now of Parry Sound, to Mary Grady, of Albion, daughter of Paul Grady and Mary Cavanaugh. Witnesses: Wm. Bingham and Catherine Sweeney. Item 3: a transcript of a marriage record from a church (Roman Catholic?) not named which reads: 7 January 1847, 3 publications of Bans and no impediment, Lawrence Cavanagh and Ann

McEvoy, both of the township of Vaughan. Item 4: a transcript of a baptismal record from a church (Roman Catholic?) not named which reads: 8 April 1849 – Mary Ann, aged 5 days, daughter of Edward Murphy and Jane Cavanagh, of Toronto Gore township, Peel County.

Kavanagh – Misc. Records

Osgoode Township Historical Society and Museum, Ontario.

Limited records from census for 1861 and 1871. Includes variations such Kavinah, Cavnagh and Cavinawe. First names include Peter, Edward, William, Garret, Thomas, James, Katherine and a female with only the initial P. Death record for a James Cavanaugh dated Dec. 1916 and a listing of the burial plot in the St. John's Church Records. Six obituary notices on file for Molly, Terence, Rita under Cavanagh and Mary William and Rita under Kavanagh. Society Newsletters, Vol. 13 No. 4, 1987 - Mrs. Sylvester Cavanagh mother of Jerome P. Kavanaugh (mayor of Detriot), and Vol. 17, No. 11, 1991- reference is to a court case involving James Kavanaugh a settler in Osgoode Township.

Kavanagh, William – Papers

West Hants Historical Society, Windsor, Nova Scotia.

Also known as the George Stanley. Kavanagh was the last man to be hanged in Hants County in 1906. Born in Roscrea, Co. Tipperary. Synopsis of the Evidence, Court Transcripts, Statements, Coroners report of Kavanaghs body, Written evidence. Sent letters. Unsent letters.

Kavanagh, Robert J. - fonds

UA RG 353a. University of New Brunswick.

Dean of graduate studies and professor of electrical engineering at UNB, Robert J. Kavanagh, the son of Alexander and Mary Elsie (Taylor) Kavanagh, was born 7 October 1931 at Whitchurch, Hants, England. He attended the Andover Grammar School (England) before enrolling in the University of New Brunswick, where he earned a B.Sc. in 1953. He continued his studies at the University of Toronto, completing a M.A.Sc. and a Ph.D. in electrical engineering in 1954 and 1957 respectively. He graduated from the Imperial College, London with a D.I.C. in 1960. On 17 September 1956, he married Millicent Constance McRae, and they raised two children, Stephen and Judith. Series #1: Graduate studies and research, UNB; Series #2: Graduate studies and research, engineering; Series #3: Research grants and research funds; Series #4: Correspondence with James O. Dineen.

Kavenaugh, James – memorial poem

Canadiana: 886025702. National Archives of Canada

To the memory of James Kavenaugh, who was wounded in the battle for freedom at Toronto, on the evening of the 5th of December, and died with the wound on the 10th, in the year of our Lord, 1837, aged 43 years, 7 months, and 2 days

Manuscripts & Papers - Ireland

Kavanagh / Cavanagh / Cavenagh Papers
MSS 5927. National Library of Ireland

Notebook 1

Inventory of some of the papers at Borris House, Co. Carlow.

Transcription of some of the letters belonging to Baron James Kavanagh.

Notebook 2

Transcription of some of the letters belonging to Baron James Kavanagh relating to late 1780's.

Notebook 3

Regiments of Imperial Austria.

Notebook 4

Irish in Imperial Regiments of Europe including Bohemia, Galicia, Croatia, Austria, Poland and Germany.

Notebook 5

Scientific notes. Notes from books related to Irish matters. Knights of Malta. Cromwell in Ireland. Maps of Ireland, Dublin and Drogheda.

Kavanagh / Cavanagh / Cavenagh Papers
MSS 8049. National Library of Ireland

Folder #1.

General history.

Folder #2.

Memorials & Relics, Murtagh Oge Cavenagh, Mabel? Daugh. Of Donough Kavanagh

Folder #3.

Coats of Arms. Mack Murrough, Nathaniel Cavanagh, Seal of von Kavanagh, Mauritium von Kawanagk, Haus? Von Kawanagk, O CAUANAGH of Berlin.

Folder #6.

Brayn Na Storake, Morgan Preussick.

Folder #9.

Ballyloo Castle.

Folder #10.

Arms of Mortoghe Oge Cavanagh of Garkhill.

Kavanagh / Cavanagh / Cavenagh Papers

MSS 8051. National Library of Ireland

Folder #1.

Kavanaghs in the Imperial Service in Austria. Extensive research for, and a copy of a paper for the Royal Society of Antiquaries of Ireland: Clan Kavanagh in the Imperial Service. By Colonel Cavenagh, Fellow. Read 27 July 1920. Paper contains notes and corrections and a pedigree of Kavanaghs in imperial service.

Notes on Lt. General Maurice Kavanagh – officer in the service of the Margrave of Ansbach Brandenberg 1702 - 1717. Reference to letters by him at Nürnberg. Appointment of Maurice Kavanagh as Major General at Liege. Lists kavanaghs serving in the Ansbach regiment in 1717 : Major General Maurice Kavanagh, Lieut Colonel Felix Kavanagh, Capt. Sylvester Kavanagh, Lieut. Arthur Kavanagh, Terence Kavanagh, Francis Kavanagh, Ignatius Kavanagh.

Contains possible copies of signatures.

Copy of coat of arms for Lieut General Maurice Kavanagh attached to his letters in the State Archive at Nürnberg, Bavaria.

Copy of arms for von Kavanagh of the Brandenberg Anspach Regt. In the Saxon service abt 1744 from the State Archives at Dresden.

Copy of unknown arms.

Small colour portrait of soldier in "Cavanahs Regt. 7th Regt Austrian Cavalry, curasiers."

2 x Small watercolour of the castle at Mali-Tabor.

Folder #2.

Extensive notes and correspondence on Irishmen in the service of Austria. Mentions a Moritz Kavanagh as Colonel in Chief of the 4th Upper Austrian Salazburg Dragoon Regt. In 1786.

Under the Army List for 1823 is listed Baron Henry Kavanagh as Lt. Colonel of the 62 Regt. and John v. Kavanagh as 2nd Lieut., 6th Hussars.

Under the Army List for 1867 is listed Henry Paul Baron Kavanagh de Ballyane Cadet 55th Regt.

Folder #3.

Notes and correspondence (Englisg, French, German) relating to Austria. Letters from Mali Tabor relating to Kavanaghs in Austria. List of Kavanagh officers by rank & regiment

Possible copies of signatures.

Letter in German from Kriegsarchiv containing family information on Kavanaghs in Austria. Names include Dermitius Baron Kavanagh, Karl Freiherr von Kavanagh, Johann Baptist Kavanagh, Moriz Grafen von Kavanagh, Jakob Freiherr von Kavanagh, Simon Henry "auch" Heinrich Ludwig Freiherr von Kavanagh Ballyane, Heinrich Paul Freiherr von Kavanagh Ballyane

Extensive correspondence (German) from the Koenigliches Kreisarchiv Nürnberg

Correspondence from James Kavanagh at Mali Tabor

Folder #4.

List of officers. Correspondence (German) with Dresden archives. Research performed into Kavanagh regiments on behalf of W. O. Cavenagh. Mentions Maurice de Kavanagh, Felise de Kavanagh, Charle de Kavanagh, Sylvester de Kavanagh, Edmund de Kavanagh, Terentius de Kavanagh, Remond de Kavanagh, Artus? de Kavanagh.

Copy of article "Irish Clan Regiments" by Demetrius C. Boulger which appeared in the Fortnightly Review Sept. 1918, p.443. Lists Colonel Charles Kavanagh and his son

Morgan at Cork; Maurice de Kavanagh & Dermot & Terence in Austria.

Copy of letter concerning the return of the Kavanagh regiment to the Margrave of Brandenburg: "We have graciously decided to give back the three Anspacher regiments Schmettan, Castelli, and Kavanagk to the Margrave of Anspach in order to relieve our War expenditure and because we do not need them any more. Warsaw 7th, January 1717. Signed Augustus Rex."

Rank List of Commisioned Officers of the Hon. Major General von Kavanagk's foot regiment: Major General Maurice de Kavanagk 12, July 1713; Lt. Colonel Felix de Kavanagk, 20, April, 1713; Captain Charle de Kavanagk, 20, April, 1710; Captain Slyvester de Kavanagk, 15, March, 1712; Lieutenant Edmond de Kavanagk, 1, November, 1712; Lieutenant Terentius de Kavangk, 1, April, 1713; Ensign Remond de Kavanagk, 2, February, 1712; Ensign Artus de Kavanagk, 11 April, 1713. Stated as a true copy of the original lying at the Royal Polish and Electoral Saxon War Office.

Folder #5.

List of manuscripts. Correspondence (French) from archives at Ostend. Notes on battles at Cork & Kinsale.

Folder #6.

unavailable due to microfilming.

Folder #7.

Lieut. Colonel Terence Kavanagh – Prince Xaviers Infantry Regt. In the service of the King of Poland & Elector of Saxony. Pedigree. Will from the Bavarian State Archives. Correspondence (German) from State Archive, Nürnberg

Felix Kavanagh. Letter mentioning the murderer Colonel Felix von Cavanagh; the search for the birthday of Johann Alexander Heinrich Gavernack and the possibility Felix is his father. Correspondence (German) from Nürnberg archives. Entry for Colonel Felix von Kavanagh from the Death Register at Swabach Vol 1735-1747 p.36

Pages from journal of the Royal Society of Antiquaries, outlining the last will of Colonel Terence Kavanagh. Also a note on John b. Kavanagh, Baron Gniditz.

Folder #8.

Cavenagh & Kavanagh in France. Correspondence (French). Arms of Cavane (de) Irlande Quarterings 1st: A tree entwined with a serpent, and an arm issuing from a cloud holding a sword whose point transfixes the reptiles jaw; 2nd: a horseman, sword in hand riding over an arm grasping a dagger; 3rd: Two lions rampant supporting a gauntlet; 4th: a tower surmounted by a flag flying and two mullets, atop a mass of masonry.

Notes on General Louis Eugene Cavaignac.

List of various Cavenaghs, Kavanaghs

Folder #9.

Misc. papers and Irish Regiments and Officers in French Service

Kavanagh / Cavanagh / Cavenagh Papers

MSS 8052. National Library of Ireland

Folder #1.

Religious houses founded by MacMurrough and Clan Kavanagh. Inscriptions from tombs at Old Leighlin, Report on Ferns by the Commissioners of Public Works. Monastery of Blessed Virgin Mary at Ferns (with watercolour). Baltinglass Abbey, Co. Wicklow (with watercolour) Nunnery of St. Mary's, Dublin. Priory of All Hallows, Dublin. Augustinian Abbey and Dominican Priory at Clonmines (with watercolour) Franciscan Friary at Enniscorthy founded by Donnell Reagh. Painiting of "Enniscorthy Friary Brooch" The Cistercian House of Kilkenny and the Abbey of Duiske. The Abbey of St. Molimgs (with watercolour). Old Leighlin Cathedral.

Folder #2.

Irish Families in Belgium. Copy of "Irish Famalies in Flanders" and "Irish Families at Bruges". Notes on various families and manuscripts at Bruges.

Folder #3.

Notes on the families of Gilligans & Redmonds. Family chart for Joseph Magennis Baron von Atter. Family chart for Garret Redmond of Fethard, Co. Wexford. Profile of Sir Thomas Stukeley – "An Elizabethan Adventurer" (8 pages)

Folder #4.

Selected index of Books & Poems relatding to Clan Cavenagh. Book of St. Moling (with B&W photos). Book of Leinster (with 2 ink Sketches) The Book of Rights – "practically an Irish Doomsday Book of the 10th Century) The Song of Dermot & The Earl. Notes on Eileen Aroon.

Folder #5

Notes on churches and saints associated with the Clan.

Folder #6.

Arms of MacMurrough. Arms of selected Irish provinces, counties & towns. Irish emblems. The Five Bloods – O'Neill, O'Conor, O'Brien, O'Melaghlins and MacMurrough. Free State stamps. Irish sea ports. Geological History of Ireland. The Irish Elk. The Rowan or Mountain Ash.

Folder #7.

Paper – "MaGennis of Iveagh" Densely packed notes (unknown) Officers in Austrian Army. Dermot MacMurrough. Roll of Casualties & Honour – The Great War. Memorial article on James Cavanagh – fives player. Quotations from various historical works related to the Clan. Trace of unknown coat of arms. Photograps of Leighlin Cathedral. Various arms - Codd, Codde, Turner, Shortall. Newspaper clipping listing pardons granted in 1601. St. Molyng. Reputation of Clan Kavanagh. Notes (unknown)

Book of Leinster - Leabhar na Nuachongbhála
MSS# 1339 (H 2 18). Trinity College, Dublin.

MSS 1367
Trinity College, Dublin.

p.118 Poem by Caroll Og O'Daly, on Elinor, daughter of Sir Murrough Kavanagh.

MSS 1361
Trinity College, Dublin.

p.22 On the hardships of Diarmid Kavanagh and Gerald O'Byrne when driven to wander in woods and Mountains. 8 lines, by the "Caillech Menntánach"

MSS 171
Genealogical Office

Pedigree of Kavanagh alias Mac Morrough, kings of Leinster c1800 BC – 1818 AD

MSS 161
Genealogical Office

Pedigree of Cavanagh, Barons Balyane 1553 – 1766 for Charles Cavanagh, Governor of Prague.

MSS 162
Genealogical Office

Pedigree of Cavanagh of Burrish, Co. Carlow, Barons Ballyane 1553 – 1751

MSS 164
Genealogical Office

pedigree of Kavanagh of Ballyleigh, of Temple, of Ugidane, of Ferns. 1553 – 1774

MSS 165
Genealogical Office

Pedigree of Kavanagh of Clonmullin, Co. Carlow, of Spain, of Nantes, France. C1575 – 1766

MSS 161
Genealogical Office
Pedigree of Cavanagh of Powermont, Co. Wexford. c1600 – c1690

MSS 471
Genealogical Office
abstracts of wills and other documents relating to Cavanaghs and allied families. C1635 – 1800

Manuscripts & Papers - UK

Cavenagh, Sir Orfeur.
GB/NNAF/P5170. Historical Manuscript Commission diaries (4 vols)

Egerton 1782
fo. 3-4. British Library

Two pieces of parchment bound into the MS at its beginning. Obit and eulogy of Art buidhe Mac Murchadha Caomhánach, who died, according to the note, in the Franciscan house at Enniscorthy, Co. Wexford, 25th, November, 1517.

Kavanagh, alias McMorogh - History
23,691. British National Library

COLLECTIONS for a history of the family of Kavanagh, alias McMorogh, by Sir W. Betham. Included are original letters from Henry, Baron Kavanagh, Major dans la suite du Prince de Schwarzenberg; Vienna, 17 Sept. [1]816. Fr. f. 9; Edmund Lodge, Lanc[aster Herald]; College of Arms, etc., 24 June, 9 July, 1816, ff. 18, 20; and W. Gregory; Dublin Castle, 29 July, 1814, f. 24. Paper; XIXh cent. Folio.

Kavanagh, Arthur MacMorrough – Papers
GB/NNAF/P15930. Historical Manuscripts Commision

1879-89: letters to Ashbourne. Corresp, travel diaries and family papers. 1882-88: letters to Laurence Parsons, 4th Earl of Rosse.

Kavanagh, Thomas Henry VC – Collection
National Army Museum, Chelsea

#1963-10-126 - Tulwar sword used Thomas used as part of his disguise while escaping from Lucknow. #1963-10-241 - Rattan dhal shield. #1958-12-42 - portrait wearing Victoria Cross. #1958-12-48 - painting of Thomas being dressed as a native before going out to cross the siege lines at Lucknow. Both paintings are by Louis William Desanges , the museum also hold a walking stick which the believe belonged to Thomas. The museum obtained the items from the Royal United Services Institute's after that it was dissolved in 1963. The RUSI received the items from United Service Museum by Kathleen Kavanagh Haynes in 1932.

Kavanagh family of Borris.

GB/NNAF/F881. Historical Manuscripts Commision

1572-20th cent : deeds, estate and family papers. Private. NRA 31152 Kavanagh

MSS 611

Lambeth Palace Library

Abstract of the division of the Kavenaghs and their lands. 1572

Manuscripts & Papers – Elsewhere

von Kavanagh, Carl Freiherr – Ennoblement

Austrian State Archive.

Ennoblement on 21st, March, 1750. No reference number available. Information received from Maria Wilflinger at the Österreichische Nationalbibliothek.

von Kavanagh, Johann Baptist Freiherr – Ennoblement

Austrian State Archive.

Ennoblement on 18th, August, 1768. No reference number available. Information received from Maria Wilflinger at the Österreichische Nationalbibliothek.

Articles, Periodicals & Journals

Carloviana

Art MacMurrough and Richard II
O'Toole, Edward
Dec 1971

The Kavanagh Kings
Hadden, W.V. Vol.1 New Series No.17

The family of the MacMurrough Kavanaghs
MacLeod, Iona. Vol. I no. 3, 1954. p.13 – 16.

Cavanah Country

Privately published and distributed by Patricia Cavanah Moore. At least 10 issues between 1993 and 1995. Contains extensive genealogical information relating to the Cavanah families of Kentucky and elsewhere.

Clann Chaomhánach

Clann Annual
ISSN 1393 1717
Chief publication of the Clann. Articles, stories, member enquiries and more.

Clann Newsletter
ISSN 1393-1733
Regular updates on the Clann, its activities and its members.

Journal of the American Irish Historical Society

Sergeant Patrick Cavanaugh - a brave soldier of the Revolution
Vol. XXI, 1922

Journal of the Old Wexford Society

Donall Spáinneach Caomhánach
 Dé Vál, Séamas S. No.1 p.43 – 45

The career of Diarmait mac Máel na mBó, King of Leinster - Part I
 Ó Corráin, Donncha. No.3 p. 27

The career of Diarmait mac Máel na mBó, King of Leinster - Part II
 Ó Corráin, Donncha. No.4 p. 17

The Ui Chennselaig Kingship of Leinster 1072–1126 – Part I
 Ó Corráin, Donncha. No.5 p.26

The Ui Chennselaig Kingship of Leinster 1072–1126 – Part II
 Ó Corráin, Donncha. No.6 p.45

The Ui Chennselaig Kingship of Leinster 1072–1126 – Part III
 Ó Corráin, Donncha. No.7 p.46

The immediate predecessors of Dermot Mac Murrough
 Furlong, Nicholas. No.4. p.59

John Kavanagh, Young Irelander -Part I
 Culleton, Edward. No.4 p.25

John Kavanagh, Young Irelander -Part II
 Culleton, Edward. No.5 p.64

Excavations at the site of MacMurrough Castle, near New Ross, Co. Wexford
 Cotter, Claire. No.11 p.33 – 49

The Right Hon. Arthur McMurrough Kavanagh M.P.
 McCarthy, R.B. No.13 p.135 – 159

Journal of the Royal Society of Antiquaries of Ireland

Clan Kavanagh in the imperial service – Part I
Cavenagh, W.O. Series Six, Vol. XII, June 1922, p.42 - 51

Clan Kavanagh in the imperial service – Part II
Cavenagh, W.O. Series Six, Vol. XV, December 1925, p.138 – 139
Outlines the fortunes of descendants of Baron Simon Henry Kavanagh at Mali-Tabor, Croatia. This line is stated as being the last representatives of the Inch branch of the Clann.

Colonel Terence Kavanagh (note)
Cavenagh, W.O. Series Six, Vol. XVIII, December 1928, p.163-164
Contains an extract from Colonel Kavanagh's will and an account of the misappropriation of his estate.

Fiacha Mac Aodha Uí Bhroin and Domhnall Spáinneach Caomhánach
Series VI, Vol. V. Vol. XLV, part II. P.109 – p.114. 30 June 1915
Inquisition at Ballinacor on 16th, January, 1605, giving the correct place and date of the death of Fiacha Mac Aodha. Also, biographical information on Domhnall mac Donnchaidh Caomhánaigh and his immediate descendants.

John B. Kavanagh, Baron Gniditz (note)
Marquis MacSwiney of Mashanaglass. Series Six, Vol. XVIII, December 1928, p.165
Summary outline of the family of Baron Gniditz and references to Brian-na-Stroaké and Murrough More Kavanagh.

Some further medieval seals out of the Ormond archives, including that of Donal Reagh MacMurrough Kavanagh, King of Leinster
Curtis, Edmund. Series Seven, Vol. VII, June 1937, p.72-76

Contains description of the arms and a b&w photograph of a seal impression facing page 76.

Journal of the Royal Society of Ireland

Diarmait Mac Murchada and Romanesque Leinster: four twelfth-century churches in context
Discusses the history and archaeology of four ecclesiastical foundations (Baltinglass Abbey, Ferns, Glendalough, and Killeshin) associated with Diarmait Mac Murchada, King of Leinster (d 1171). Their context in the architectural traditions of south-eastern Ireland is also assessed.
#127, 2000, 52–79, figs, pls, refs, ISSN 0035-9106

Nova Scotia Historical Review

Lawrence Kavanagh I: an eighteenth-century Cape Breton entrepreneur
Wagg, Phyllis. Nov. 1990 Volume 10 No 2, p.124 – 132.

Proceedings of the Royal Irish Academy

Dermot and the Earl: Who wrote "The Song"?
Long, Joseph. Vol. 75, Sec. C, No.13. 1975
Investigates the role of Morice Regan in the poem.

The Irish Genealogist

The Kavanaghs, 1400 – 1700 – Part I
Nicholls, Kenneth. Vol.5 No.4 p.436 – 437
An extensive analsysis of the major septs of Clann Chaomhánach.

The Kavanaghs, 1400 – 1700 – Part II
Vol.5 No.5 p.573

The Kavanaghs, 1400 – 1700 – Part III
Vol.5. No.6 p.730

The Kavanaghs, 1400 – 1700 – Part IV
  Vol.6 No.2 p.189

The Kilkenny Archaeological Journal

The Clan Kavanagh
  Hore, Herbert Francis. Ser. II, vol ii, p.74

Tipperary Historical Journal

Julia Kavanagh (1824–1877) - a novelist from Thurles
  Higgins, Noreen. No 5, 1992.

Labour / Le Travail

Rebel of Revolutionary?: Jack Kavanagh and the Early Years of the Communist Movement in Vancouver, 1920-192.
  Akers, David. Vol.30, Fall 1992. Published by the Canadian Committee on Labor History.

Field & Laboratory

Benjamin Taylor Kavanaugh, and the Discovery of East Texas Oil
  Geiser, Samuel Wood., vol. XII, no. 2, June, 1944, pp. 46-55

Miss Laura Cavanaugh. c1901

Bernard Cavanagh

Between late 1840 and early 1842 Bernard Cavanagh rose from obscurity to become a major celebrity in Ireland and at one point began to rival Daniel O'Connell, The Great Emancipator, in popularity and newsworthiness. His reputation was based on the remarkable claim of being able to abstain from food and drink, and also to be able to control all his body's excretions. Consequently he became known as the "Fasting Man" and he regularly attracted audiences numbering in the thousands at the Adelphi theatre in Dublin. For the privilege of seeing him attendees were charged between 6d (£1) to 2s (£6) on entry and for their money they were treated to a spectacle similar to a modern day television gospel preacher. The sick, the blind, the lame and the desperate gathered from miles around in the hope of a miracle and to receive his blessing. Obviously a showman, Bernard recalled the words of Jesus himself and was heard to say "Arise, and walk". Thanks to the attention of the media he quickly became a topic of discussion within the medical profession and the public generally.

When asked to describe the source for his extraordinary powers Bernard explained that it began as a result of the penance imposed on him by his parish priest. Gradually he found himself able to endure longer and longer periods without nourishment until finally, he could abstain completely. Indeed, he claimed that rather than being a hardship he now enjoyed such an ordeal and that he lived not by the bread of man but by the word of God. The local authorities were unable or, unwilling to put a stop to his activities though he quickly attracted the attention of the church and was denounced from the pulpit.

In August 1841 Bernard left for England and on arrival he was again the subject of much speculation by both the popular press and the medical world who debated the authenticity of his claims. While most doctors were skeptical, some argued that his claims might be possible. When questioned by a reporter Bernard produced a testimonial:

> *"We, the undersigned, certify that Bernard Cavanagh, who is now on his way to London, is the same person who underwent the ordeal of fasting during the space of seven days and nights, in the town of Claremorris, in the county of Mayo."*
>
> *Signed*
> *George Gore, Dean of Killala*
> *John Coleman, Parish Priest*
> *Edward Dean, Justice of Peace*

As Mr. Gore was a brother to Lord Arran and also to the Duchess of Inverness there was a distinct reluctance to accuse Bernard of being a charlatan and a liar. The ability to abstain from food and drink was apparently a popular boast at the time and the claimants were usually revealed as impostors after an elementary investigation of the facts. In Bernard's case his physical appearance did little to persuade the doubters for he seemed to be in full health with no trace of malnourishment. He responded to all doubters by offering to seal himself in a room and therein, to be deprived of any provisions. Eventually a gentleman took him up on his offer.

It was suggested that Bernard be locked in a room for ten days and nights to demonstrate his powers beyond doubt. A room was found measuring fifteen feet by nine feet by seven feet high. Bernard himself requested that the window and fireplace be sealed shut but this was refused on the grounds that there might be insufficient air in a room so small. He was stripped, searched thoroughly by a Dr. Kenney in the presence of an observer and finally sealed in the room. On the seventh day of the fast Bernard was released temporarily to attend mass being accompanied at all times by a physician and a solicitor. On his return he was again stripped and searched before returning to the room.

On the eleventh day of the fast the seal on the door was broken in the presence of a number of witnesses and Bernard emerged triumphant. The only outward sign of the ordeal was that he looked a little thinner than when he had entered, and this he cheekily put down to a lack of exercise. The room was examined closely but no sign of food or excretions could be found. A barrage of questions followed but he offered no information that could shed any more light on his performance. Slowly he was winning over some of the skeptics; many now accepted that Bernard could fast for anything up to two weeks but few believed his claim of being able to endure for five years.

Within days of completing the fasting experiment, its result was thrown into doubt. Serious questions were raised over the failure to seal the window and it was suggested that an accomplice, or other third party, could have taken advantage of the opening to supply food. Those in charge of experiment were confident that nothing of the sort had occurred but accepted that there was room for doubt and so, a second experiment was quickly arranged. A larger room was found so that all openings could be sealed without depriving the occupant of a suitable supply of air. On October 12th Bernard was again stripped, searched and sealed in a room. A certificate was drafted and signed:

> *"We, the undersigned, saw Bernard Cavanagh, the fasting man, generally so called, entirely denuded of his clothes, and examined in our presence as to the possibility of concealing any food about his person, and are of opinion it was not possible that any food, even in the smallest quantity, could have been concealed on his person. We also state that a fresh suit of clothes, which had been substituted without his previous knowledge for those he wore when he entered the room, were put on by him."*

> *"He was subsequently confined in a room, and our seals affixed to the door, and the keys*

delivered to Dr. Edward Blundell. We also observed that the window, doors and chimney were all sealed."

E.S. Blundell M.D.
J.T. Reeve, Surgeon,
Peter Kenney, M.D.,
J. Spencer, Druggist,
J. Eyles, Surgeon-Dentist

On Thursday, October 21st, the seals were broken and the door opened in the presence of approximately thirty-five witnesses. The seals on the window, fireplace and doors were meticulously examined for tampering but none could be found. The bed and all corners were examined for traces of food and excretions and again none could be found. At first Bernard appeared a little sluggish but after stretching his legs for a minute or two he was soon back to his usual self. He had once more placed himself under the microscope and emerged to silence his critics and detractors. A journalist was moved to write "*...his powers are extraordinary, that to physiologists he presents a singular case...*"

One of the witnesses present asked if Bernard would mind submitting to scrutiny on a third occasion in St. George's hospital. At first he accepted but then, whether due to genuine fatigue or the thought he might be pushing his luck a little too far, he subsequently declined the offer saying he would rather be locked up.

By November 12th Bernard, accompanied by a friend, found his travels had taken him to Reading in Berkshire where he lodged in the "Black Boy" public house. The companions were later joined by Bernard's bother. The following morning notices and leaflets were appearing all over town to announce his arrival:

"EXTRAORDINARY PHENOMENON

The celebrated Bernard Cavanagh, from the county of Mayo, who has excited so much attention from the medical and scientific world, on account of his excessive powers of abstinence, which are attested beyond all doubt, is now in this town, and invites all inquirers into this case of so singular a phenomenon to pay him a visit at the Black Boy, Reading during his stay. A few of his philosophical friends in London, wishing to gain some additional light upon this case, have advised him to give this general invitation, and make no distinct charge for admissions; but as the expenses of travelling about the country with his brother, who eats like other men, will be beyond their means, any friendly donation will be thankfully received."

In the following week Bernard proved to be a popular hit and large crowds gathered to see him. However due to a "no distinct charge for admission" policy little revenue was generated. During each session the audience repeatedly quizzed him on the length of abstinence and the source of his powers. He was reluctant to answer their questions but one woman in particular, a Mrs. Hatt, was determined to get to the bottom of the matter; in reply to her questioning Bernard finally stated he had abstained for 5 years and 6 months.

The next morning, November 18th, Mrs. Hatt was shopping in town and stopped for a chat with the shopkeeper of a provision store. During their conversation a man entered with a handkerchief across his eyes and a black patch on his nose and requested a quarter pound of ham, a saveloy and three-pennyworth of bread. Despite the comical attempt at disguise Mrs. Hatt recognised the man immediately as "The Fasting Man", Bernard Cavanagh.

Hatt did not say anything immediately but watched the man pay for his goods and leave the shop after which he would presumably consume the feast. Angry at what she had just witnessed she then made for the Black Boy and enquired of Mr. Cavanagh, where she was informed that he gone out for a walk. Obviously a woman of patience as well as determination she took a seat and waited for his return. An hour and a half later Bernard appeared and Mrs. Hatt confronted him, notified the landlord of events and the police summoned. Some time later Bernard was brought before the Mayor for questioning.

During the investigation that followed, Mrs. Hatt was adamant that she had made no mistake in identifying Bernard Cavanagh as the man in the shop. Bernard was then requested to make his defence to which he replied, "If he did say anything it would not be believed, and he might, therefore, as well say nothing." As matters progressed however Bernard realised the tide was against him and he finally admitted "the Lord caused me to be hungry, and I did eat."

Bernard was convicted of being a "rogue and a vagabond" and was sentenced to three months hard labour. As he was led away he said that, while it was true he had told that woman he had fasted for 5 years and 6 months he had omitted to say that he now ate and drank like any normal man. In the days following, there was some debate as to the manner of his conviction. Although Bernard had admitted purchasing the food no one had actually seen him consume it and, while he claimed to be able to abstain for extended periods he had not actually claimed to be currently abstaining.

In prison Bernard refused to take the daily food and drink rations provided. Prison officials began to carefully weigh the food before placing it in Bernard's cell. When they removed the food it was again weighed and on each occasion no discrepancy could be found; the weights always tallied exactly. After three days without rations the prison surgeon, a Mr. Bulley, excused Bernard from hard labour. The prison governor and some visiting magistrates overturned the decision however, and Bernard was back on hard labour Monday morning. Events turned a little comical when, in the afternoon, the mayor overturned the decision once more and Bernard was again excused hard labour.

After eight days Bernard received a visit from a correspondent of the London Times who found him *"in excellent health and very good spirits (not at all "down" at his present situation), but there was colour upon his cheeks, clearly indicating (that) there were no symptoms of starvation visible."* The prison surgeon handed a written statement to the correspondent that added weight to Bernard's claim:

> *"Bernard Cavanagh, at this date, completed his 9th day of entire abstinence from food and drink.*[2]
>
> *After the closest watching and the strictest care on the part of myself and the turnkeys of the prison to prevent the possibility of his clandestinely taking food, I feel satisfied and convinced, in my own mind, that Bernard Cavanagh has not tasted food or drink during the nine days he has been an inmate of the gaol. He remains, notwithstanding the privations he has voluntarily endured, in a state of perfect bodily health, and I cannot detect the slightest alteration in his appearance or spirits."*

Bernard was again demonstrating his extraordinary powers but within two days matters had taken a dramatic turn for the worse as he began to show adverse reactions. His pulse was weak, he could barely walk and generally he had the appearance of a very sick man. On the Saturday morning he admitted defeat. When prison officials measured his daily ration they discovered that a small amount of the gruel was missing. The prison surgeon Mr. Bulley was immediately

---

[2] The surgeon later corrected this to eights days abstinence

called and when he saw Bernard's state sent for more gruel and a glass of port wine.

Following his release from prison Bernard continued to tour England, advertising himself as the Fasting Man. Eventually he settled down and opened a shop. It is difficult to know whether he was a crank, a conman or if he genuinely believed he had a gift from god. In his description of Bernard the prison governor stated that he was a reasonable man in most things except when it came to religion. Bernard's repeated offers to submit him self to scientific examination would seem to indicate that he was not a normal run of the mill confidence trickster.

The following notice appeared in The Armagh Guardian on August 19th, 1845:

> *DEATH OF BERNARD CAVANAGH, THE FASTING MAN.—This individual, who three or four years since excited some attention in the metropolis, by professing to exist without sustenance, liquid or solid, expired on Sabbath last, in rucoat's-lane, in his 32d year. He had recently kept a huckster's shop, in which he had failed. He had gone by an assumed name, and his right one did not transpire till shortly before his death. His brother, who was with him when he exhibited in London, was present. The deceased was of parsimonious habits, and often reduced to great extremities, but has left money in bank.— Dublin paper*

Thomas Henry Kavanagh VC
(1820 – 1882)

Thomas Henry Kavanagh was a man impatient to meet with destiny. He possessed a level of self-confidence which to some who met him bordered on arrogance. Born in Ireland it would be in the service of the British Empire that an opportunity would finally present itself. He seized it with both hands and fully justified his confidence in his own abilities.

Thomas was born in Mullingar, County Westmeath on the 15th of July 1820, the third son of the bandmaster of the 3rd foot. From the earliest days of his childhood he longed to perform deeds that would bring fame and fortune. His family however paid no heed to his daydreaming and one of his uncles went so far as to inform him that he was more likely to be hanged.[3]

Thomas moved to India in 1839 where he worked for the British civil service. He spent some years in the Punjab as head clerk in the Revenue and General Department of the Board of Administration. Following the annexation of Oudh, a province in the north of India he was offered the position of Superintendent of the office of the Chief Commissioner. India was the crown jewel of the British Empire and it was ruled and policed by the Honourable East India Company. Formed

---

[3] How I Won The Victoria Cross – P.73, Kavanagh, Thomas Henry

in 1600 by Queen Elizabeth the company was one of the most powerful economic forces that the world had ever known. It maintained its own army which outnumbered the official British Army on the Indian subcontinent. This private army was comprised of Europeans and over 250,000 native soldiers, known as sepoys. The sepoys were drawn largely from Hindus but there were also Muslim and Sikh contingents. They were drilled in the European fashion and well armed. Thomas Henry described the native army thus:

> "Its proportions had grown great – its courage unquestionable – and its temper excitable"[4]

In the early years of the empire the native soldiers had enjoyed a close relationship with their British commanding officers but over time this relationship began to decline and the sepoys became more and more unsettled. They also mistrusted British missionaries who they suspected were trying to convert them to Christianity. Relations generally between the British rulers and Indian natives were at their lowest point since the arrival of the colonists. At all levels of Indian society British customs and values were being introduced that eroded local traditions. Bills and laws were passed that allowed Hindu widows to remarry and Hindus that converted to Christianity could share in the inheritance of family estates. A "Doctrine of Lapse" was passed that resulted in the province of any Indian ruler who failed to produce a male heir being forfeit to the British crown. Superstition and ancient prophecies added to the mixture to create a volatile atmosphere.

The spark that ignited the conflict which threatened to engulf the entire sub-continent was a humble rifle cartridge. The latest Enfield rifle was being issued to the East India Company army and it contained a new type of self-contained cartridge. This cartridge contained both the powder charge and the ball or bullet. A soldier needed to bite off the end of the cartridge and ram it down the muzzle. To make its

---

[4] How I Won The Victoria Cross – P.VII, Kavanagh, Thomas Henry

progress down the gun muzzle as easy as possible the cartridge was lubricated with grease. Rumours began to spread among the sepoys that the grease was made from cows which are sacred in the Hindu religion, and pigs which are unclean in the eyes of the Moslem religion. A number of factors compounded the problem. First a number of British commanders were unsure of the composition of the fat themselves and second many of the officers could not understand what all the fuss was about and dismissed the problem as religious hysterics.

At the end of April 1857 the sepoy troops at Meerut refused to accept the new cartridges and were sentenced to 10 years hard labour. A number were also publicly humiliated, stripped of their uniforms and shackled in irons in front of the entire garrison. The following day those who had not been punished rose up in support of their comrades. In a frenzied attack they shot the British officers and then murdered the women and children of any European or Indian Christian families they could find. Then they marched to Delhi where they joined up with other sepoys.

The Sikhs remained, for the most part loyal to the Empire and so too did a small number of the Hindus. Nevertheless the mutiny spread rapidly throughout northern India repeating the scenes at Meerut. The response of the British commanders in those areas that remained unaffected was varying. Some officers refused to believe that the sepoys under their command could be affected by the madness and rise up against them, while others immediately began to withdraw weapons and draw up defence plans.

Thomas was stationed in Lucknow a city to the southeast of Delhi while his family was staying in Cawnpore. Following a dispute with friends Thomas' wife and the children followed him to Lucknow. This was a fortunate moved because shortly after their departure the sepoys laid siege to Cawnpore. Sir Henry Lawrence was the commanding officer at Lucknow and he had decided that the most suitable defensive position was inside the British Residency compound. Constructed in 1780 the Residency occupied the highest point in the city but was hemmed in to the south, east and west by tightly packed city streets and native buildings that provided excellent positions for snipers.

By the 30th of May the sepoys at Lucknow had mutinied though a small number including the Sikhs remained loyal. That night Sir Henry Lawrence stared into the darkness of the night and contemplated the fate that awaited his men and the civilians in his care. From around the city came the cries of the mutineers. One by one the buildings surrounding the Residency were set ablaze and the sound of timbers burning and foundations falling filled the air. Lawrence's heart was full of foreboding knowing that when the attack finally came there was no hope of resisting for more that a couple of hours. However fortune smiled on the occupants of the Residency as the natives retreated instead of trying to force an entry. This gave Sir Henry some precious time and he immediately set about reinforcing the defences. Thomas was now in charge of the compounds civilians and he set about organising them into a fighting unit. He arranged their accommodation and issued them with arms. Some felt that this was a foolish move; that armed civilians were a bigger threat to themselves than the enemy.

Thomas took great pride in ensuring these new civilian units behaved with as much military discipline as was possible given the circumstances. Some of his charges found his methods overbearing and some openly questioned his authority. He worked day and night and the exertions slowly began to take a toll on his health. In spite of this he continued to participate in the convoys and escorts that brought women and children from outlying districts to the safety of the Residency.

When word arrived of events at Cawnpore it left the defenders of Lucknow appalled and sickened. General Sir Hugh Wheeler and his troops at Cawnpore had held out for three weeks. On June 25th Nana Sahib the leader of the sepoys offered General Wheeler safe passage to all in the city if he surrendered. With the lives of women and children at stake and no prospect of a relieving force the general was forced to accept the offer. Some of the British were escorted to the river where they were then loaded onto boats.

As they prepared to leave the riverbanks were suddenly filled with gunfire. Terror struck the women as round after round of deadly metal rained down. The river turned red and except for four survivors, all perished. The sepoys then turned their attention to those still left in the city. They killed the men on sight but led the women and children to a building called the "Bibi-Ghar" where shortly after they were hacked to death with knives and hatchets. At Lucknow the defenders resolved to avenge the dead and "Cawnpore" was to become the battle cry from that day on. Indeed it became the justification for many atrocities committed by the British later in their campaign to quell the revolt.

Thomas finally succumbed to exhaustion and fatigue. Unable to rise from bed he relied on others to bring news of the siege and the daily skirmishes. The news was not good. The sepoy army had emerged victorious in a number of small encounters and was beginning to appear unstoppable. On one occasion when Thomas did manage to leave his bed he found utter confusion. Preparations were under way for an imminent attack and panic did not seem to be too far away. Unable to lend support in any meaningful Thomas sat for a while with his face buried in his hands and finally returned to his bed. An attack of erysipelas in his left leg left Thomas in constant pain but by the 20th of June he had recovered a little and he eagerly sought news of events. Each report in the rise and fall of the defenders fortunes caused Thomas more and more anguish and agitation until eventually those tending to him considered it best to keep him ignorant of proceedings.

Thomas was now utterly dejected. Here was the moment he had waited for all his life. A time for heroes, a chance for glory and he was helpless in his sickbed! He had toiled for twenty years without recognition and now his great chance was passing him by. He quietly made a promise to himself: to emerge from the siege with a reputation and fame or to die in the attempt. When Thomas finally recovered sufficiently to leave his sickbed he found the Residency in high spirits. They had spent the morning and day of July 20th in continuous battle and had survived the onslaught. Listening to the tales of gallant deeds only served to increase Thomas's resolve to play his part.

By the end of July the sepoy army outside the gate was not the only enemy the Residency faced. In the constant heat and unsanitary conditions cholera, fever and small pox now stalked the streets bringing death just as surely as a snipers bullet. Thomas lost his eldest child Cecil to sickness and was haunted by the fear that a similar fate awaited the rest of his children. It was almost impossible to keep the healthy completely separate from the diseased so Thomas encouraged his children to play outside. He preferred to keep them away from the threat of infection even if it meant they were exposed to enemy snipers.

On the 4th of August Thomas had a close escape while walking through the compound to report for duty. He came under fire and had to be rescued from almost certain death by two comrades. Reporting later to Captain M'Cale Thomas declared he was healthy enough to return to duty. M'Cale took one look at the sickly form standing before him and immediately refused. Shortly thereafter Thomas managed to provoke the ire of M'Cale by firing into the night at suspected mutineers. In order to curb his exuberance M'Cale had Thomas arrested and then released the following day.

Eventually Thomas was fit enough to return to full duty and tried to arrange a position in charge of the mortars, having realized how effective they were at inflicting damage on the enemy. Unfortunately there were others more able and qualified than him and this avenue was closed. In the end he had to settle for rooftop observation duty, reporting on the enemy as they gathered in the surrounding streets for each attack and again as they retreated. Although there were occasional moments of drama it was for the most part, a dull and uninteresting duty.

Throughout August there were constant rumours of imminent relief. Time and again it was imagined the sound of British artillery could be heard on the outskirts of the city but on each occasion excitement gave way to despair. One dispatch that reached the Residency had promised help within four days but none arrived. The situation inside was getting more desperate. The heat was stifling, food was low, rats swarmed everywhere and disease continued claim lives.

Thomas began to explore other ways of involving himself in the action once he was fully recovered. One of these was to engage in what he called "Man-Shooting" For this Thomas would climb onto one of the defence batteries and take pot shots and the enemy one hundred yards away. During one of these episodes he had another close encounter with death. As he was mounting the barricade a canon shot raced past his head badly burning the side of his face.

September brought some relief from the scorching sun in the form of rain showers. Cool and refreshing they helped revive the spirits and also had the more practical effect of cleansing the streets of dirt, blood and decaying flesh. The monotonous nature of their position soon returned however and was trying the tempers of many of the Residencies inhabitants. Fortunately good news was close at hand.

Under the command of Sir Henry Havelock and Sir James Outram the British were fighting their way from Cawnpore which they had retaken, towards Lucknow. On the 25th of September they were on the edge of the city and were about to make the final push. Inside the Residency word spread that salvation was at hand and many climbed onto the rooftops to glimpse their saviours. In the distance canons roared and rifles cracked as the dash began.

During their advance the relief force came under close fire from doors, windows and rooftops as they passed. In the twisting streets some men got lost but managed to reunite with the main party. When the battling soldiers came into view of the Residency the defenders on the roof erupted with cries of joy and support to those who had come to their aid. When the gates were at last opened and the ragged troops poured through, men and women alike were reduced to tears of gratitude. Over 200 of the 1,000 that attempted the perilous dash to the Residency were lost.

Almost as soon as the gates were closed the cheers subsided and spirits sank a little when everyone realised that, welcome as the relief force was, it was not large enough to turn the tide. Inside the walls the defence now numbered around 1500 while outside there were still around 10,000 sepoys thirsting for blood. They were still prisoners but now had even more mouths to feed.

Thomas was beginning to enjoy his part in the siege and with increasing enthusiasm volunteered for the more dangerous assignments. His intimate knowledge of the buildings and streets surrounding the Residency was particularly valuable. As a result he was called on to guide many sorties into enemy positions in order to knock out their artillery or to gather intelligence. Each evening he would look back on the day's adventures with quiet satisfaction.

At the end of October Thomas was made Assistant Field Engineer which he felt was in recognition of his endeavours. He began changed the focus of his attention to below ground level. The sepoys were digging tunnels beneath the compound in which they hoped to plant explosive charges. Thomas was responsible for the discovery of the explosives and their destruction through countermining. He found crawling through cold dark tunnels a frightening experience; at any moment he might run into sepoys or the tunnel could collapse and bury him alive. Many times he had to urge himself forward with quiet words of encouragement.

There was still time for the pastime of "Man-Shooting". Whenever he discovered an enemy tunnel about to open he would wait in the shadows for a sepoy to emerge and then step forward and fire. On one occasion after shooting a poor wretch he crawled into the enemy tunnel in order to recover their mining tools. Unable to locate the tools he crawled further and further into the tunnel until he could hear the sepoys on the other side calling to their dead comrade.

Realising he had crawled too far into the tunnel Thomas lay still to see what would happen next. Suddenly another sepoy appeared and Thomas shot him in the stomach. There was just one round left in his revolver so Thomas quickly reversed his way out. And not a moment too soon! For the tunnel was quickly filled with gunfire and the acrid smell of gunpowder. For the next couple of minutes abuse and insults were thrown back and forth from one end of the tunnel to the other.

Thomas wagered with the enemy that he could retrieve the digging equipment. The sepoy commander replied he was welcome to them if he could take them. With as much confidence as he could muster Thomas spoke at length on the excellent state of their provisions and of the rapidly approaching British relief force that would soon break the siege. So confident and fanciful were his tales that the enemy was distracted for a moment. Quick as lightning Thomas jumped into the tunnel and safely retrieved the tools. It was such a daring and audacious move that even the sepoys were moved to applaud it. Inside the residency the Sikh soldiers who had remained loyal nicknamed Thomas "Burra Surungwalla" – the Great Miner.

On the 29th of November Thomas learned that an Indian messenger by the name of Kunoujee Lal had managed to get inside the Residency. Lal carried with him a dispatch from Sir Colin Cambell at Cawnpore who hoped to reach the Resdiency and break the siege within a week. In the preceding few days officers at the Residency had drawn up a plan to assist such a force outlining the best route through the city.

It occurred to Thomas that the city plan on its own was of little use without someone to explain it. Thomas was convinced that someone with local knowledge of the city layout and of the enemies' positions should meet Cambell before he arrived at the city limits. If the route outlined in the plan should be blocked by the enemy or otherwise inaccessible what would Cambell do then? Hesitation could be fatal and might result in more losses than the 200 suffered by Havelock. Should a mishap occur then a guide could minimise the time spent finding an alternative route. The Residency could not afford the luxury of a third attempt – the food was almost exhausted and the sick and wounded were dying for want of medical supplies. It was a matter of relief now or disaster later.

Thomas was determined that he should be the guide to meet Cambell. He met with the Kunoujee Lal and outlined his plan to accompany him on his return journey. Lal refused point blank due to the added risk of having to care for an accomplice especially a white European one. In the end Thomas convinced him by hinting at the possibility of a great reward. Having convinced the messenger he now faced a more difficult task – that of convincing his superiors.

Thomas approached Colonel Napier an officer with whom he enjoyed a friendly rapport and outlined his idea. It took no more than a couple of seconds for Napier to realise the absurdity and absolute folly of such a mission. How would any European manage to slip undetected though the many enemy patrols and checkpoints, never mind one who was over 6 feet tall, had blue eyes a shock of red hair and freckles! Nonetheless Napier was impressed with the courage shown by Thomas and believed that Sir James Outram should be made aware of the offer.

In front of Outram Thomas again outlined his audacious plan. With arms outstretched he pleaded with Outram to balance the loss of one life against the saving of thousands. Like Napier before him Outram was astonished and impressed by Thomas' determination to undertake such a hazardous and surely fatal adventure. Outram confessed that he also saw the benefit of a guide but the odds of making it through enemy lines were practically zero and so he politely declined the offer.

Thomas did not give up easily and two strong forces were urging him on. The first was his strong sense of duty and the desire to ease the suffering of his family and comrades. The second was the knowledge that this might be his only chance to demonstrate clearly the courage he admired so much in others. Eventually his persistence and determination paid off when his offer was finally accepted.

On returning home to his family Thomas began to feel utterly miserable. He had been married for 12 years and his wife Agnes had stood by him through many ordeals. He knew that if he revealed his plans to her she would beg him not to go and that he would probably surrender to her pleading. Unable to look her in the eye and distressed with having to keep such a secret from her he left the house and tried to convince himself once more that he was doing the right thing. But if he should fail the test now then who would look after his family and ensure their safety?

At 6 o'clock in the evening he kissed Agnes and his children giving them the impression that he was heading for mine duty as usual. He found a small deserted room and with the aid of a colleague put on a disguise made from native clothing he had acquired earlier. He then applied black colouring to his face and hands to give the appearance of native skin. At first Thomas was not convinced that the colouring was natural but after a quick discussion it was agreed it would be good enough in the darkness of the night. To be sure a test was needed in order to judge its effectiveness.

It was forbidden for natives to enter the house of Europeans without first removing their footwear, or to take a seat without being invited to do so. When the disguised Thomas entered the quarters of Sir James Outram he did so with his shoes on and immediately took a seat. All of the staff on duty that evening knew Thomas quite well but it appeared none of them recognised him. Indeed the atmosphere was one of agitation that a native would be so impudent. They called for Sir James who would soon put this insolent wretch in his place.

When Outram entered the room he also failed to recognise Thomas immediately. Having past this simple test Thomas was feeling more a little more confident in his disguise. Outram and the other officers present then made some final adjustments and alterations to complete the deception. Captain Sitwell presented Thomas with his revolver which was not to be used for shooting his way out of trouble, rather to be turned on himself should he be threatened with capture. If would be far better that Thomas died quickly of his own hand rather than slowly and agonisingly at the mercy of the sepoys. At 8 o'clock the farewells were made and Thomas left to meet with Kanoujee Lal.

The first task the pair faced was to cross the river Gomti. Thomas removed his clothes gathered them into a bundle on his head and slipped into the icy cold water. Though the skies were clear and the moon shone there was little light to illuminate the swimming party. As the cold took hold of his body Thomas began to have serious doubts. He was about to call to Lal and abandon the enterprise when he realised that the distance between them was too great. Lal was almost at the opposite bank and to call out loudly now would surely attract the attention of the enemy. So Thomas was forced to complete the crossing and catch up with his companion.

Dry and in warm clothes again Thomas felt a little better so the pair made their way a hundred yards or so inland. Encountering a matchlockman[5] Thomas decided it was time to try out his native Hindu accent. He casually remarked on how cold the night was to which the matchlockman replied that it was indeed cold. As he departed Thomas commented

---

[5] A member of an artillery crew

further that it was likely to get even colder as the night wore on. Again the matchlockman suspicions were not aroused and Thomas began to feel ever more confident in himself.

A little further along the companions came to an Iron bridge where they were called over by a sepoy officer. Recognising the danger of the situation Thomas remained in the shadows while his Lal approached and explained that they were returning to their homes in the city. This satisfied the sepoy and he allowed them to continue on their way. Their journey now took them back over the river and into the heart of city; a city filled with the possibility of discovery and danger at every corner. Though the guide wished to use the small side streets Thomas thought it best to stay on the main thoroughfares and mingle with the larger crowds.

Thomas' gamble paid off. They were stopped and questioned only once and they now found them selves in open country. The vivid green fields had an immediate and resuscitating effect on Thomas. His spirits were lifted and he even managed to find a carrot, which tasted fresh and delicious as only a carrot can taste after months without fresh produce of any kind. The pair continued on for five miles brimming with confidence not realising that they were heading in the wrong direction.

When the Kanoujee Lal finally realised his mistake Thomas decided to make the most of the situation and wandered off to gather some intelligence about enemy positions. On his return he found the guide on the verge of panic and asked him the reason for his state. Lal explained that he was convinced Thomas suspected him of deliberately taking a wrong turn. Thomas reassured Lal that he readily understood how such a thing could easily occur in the dark. With the guides nerves soothed they then set off in search of help and eventually found an old woman who pointed them in the right direction.

After a couple of hours travel they came across a man singing at the top of his voice. Despite the noise he was making the stranger heard Thomas and Lal approach and immediately sounded the alarm. A party of sepoys came rushing out of a hut and began to ask questions. It was a very dangerous situation and for the first time since they had begun Kunoujee Lal lost his nerve. Not wishing to be captured as a spy he threw away the despatch he was carrying for Sir Colin Cambell.

Thomas stepped forward and assumed control of the situation. He protested that the behaviour of the soldiers was frightening his poor companion and explained that he and Lal were travelling to meet a mutual friend. They would have to explain to their friend that the British had shot and killed his brother. Accepting the explanation the sepoys allowed them to proceed and even advised them on the best route.

After a time they companions came across one of the many marshes that are common in the area and before they knew it were too far in to turn back. The water was cold and dirty, heavy mud sucked on their feet and their clothes grew cumbersome. Progress was slow and Thomas became more and more irritated. He cursed at everything- the natives, the swamp and the weeds. It took almost two hours to traverse the marsh and Thomas was so exhausted by the effort that he rested for 15 minutes.

Around 4 o'clock Thomas succumbed once more to fatigue and decided to lie down and rest for an hour. Kanoujee Lal was not pleased but agreed to try and find some assistance while Thomas slept. But the guide managed to walk just a few yards before a challenge of "Who comes there?" rang out. Thomas immediately sat up and listened intently. He heard the guide in conversation with some native soldiers and attempted to determine where their loyalties lay. It quickly became apparent that the soldiers were under the command of the British and within minutes Thomas and his companion were being escorted to meet with Sir Colin Cambell.

At 5 o'clock they were standing in front of the commander-in-chief. Their reception was not what Thomas had imagined it to be. Cambell was having great difficulty believing the tired and dishevelled man who claimed to come from Lucknow. Thomas removed his turban and took from it a piece of paper which he then handed to Cambell. The message it contained was from Sir James Outram and it was addressed to Cambell personally. As he read the paper Campbell's gaze moved from the note to Thomas and back to the note again. Finally he accepted Thomas as genuine and pressed him for an account of the journey.

Thomas was physically and mentally drained and begged that he be allowed to sleep first. Cambell agreed and he was assigned a tent in which to rest. Before laying down Thomas knelt and gave thanks to heaven for the success of his enterprise and the courageous and intelligent guide who had assisted him so well. Lying in bed his thoughts drifted to the great heroes of history and his own place among them.

Later that morning over breakfast with Cambell Thomas rediscovered the simple, delightful pleasures of bread and butter. It had been months since he had tasted coffee with sugar and the flavour of it too was wonderful. He recounted his adventures to Cambell and the other commanding officers who were full of admiration for him. When the officers left some time later Cambell outlined his impressions of the plan contained in the message from Outram.

The next day the relief force set out for Lucknow. The sight of four thousand soldiers advancing with a determined purpose was impressive and left Thomas felling confident of their success. En route word reached the Residency that Thomas had succeeded in his mission and the spirits of the besieged were lifted. Agnes was finally informed of her husbands' successful adventure. She was full of pride for her husband although she was in considerable pain, having been shot and severely wounded in the leg.

On the 14th of November the second attempt to break the siege of Lucknow began. Arriving on the outskirts of the city Cambell's force came under sporadic fire from the sepoys.

Their progress was checked when they came to a canal that was crossed by a stone bridge. Unsure of its condition Cambell requested a report. Thomas volunteered and rode as close to the bridge as he dared. On his return he reported to Cambell that the bridge appeared to be intact but that he could not be absolutely sure since he had not been close enough to see to the roadway on the other side. One of Cambell's officers was unhappy with this news and suggested, "Why not assure yourself of it?"

The remark injured Thomas' pride a little and he set off once more for the bridge. He rode nearer on the second attempt and came under close fire from the enemy. His horse was badly wounded but he had seen enough to determine that the bridge was indeed damaged. On receiving the updated report Cambell decided it was unsafe to cross and ordered his troops to camp for the night.

The following morning Thomas found Cambell on high ground surveying the city for weaknesses and potential trouble spots and confessed to him that he was unhappy with the route chosen by Sir James Outram. It was the same route taken by Havelock and he was sure it would be heavily defended. Thomas proposed an alternative route that was more likely to offer the opportunity of surprise. The omens were not good however for shortly after the sepoy army advanced along the very road Thomas had suggested.

There seemed to be no coordination or plan to the movement of the sepoys. Here and there small groups broke off and halted as they saw fit. When their cavalry arrived they contented themselves to waving their swords at their enemies from a safe distance. The only threat came from the sepoy artillery who from the cover of some woods were managing to make themselves a nuisance. They were soon sent running when Cambell ordered a combined infantry and cavalry charge. Cambell pursued the retreat for some distance in order to gain intelligence about the route. On his return to camp he announced his agreement with Thomas' choice and announced that would they would set out the following morning. In order to maintain the illusion that they would follow Havelock's advance Cambell ordered the artillery to bombard the original route throughout the night.

The advance the next morning was swift and silent. They met no resistance as they navigated the narrow twisting streets and were soon at the Secunder Bagh, an enclosed garden. Thomas apprehended a native and learned that although there were many defenders inside they had been surprised by the route taken by the British. Approaching the walls they were greeted with a volley of rifle fire killing the first soldiers brave enough to try and storm the gate. Time and again the British attempted to breach the gate and a hail of deadly metal rained down on them. Many lives were lost.

The air was filled with the thunder of booming artillery and the crack of rifle fire. The noise was deafening and the ground trembled underfoot. Amid the racket the British rushed forward with a bayonet charge but were stopped again so Cambell urged his men to try the roof. Roof tiles were ripped off and timbers discarded to enable a small number to gain access. At the same time a breach in the wall was created and Cambell ordered the Sikhs and Highlanders to secure it. A race ensued between the two regiments to see who could get there first and the first half dozen men to reach it were killed. Oblivious to flying bullets and the pile of bodies building at the wall the relief forces continued to race forward, took control of the critical position, and then pursued the natives inside.

Meanwhile the Sikhs had managed to force open the entrance gate and a terrible rage of bayonets was unleashed as they poured in. Bullets flew from friend and foe alike. The cry "Cawnpore" rang out from every quarter and total carnage followed. Bodies were dragged out dead or dying and piled up one on top of the other. Drenched in native blood, the British trampled over the bodies of their enemies to reach those still offering resisting inside. No mercy was shown and they exacted a terrible revenge for the atrocities their women and children had suffered. A red mist descended on the British and everyone regardless of rank was blinded by it.[6]

With the brutal battle for the Secunder Bagh won the relief force moved on to the next objective; the Shah Sujjif mausoleum. Artillery pounded the walls with round after round but the dense wall refused to yield. The British advanced with bayonets and the sepoy defenders repulsed them. Wave after wave followed but each attempt failed and the casualties and the fatalities were mounting at a terrible rate. Then just as the situation appeared lost the Highlanders poured in through a small breach in the wall and the sepoys quickly retreated. It was now nightfall but no one could rest as the threat of a sudden counter attack forced everyone to stand at arms.

The next morning Thomas was ordered to proceed with an advance party under Colonel Hale and secure any British buildings along the advance route. There was only light resistance and the objective was quickly achieved. Thomas decided to take the opportunity to gather intelligence on the enemy's position from one of the captured buildings. Unknown to him Colonel Hale's party had been relieved by another detachment. This new detachment was unaware of Thomas' identity and became suspicious of him as he moved about the building. Dressed with various donations from Sir Colin Campbell's officers he looked even more suspicious. Thomas was just about to advance further into enemy territory when he decided it would be better to return and obtain a telescope. When Thomas reached the commander of the new detachment he was informed that he had had a lucky escape. An order had been given that the suspiciously dressed stranger was to be shot should he advance any further towards the enemy.

News of the British advance and their successes quickly spread throughout the city. The result was an exodus of native civilians and sepoys. Three key buildings were targeted en

---

[6] How I Won The Victoria Cross – P.109, Kavanagh, Thomas Henry

route to the Residency where inside the besieged played their part with constant artillery shelling of the enemy. The Residency compound was now in sight and Thomas decided to try and reach Sir James Outram alone. Running haphazardly through the streets he managed to dodge the enemies' fire until he met with a soldier from the Residency. Together they ran at full tilt until they reached the Steam Engine House where some officers from the Residency were taking cover. Only when Thomas was upon them did they recognise him. "It is Kavanagh! Three cheers for him! He is the first to relieve us!"

Thomas was quickly shown to Outram receiving thanks and praise from all he passed. He then escorted Outram and Havelock back through enemy fire to Sir Colin Campbell's command post. Finding Cambell inside Thomas announced "Sir James Outram is waiting, sir, to see you." Campbell was incredulous - "The devil he is! Where is he? Where has he come from?" Thomas outlined his quick visit to the Residency and led him to meet with Outram where they congratulated each other on their achievements. Leaving them to organise the evacuation of the Residency Thomas then set out to find his family. Agnes squeezed him tightly to her breast and with tears of affection and admiration running down her cheeks chastised him for being so foolhardy.

In the moments that followed Thomas slowly began to realise the extent of his accomplishment. The daring journey to reach Cambell and the courage he displayed during the advance through the city had finally brought the recognition and adulation that he had craved since boyhood. His comrades in the Residency called to his house just to catch a glimpse of the man who had stepped into the pages of history. As word of his deeds spread throughout the territory he became known as "Lucknow Kavanagh". He had risked his life and the comfort of his family, but as Thomas himself put it:

> *"Nothing is comparable to the glory of a good deed, and few things are more gratifying then the*

sound of manly voices applauding it. Were not greetings like those worth striving for?" [7]

But Thomas had promised himself two things during the siege. He had now achieved the first: fame. But the second desire of fortune was not filled to his satisfaction. In return for his services during the relief of Lucknow the Indian government awarded him £2000[8]. Thomas felt this to be a miserly sum considering that his actions had also saved the public treasure which he estimated at around £300,000.[9] This was to be a sore point that stayed with Thomas until the day he died.

When Thomas was first nominated for the Victoria Cross the application was refused by the award review board. There were two issues that weighed against him. Firstly the board observed that Thomas would in all likelihood receive a special medal that the Queen would award to the garrison and relief force of Lucknow. Secondly, the Royal Warrant which outlined those eligible to receive the Victoria Cross stated that it could only be conferred on military personnel. A second civilian, Ross Lowis Mangles, had also been nominated for distinguished conduct during the Indian mutiny and many thought that they both fully deserved the award. A tribute from Sir Colin Cambell must also have contributed significantly;

> *"This escape at a time when the entrenchment was closely invested by a large army, and when communication, even through the medium of natives, was almost impossible, is in Sir Colin Cambell's opinion, one of the most daring feats ever attempted"*

After much lobbying the Royal Warrant was amended to allow nominations for anyone who "was serving under the orders of a General or other officer in command of troops in

---

[7] How I Won The Victoria Cross – P.121, Kavanagh, Thomas Henry
[8] Approximately STG£9,500 today
[9] Approximately STG£1.4 million today

the field" (THE LONDON GAZETTE, JULY 8, 1859) Thomas was presented with his medal by Queen Victoria on January 4th, 1860. He also received the Medal for the Relief and Siege of Lucknow. Thomas left for India with the impression that the VC had only been awarded grudgingly and wrote:

> "I shall probably be on my way back (to India), reluctantly to resume my duty under a Government that thinks me undeserving of the honour, and to labor hard in a climate from which I cannot hope to escape again to Europe"

Back in India Thomas was unwilling to sit back and trade on his reputation. He volunteered to act as a mediator between the rebels and the British but the authorities were unwilling to expose him to danger. At Birrwa he offered the rebels the chance to escape with their lives if they surrendered immediately. The mutineers were not sure if they could trust him so he put down his revolver, walked in to the middle of the fort and placed himself at their mercy. Impressed by his courage and willingness to sacrifice his own life the mutineers surrendered.

Thomas died in Gibraltar on November 11th 1882. There is no doubt that he was a man of great personal courage. Though the wrangling involved securing the Victoria Cross soured his attitude towards the British government he served it willingly and selflessly throughout the rest of his career. At the time of his death he had earned the respect of an empire, the admiration of both the common foot soldier and lords of the realm. He also enjoyed the loyalty of the Indian natives whom interests he continued to protect and the devotion of his friends and family.

Thomas' medal is currently in private hands in Ontario, Canada. The disguise Thomas wore during his adventure is held by the National Army Museum in Chelsea, England.

Hobart Cavanaugh
(1886 – 1950)

Born on September 22nd 1866 in Virginia City, Nevada John Hobart Cavanaugh was making the newspapers from the very first day. His father Jack announced the birth of his son in the Virginia Evening Chronicle:

"New Today

Under this heading Professor J. A. Cavanagh announces that he has made an addition to his stock of earthly goods. The little joker (a 10 pound son) was born early this morning, and mother and child are doing well. Jack is as proud as a peacock, and struts around town as if he was the only father of a bouncing baby boy."[10]

The title "Professor" is a bit of a puzzle for Jack was a railroad engineer. His wife Alice May Galloway was the daughter of James Galloway a prominent lumberyard salesman in the area. Within a year or two of Hobart's birth the family moved from the Comstock area of the city to the Bay area probably for economic reasons, and Hobart was soon something of a minor celebrity. By the age of three the family had moved again to San Francisco where around the age of twelve, he made his first outing on the stage at the California Theatre in a juvenile operetta entitled "The Brownies." Also in the production was Hobart's childhood friend Walter Catlett. The two boys soon found that they worked well together and formed a vaudeville act called the "Irish Boy Comedians." At the age of forty-two Hobart was invited to join Richard Jose's production of "Silver threads among the Gold" and when the show moved to New York the Broadway establishment quickly recognised his talent.

---

[10] Virginia Evening Chronicle (Sep. 22nd 1886)

Hobart spent the next couple of years honing his skills and with each year that passed his performances gained him wider recognition. While performing in "Bought and Paid" Hobart met Florence Heston and they were married in 1913. They had one child, Patricia born in 1919. The production of "The Show Off" seems to have been Hobart's big breakthrough and his performances garnered great reviews. The precise moment of his first appearance on the silver screen is unsure but it may have been in a short film called "San Francisco Nights" around 1928. His film career began proper in 1932 when he was offered a contract and moved to Hollywood. But the adventure was almost over before it had begun when the film he was contracted to appear in was promptly cancelled. Fortunately Hobart won a role in "I Cover the Waterfront" which starred Claudette Colbert and Ben Lyon and was released in 1933. With a major feature film behind him Hobart wasted no time in establishing himself as an onscreen regular; within one year of the release of Waterfront he had made over twenty more movies including: "Death Watch", "Broadway Through a Keyhole" and "Mandalay"

That hectic first year set the tone for a career which eventually comprised over 170 movies, a total which few of his contemporaries can match. Despite the large list of credits the quality of Hobart's work never suffered and he earned almost universal critical praise for both his film and stage performances. Although he enjoyed considerable onscreen success Hobart may have found it a frustrating experience for he never quite made top billing, something he had often done on Broadway. Hobart also suffered from typecasting, so much so that almost every movie guide describes him as a character actor portraying "a hen-pecked husband" or a "nervous" or "mild mannered clerk." Many of his roles were beside artists that would go on to attain worldwide fame such as Ronald Reagan (Santa Fe Trail, 1940) and Clark Gable (Idiot's Delight, 1939). Hobart also performed a song and dance duet with the legendary Al Jolson in the 1939 film "The Rose of Washington Square" and he also made three appearances in Busby Berkley extravaganzas.

Hobart was the embodiment of the Hollywood support actor. His performances were both effortless and flawless, never drawing attention away from the star of the picture but always contributing to the essential fabric of the film. This was a rare talent valued by many Hollywood directors who knew that there were many pitfalls in movie making but that they could always depend on a Hobart Cavanaugh performance.

Hobart died in 1950 aged of sixty-three at the Motion Picture Country Home hospital and is buried in Holy Cross cemetery, Culver City, California.

James Kavanaugh
(1826 - 1885)

James was born at Deer Park Parish, County Wexford in 1826. Little is known about James' early life but his habit of writing Latin verse indicates that he enjoyed a quality education and was probably a member of a reasonably wealthy family. Prior to 1849 James left Ireland with some relatives for America and settled at New Orleans in Louisiana. Accounts of the riches to be found in the goldmines of California tempted him to move west. He sailed to San Francisco via Cape Horn which though a potentially hazardous route was the easiest way to travel from coast to coast at that time. James arrived sometime in 1849 and spent the next nine years working the mines of Sacramento with little or no success. During this time he met a man by the name of Hiram March and he and James quickly established a close and enduring friendship.

Despite his failure to strike gold in California James never gave up hope but with each year that passed the number of miners successfully finding gold continued to diminish. In April 1858 word reached California that gold had been found in the sand bars of the Fraser River in British Columbia and almost overnight miners began to make their way north. James and his good friend Hiram bought themselves a steamship ticket and arrived in Whatcom, Washington in May. Like thousands of other miners they were temporarily stuck in Whatcom as a road to the Fraser River had not yet been completed. In order to feed himself James took a number of construction jobs and was also employed for a time by the Canadian Government as a boundary commissioner. James eventually gave up on the dream of striking gold and decided to settle down in Sehome at Belingham Bay.

James was the first US marshal to be appointed in the Northwest and was later elected the first Sheriff for Whatcom

County. During his free time he helped to educate the children of Whatcom's early pioneers. Around this time he met a native Indian widow by the name of Tol Stola. Tol was renowned in the area for her intelligence, beauty, charm and grace. She was the daughter of Sil-Wis-Os a sub-chief of the local Swimonish tribe and Guil-a-Can. When Tol was still a young girl her mother died and Sil-Wis-Os placed her and a sister into care of others. A white family by the name of Eldridge learned of the children's misfortune and offered to raise the children as their own. Her father Sil-Wis-Os appears to have been a man of great character and foresight. He held no animosity towards the white settlers and saw that the future of his own people lay in closer ties with them. At one point he held a potlatch[11] and announced that his men were to stop killing white men, adding "You may be spilling my grandson's blood."[12] Around 1858 Tola married a Lieutenant Davis and bore him a son by the name of Samuel. At the outbreak of the Civil war Davis joined the Southern army and never returned home.

James was quite taken with the beauty of the Indian princess and they were married though no record of the ceremony, if one did take place, has been found. James and his new bride whom he called Caroline lived for a while in Sehome before moving on to Unionville on October 28th 1862. James managed to keep possession of the house in Sehome and would later rent it out for $2 per month.

In his role as Sheriff James was expected to perform a wide variety of duties. In August 1863 he travelled to the island of San Juan with the intention of collecting taxes. He was frustrated by the British Garrison stationed there when they refused to recognise his authority. In June he was investigating the murder of O.V. Russell who had been "cruelly and barbarously murdered on the beach at his residence on Perry's (Fidalgo) island." On November 26th he got into a fist fight with a man known to be selling whiskey to

---

[11] A ceremonial feast of the American Indians of the northwest coast
[12] Told by the Pioneers, Vol.III, 1938

the Indians; "Had quite a fracas at Sehome with Bill Smith (Indian Whiskey Smith). I whipped him though." He later arrested Smith and his wife and charged the pair with selling liquor without a license.

At home James decided with tobacco plants to see if they would prosper in the damp environment. Rain played a large part in the weather of Washington as can be seen by entries in a Diary that James kept:[13]

April 7, 1864 – It rains this afternoon as usual. It is the wettest spring so far I ever experience.

April 9, 1866 – Rain all last night. Rain all this day and yesterday – pouring. It has rained pretty nearly constant since the middle of March.

June 15 – It is pouring rain today as it did yesterday and for a week back in has done little else; indeed the whole spring as well as the past winter has been remarkably wet.

June 17 – Still it rains. Dull, dark and cloudy.

July 20, 1867 – It has been raining and blowing for the last 8 or 10 days.

May 14, 1876 – Heavy rain, rained all last night. About nine months of the year it rains. I am of the opinion that this county will soon have to be abandoned and left with the Indians and wild water fowl for whom it is admirably adapted. No white man can succeed amid so much rainfall.

The tobacco experiment proved successful and he harvested his first crop on August 31st considering it to be of very good quality. Meanwhile Hiram March had staked a claim to land on Fidalgo Island and was busy establishing a farm. On December 13th, 1863 James and Caroline were enjoying the hospitality of Hiram's new home when Caroline gave birth to a baby boy. Tragically their joy was short lived

---

[13] Anacortes American, 1913

when the infant died just eighteen days later and was buried in Unionville on the first day of the New Year.

The year 1864 began with James sowing a second crop of tobacco and also planting cabbage, turnips and peas. He supplemented the income he earned as an officer of the law in a variety of ways such as selling lumber and constructing boats which could fetch up to $30 in gold. In his official capacity he arrested an army deserter by the name of George Hughes at Utsaladdy and claimed a $30 reward, placed Vincent Silcock in jail for non payment of fines and attended the district court at Olympia.

1865 opened with bitter cold and heavy with snow for the first three months of the year. There was good news on March 16th with the arrival of the first telegraph operator to the area and everyone looked forward to being able to communicate with the wider world. James managed to keep himself occupied building a schooner for himself which he proudly launched on April 3rd. The following day a telegraph link was established between Sehome and New Westminster in British Columbia. Later that month James was on the trail of a band of thieves who had stolen a canoe. He pursued them north to Semiamhoo close to the Canadian border where he recovered the canoe. He continued the chase across the border to New Westminster where he arrested the thieves and placed them in jail. The pursuit and return journey took three days to complete.

In June James took time out to take stock of his financial affairs; he recorded that the cost of provisions for the year to date had come to $140 and that his boat had cost almost $59 to construct. On the twelfth day of the month Caroline gave birth to a baby girl. After the experience of their first child she and James must have spent the hours and days following the birth in a state of nervous excitement. All was well until the middle of August when fate dealt a cruel blow to the Kavanaugh family a second time; on August 23rd the infant died.

In October 1865 James and Caroline moved to Fidalgo Island and settled on a plot of land next to Hiram March. The move may have been sparked by a desire to leave behind a house filled with memories of loss and to make a fresh start. The family immediately set about adapting their new home; wild cherry trees were planted on the beach and a small apple orchard as created.

On June 7th 1866 James left the Sheriff's office for the last time. Relieved to be free of the burdens of office he began to concentrate his time and energy on the family farm. He and Hiram worked closely together and helped each other out when required throughout the year. In August James decided to return to Sehome and work in the coal mines in order to raise extra money. Working in the coalmines was demanding and dangerous work; the mine caught fire the day after James' arrival and he had to wait six days before he could start. On September 16th James returned home to find someone had broken in and stolen some items. An inventory showed that two muskets, a tin-lined kettle, a frying man, a knife and a spoon had been taken. It must have been very frustrating for James to have to leave the investigation and pursuit of the offenders to his replacement in the sheriffs department.

James spent the following year dividing his time between the farm and the coalmine in Sehome. He travelled with Hiram to Utsalady to sell oil, potatoes and cut hay on the Swinomish flats. In August he was back in the mine where one man was later killed by the explosion of two kegs of blasting powder. By the middle of November his stint at the mine had finished and he returned home to Fidalgo Island. There he started construction of a kitchen building which after a number of interruptions was completed at the end of January.

By 1868 the farm was in full swing. In April James travelled to Whatcom where he sold 981 lbs of potatoes at one cent per pound. In May he planted tobacco and sugar cane, tomatoes and corn. In July he was on the Swinomish flats with Hiram once more cutting hay. In September he made $16.40 selling potatoes, onions and peas. 1869 brought both good fortune and bad; in April James shot one his own heifers in the mistaken belief it was a deer while October brought a letter enclosing $10 dollars he was owed for his services as a US Marshall.

Through James and Caroline efforts the farm grew steadily. By 1870 others had taken notice of the excellent opportunities on Fidalgo Island and new settlers began to flood in and occupy every piece of available land. In February 1872 James' property was assessed for $3.35 tax and by March 1874 the assessment had risen to over $4. On April 27th 1881 James made the final proof[14] on his homestead

Despite the tragic loss of two infants James and Caroline never gave up hope of extending their family and she eventually bore James two sons – Francis .J. Kavanaugh and Sarsfield John Kavanaugh who was born on February 13th, 1867. But tragedy did revisit Caroline on one more occasion on January 17th 1883 when Samuel, a son from her first marriage was lost in a riverboat explosion.

James had a cousin named Morgan Kavanagh in Canada and he also corresponded with a Laughlin Kavanaugh in Jackson, Mississippi. It is also likely that he had a sister living in Jackson. A well educated man, James took a keen interest in the political events of the day both domestically and in Europe. To keep up to date with events he subscribed to and corresponded with a number of national newspapers and journals. He was also a committed Catholic and a staunch supporter of the North's cause during the civil war. He played a prominent role in the advancement of local society in his capacity as Sheriff, teacher, US Marshall and a clerk during local elections. He also helped to form a debating society which met once a week and he was held in high regard throughout the community. James died on June 19th, 1885.

---

[14] Homesteaders were required to make continuous improvements to their lots in order to hold on to them.

Caroline remained on the homestead they had built together until she passed away on February 9th, 1919.

Lawrence Kavanagh II
(1764 – 1830)

Lawrence Kavanagh II was born in Louisbourg, Nova Scotia in 1764. There is some confusion about how his family arrived in Louisbourg. It is widely believed that his grandfather, Morris had emigrated from Waterford in Ireland with three sons; Lawrence, Morris and Edward and that they arrived in Louisbourg shortly after the British took that town from the French in 1758. Another suggestion is that it was Lawrence's father Lawrence I who had sailed from Ireland and that he carried with him significant assets of 9,000 pounds[15]. Regardless of their exact origin various documents record the family as being in Louisbourg from 1763 onwards and they were probably resident as early as 1760.

Lawrence I established himself as a gentleman of some note in the region and by 1772 could probably be considered as the most powerful private citizen in Louisbourg employing over fifty percent of the towns' available workforce. Lawrence had his fingers dipped in every area of local commerce such as agriculture, retailing and fishing. He also imported large quantities of alcohol which was considered an essential antidote to the unpleasant climate.

While residing in Louisbourg Lawrence married and again there is confusion surrounding this event. Some sources state that he married a widow named Felicité le Jeune[16] while others state the he married Margaret Farrell[17]. Together he and his wife had six children – James, Catherine, Lawrence II, Elizabeth, Marie and Edward. A catholic in a protestant outpost of the British Empire Lawrence I had to wait seven years for the arrival of a priest to baptise four of his children at one time. In 1775 Lawrence I was lost at sea while

---

[15] Lawrence Kavanagh I: An Eighteenth Century Cape Breton Entrepreneur, Wagg, Phyllis MacInnes, Nova Scotia Historical Review, Vol.10 No.2
[16] Laurance Kavanagh, Rankin, Rev. D.J., reprinted from the Annual Report of the Canadian Catholic Historical Association 1940 -1941
[17] Laurance Kavanagh – His Life and Times, Traboulsee, Anthony, 1962

travelling to Halifax on one of his ships. The management of the family business fell to his wife and to the eldest son James.

In 1775 the conflict between the British Crown and American rebels who sought independence brought trouble to the families' doorstep. American privateers began to carry out raids on the stores and goods of loyalist traders such as the Kavanagh's. Matters degraded to such a point that in 1777 the family decided to leave Louisbourg and head south to St. Peters. James then moved on to Halifax where he opened another branch of the business that flourished initially but eventually failed with huge debts. James died in Halifax at the age of fifty-four.

When James left St. Peters the fortunes of the family were placed on the shoulders of the young Lawrence II. Having observed his father and absorbed many of his skills Lawrence II wasted no time in expanding the Kavanagh Empire through shipping and fishing. And like his father the young Lawrence developed into a major influence in the social and economic circles of local society. His house, the largest in the area was always open to guests regardless of their religion. In 1799 a Presbyterian minister called to the house noting "that night we reached St. Peter's where, Mr. Kavanagh lodges us all with great kindness and generosity" and "he readily offered us his own oxen to haul our boats"[18]

Lawrence's wealth and influence grew with each passing year. He became so powerful that he could afford to extricate himself from practically any adverse situation that presented itself. On one occasion a man by the name of Francis Murphy threatened legal action against him. Lawrence promptly called on every lawyer in Cape Breton and retained their services for any action that might arise from the matter. This left no one available to prosecute a case on Murphy's behalf. A petition was raised in the court requesting that one of the lawyers be released and allowed to represent the plaintiff. It is

---

[18] Laurance Kavanagh – His Life and Times, Traboulsee, Anthony, 1962

unclear whether the petition was granted or whether Murphy's case was frustrated for lack of legal representation. The incident clearly demonstrates the financial resources and ruthless determination of Lawrence. The English authorities appointed him as a Justice of the Peace and later Custos Rotulorum which was the highest possible civilian post in the county.

In 1820 Cape Breton was reannaxed to Nova Scotia after forty-six years of independence. The island was declared a constituency for the purpose of elections to the Nova Scotia Assembly. An election was called with the intent of sending two members to represent Cape Breton. When the votes were tallied Lawrence Kavanagh and a man by the name of Richard John Uniacke were elected. Richard travelled to Nova Scotia and duly took his seat on December 12th 1820. Lawrence Kavanagh remained at home.

To serve in the elected chamber of the English Crown or any of its colonies an elected member was first required to take a series of oaths. One oath in particular was crafted so that Catholics found it impossible to take and yet remain true to their convictions:

> "...that I do believe that there is not Transubstantiation in the Sacrament of the Lord's Supper, or in the elements of Bread and Wine, at or after Consecration therof by any Person whatsoever."

The belief that wine is turned into the blood of Christ and bread into the body of Christ is central to the Catholic faith and as a Catholic Lawrence could never take such an oath. He refused to attend the assembly and by August the following year the situation had not been resolved. At that time the British government wrote to James Kempt, the Lieutenant Governor enquiring if there were any local laws that might apply. Kempt replied in November stating that there were "no laws in this Province imposing restrictions upon the admission of Catholics to either House of the Legislature, but that as far as I can learn no Catholic has, in point of fact, ever sat as a Member either of the Council or the Assembly." He indicated that Lawrence was a man of the "highest Character and respectability" and went on to write "I do not think any evil can arise from his Admission into the House"

In 1822 Lawrence travelled to the Assembly which was then meeting at Halifax and declared that he was willing to swear all oaths except the one against transubstantiation. Kempt made it known that the oath in question could not be overlooked. The assembly itself debated the issue and tried unsuccessfully to resolve the impasse. They requested that the Lieutenant Governor determine if the British Crown might quickly modify its procedures and regulations so that Catholics might take their place in "the Legislature, the Bar, and all offices under Government." Kempt wrote to the British Government in March asking for their advice. On May 8th the Colonial Secretary replied that you have "His Majesty's Authority to admit Mr. Kavanagh to take his Seat in the Assembly on taking the State Oaths and to dispense with his making the declaration against Popery and Transubstantiation."

The news was communicated to the Assembly on the 2nd of April. The House spent that day and the next debating the mechanics of how the Assembly should adopt the Crowns decision. A motion was eventually adopted "expressing its gratitude to the King, and its determination to admit Kavanagh and any other elected Catholics, on the conditions now appointed by His Majesty"[19] Quite why the members decided to admit any other elected Catholics is unknown for, in the strictest sense the decision of the British Crown applied only to Lawrence Kavanagh. On April 3rd 1823 Lawrence Kavanagh entered the House of Assembly, took the State Oaths and then took his seat as a parliamentarian. It was a truly historic event as Lawrence had achieved emancipation

---

[19] Laurance Kavanagh, Rankin, Rev. D.J., reprinted from the Annual Report of the Canadian Catholic Historical Association 1940 -1941

for the Catholics in Nova Scotia. It would take Daniel O'Connell another six years to achieve the same goal in Ireland.

Lawrence continued to serve in the Assembly until his death, taking a keen interest in the welfare and education of the people of Cape Breton. He married a woman by the name of Catherine Murphy and together they had eight children; Lawrence III, Edward, Maurice, Wallace, Margaret, Catherine, Frances and Anne. Lawrence died in his sixty-sixth year on August 20th, 1830 at St. Peters.

Hubbard Hinde Kavanaugh
(1802 - 1884)

Hubbard's predecessors had first set foot on American soil in 1705 when two brothers named Philemon and Charles arrived from Ireland. It is likely that a third unnamed brother also travelled to England. Shortly after arrival Charles moved to New England where all communication with him was subsequently lost. Philemon set out for Virginia, spending a short time in Essex County before finally settling down in Culpepper County, north Virginia. Philemon married twice, the second union producing a son named Williams, born in February 1744 and whose line would eventually lead to Hubbard. By 1775 Williams had moved to Kentucky which was at that time a hostile frontier state. During the migration Williams junior was born on August 3rd close to the border of Virginia and Tennessee. From an early age Williams junior attached great significance to the role of religion in everyday life and was convinced of the importance of spreading the word of God.

Williams junior enrolled in the Methodist church in Jessamine County, Kentucky in 1794 and began to tour the frontier bringing the good news to every outpost that he could reach. It soon became apparent to the elders of the church that Williams was a powerful orator and a great theologian and that many considered him to be the finest preacher in Kentucky. In March 1798 Williams married Miss Hannah Hubbard Hinde, daughter of Thomas Hinde then a prominent preacher in the Methodist church. The church elders were reluctant to lose such a young talent to the travelling circuit but accepted that it was Williams' most fervent wish to marry Hannah and gave him their blessing. Shortly after marriage Williams came to the attention of Dr. Harfield a vestryman of the Protestant Episcopal Church in Lexington who had also noted his potential. Harfield lost no time in offering the post of minister to Williams on condition that he take orders from the Episcopal Church. After examining his conscience and the scriptures of that church Williams concluded that there was no violation of his Methodist principals. Though Hannah was devoted to the Methodist church and considered it "the more excellent way" she voiced no concerns to her husband and Williams accepted the position. After serving for some time in Lexington Williams moved his family to Louisville and then later to Henderson where he died, aged 62 on the 16th of October 1806.

Williams' death left his wife Hannah struggling alone to raise six children; Thomas Williams born January 5th 1792, Leroy Harrison born May 29th 1800, Hubbard Hinde born 14th February 1802, Mary Jane born 16th November 1803, Benjamin Taylor born April 23rd 1805 and Williams Barbour who was born February 17th 1807 some months after his father's death. Hannah was as committed to her faith as Williams had been and she resolved to raise and educate all of her children in the ways of the church. Such was her determination and spirit that she succeeded and each one of them entered into the church in one capacity or another. Hannah also recognised the value of instructing her offspring in the way of business and as each of the boys reached a suitable age they were apprenticed in some practical profession. When Hubbard had reached the age of thirteen he was placed in the service of a Presbyterian minister by the name of Rev. John Lyle to study printing.

Reverend Lyle was appreciative of the industriousness with which the young understudy performed his duties and a deep affection soon developed between them. Hubbard began to accompany Lyle on his Sunday appointments and on these trips Hubbard gained some insight into life and the role religion played within it. On one such trip on November 3rd 1817 God called to Hubbard as he had done to St. Paul on his journey to Damascus. The revelation Hubbard experienced was clear and moving and it left him "inexpressibly happy." He gave thanks and praise to him who "had taken his feet from the miry clay and the horrible pit and set them upon the Rock." Having witnessed Hubbard's calling the Rev. Lyle expressed that it was his wish that Hubbard join the

Presbyterian Church where he would enjoy a classical education, something that Hubbard was otherwise unlikely to experience. Hubbard's mother Hannah exerted a strong influence on his decision making and he politely declined the generous offer. Lyle graciously accepted the decision and released Hubbard from his seven-year apprenticeship two years early so that he might begin his studies.

Hubbard joined the Methodist church, the beloved church of his mother in January 1818 and four years later he was recommended and accepted as a person suitable to be licensed to preach the gospel. Despite his small height of 5'2" Hubbard possessed a booming voice and this combined with a fine intellect promised much for his future as a minister. Hubbard moved his family to Augusta where he helped to edit and publish "The Western Watchman". The town church of Augusta was at that time served by John P. Finlay while Hubbard contented himself with ministering to the surrounding countryside. Finlay was respected and liked by his congregation and was held in such high regard that it was considered unwise for any outsider to attempt a sermon in the town. Hubbard established his reputation in the countryside and when Finlay himself witnessed one of Hubbard's sermons he too recognised that he was in the presence of something special. Keen to see Hubbard preach in town but knowing the frosty reception that waited for any outsider, Finlay devised a plan in partnership with James Armstrong the editor of The Watchman. Armstrong arranged for Hubbard to deliver a private sermon in front of a small audience in one of his rooms. Influential members of the town congregation were invited but neither party were informed of the others presence. Blissfully unaware that he was being put on show Hubbard proceeded to give a sermon full of intense passion and power that the spectators clung to every sound and gesture. When Hubbard had finished his presentation the audience had been fervently won over and from that day forward he had an open invitation to preach in the church of Augusta whenever he so wished.

Following the Kentucky conference of the Methodist Episcopal Church of 1823 Hubbard was appointed junior preacher on the Little Sandy Circuit where his presiding elder was Andrew Monroe. In preparation of the life ahead Hubbard gathered the standard issue of the day: a horse, a hat, an overcoat, a comfortable suit of clothes, a change of underwear, a Bible and a hymnbook. The circuit comprised twenty-four preaching locations ranging from simple log cabins to churches all dispersed over a large range of mountainous territory. Though the people he met on the circuit were quiet and simple folk Hubbard's friendly character and his visible passion for God soon won him a place in their hearts. Hubbard found his first year a tough and lonely experience and his inexperience as a travelling preacher sometimes caught him out. It was common practice for roaming preachers of the day to carry a small six-inch marking iron which they used to mark trees at the fork of a road. The mark would serve as a guide for future trips but on a number of occasions during his first tour of the circuit Hubbard marked the wrong tree. On his second tour Hubbard was accompanied by a guide who marked the correct tree. On subsequent trips Hubbard found it difficult to remember which mark was correct and which was incorrect and this resulted in a number of unintentional detours into the countryside.

Returning to his family after a year on the road Hubbard recounted to his mother the long hours of solitude on horseback riding from one location to another, the less than generous reception he had received from some quarters and the perils of travelling alone through frontier country. His mother asked if Hubbard had tired of the work and the reply she received must have filled her heart with joy for Hubbard said "I sometimes get tired in it, but never of it. I have enlisted for life." Here truly was her mother's son for she too had experienced the hardship of challenging life alone as she struggled to raise six children following the death of her husband. The strength and resilience Hannah had so ably displayed was present in equal measure in Hubbard.

Following the conference of 1824 Hubbard was assigned to the more established circuit of Newport and in 1825 he moved on to the Salt River circuit. His reputation and that of his church were growing steadily. Such was his eloquence that he drew large audiences and won many converts in the town of Bardstown which was then a Roman Catholic stronghold, and had proven barren ground for the Methodist church before Hubbard's arrival. In recognition of the breakthrough and his successes generally Hubbard was reappointed to Salt River for a second year. As the fourth year of Hubbard's wandering ministry drew to a close he had been appointed a deacon and an elder of his church.

Towards the end of 1827 Hubbard was assigned to the Lexington circuit and with each year that passed he matured as an individual and grew in stature as a minister of the church. His sermons were a truly wonderful experience for his inner strength could command the attention of an audience for hours, while his eloquence in describing the joys of heaven could reduce the most hardened of souls to tears. On the 24th of July 1828 Hubbard married Margaret Greene, a daughter of one of Kentucky's most powerful families and at the conference that year was then assigned to serve Russelville. Louisville followed in 1829, Danville in 1830 and then a return to Bardstown and Springfield. The year 1831 brought new honour upon Hubbard as he was elected to represent the church of Kentucky at the general conference held in Philadelphia in May of that year. In 1832 he was assigned to the capitol Frankfurt where his congregation was filled with the great and the good from all over the state. Performing in front of this more sophisticated audience held no terrors for Hubbard and his powerful voice and impassioned oratory won over a whole new audience. In fact the Methodist church had never previously commanded such large and enthusiastic audiences as they did under Hubbard's guidance. When his term in Frankfurt had finished Hubbard returned to Lexington.

In 1836 Hubbard was once more in the rapidly expanding city of Louisville where he was assigned to the central church on Fourth Street. Though his fervour was undiminished and his abilities continued to develop there were few conversions or awakenings in reward for his efforts. As a result for the first time in his life he began to doubt his effectiveness as a minister and he considered retirement. As the doubts took hold he shared them with his wife Margaret – "Perhaps I am mistaken in thinking I am called to the work of the ministry." Margaret tried to reassure her husband by pointing to the success he had enjoyed throughout all of his travels. Unconvinced Hubbard asked her why he was enjoying so little success now. Margaret responded, "It is not always harvest time. You must sow before you reap. Have you not sometimes thought that you entered upon the labours of those who succeeded you and reaped a harvest from their toils? This year may be seedtime for your Church, and the harvest may come hereafter. On our itinerant system such results may frequently occur."[20] These simple words of truth from a devoted wife lightened Hubbard's heavy heart, filled his eyes with tears and after a private prayer he was once more ready to spread the word of God.

In February 1837 Hubbard was appointed to the position of superintendent of public instruction by Governor Clarke and was so successful in his duties that he was reappointed to the post by the successive administration of Governor Wickliffe. In 1838 the conference assigned Hubbard to Bardstown and he was also appointed as the conference liaison to the newly created Augusta College. For a while Hubbard's time was occupied with the promotion of the college and to fundraising on its behalf but by 1840 he had resumed his normal duties when he was assigned to Maysville. In that town he continued to be successful in harvesting new blood to his church serving two years there before moving on to Shelbyville for another two-year term. In 1842 Hubbard ministered to the needs of the city Louisville and its surrounding districts.

---

[20] Life and Times of H. H. Kavanaugh, D.D, Redford, A. H. (P.174)

In May 1844 Hubbard represented Kentucky at the General Conference held in New York. This particular gathering marked the beginning of some years of trouble for the Methodist church when the issue of slavery arose. From its inception in the early 1700's Methodism had been opposed slavery but as the church grew in popularity in America the attitudes of its various conferences began to reflect the opinions of the local populace from which they were drawn. A division based roughly along north and south lines developed with regards to slavery and at the General Conference of 1843 the division widened significantly. The matter of Bishop James O. Andrew, who had acquired slaves through marriage, was debated by the conference. Although Andrew had legally inherited the slaves he did not hold them in servitude and under the laws of his home state of Georgia it was illegal to free them. Although he offered to resign over the issue the Southern churches, which were in the minority, would not allow him to do so as they resented what they considered interference in local matters. The slavery issue had forced Hubbard to choose between his loyalties to the Methodist church and his love for the Kentucky church in which he grown up and in the end he chose to stand with the Kentucky. After a heated debate the General Conference voted to suspend Bishop Andrew and as a result the southern representatives decided to separate and subsequently formed The Methodist Episcopal Church, South in 1845.

In 1846 Hubbard took the next step in his church when he was elected the presiding elder to the Lexington circuit where he remained as a preacher for the next three years. Much of his energy, and that of the church generally, were devoted at this time to averting a split on the issue of slavery. The slavery question was still a cause of division in the Methodist Church, South and the circuits on the border of Kentucky were under particular pressure to re-enter the fold of the Methodist Church. In 1848 Hubbard was appointed as corresponding editor to the "Methodist Expositor and True Issue" newspaper where it was hoped that he could argue the cause of Southern Methodists, and while Hubbard was always more comfortable addressing his audience personally, nevertheless he fulfilled his mission admirably. In 1850 he moved to Clarke County, his childhood home for a period of two years stint and then onto Versailles where he and his wife had established their home. An incident at the Kentucky conference held in Versailles in 1853 serves to indicate just how far Hubbard had progressed in his church and that despite his determination he always maintained a sense of humour. Bishop Capers, whose habit it was to politely invite a speaker to take their seat whenever he considered that they had appropriate time to make their point, chaired the conference that year. During a debate Hubbard was placing his case before the audience when Bishop Capers interrupted him mid flow.

"Brother Kavanaugh, you will please take your seat."[21] "I must respectfully decline," replied Hubbard. "But I tell you to sit down," commanded the Bishop. "For what?" Hubbard enquired. "You have spoken long enough," was the response from the chair. "I prefer to be the judge of that myself," said Hubbard to which the bishop once more commanded him to take his seat. "Am I out of order?" asked Hubbard. The bishop, now a little excited said, "Nobody said that you were out of order." Hubbard insisted that if he were not out of order then he would finish what he had begun to say. Bishop Capers, perhaps surprised by the dogged resistance of the preacher, relented a little and said "You will proceed and hurry through, for it will soon be time for dinner." "I am not in the habit of hurrying and do not propose to do so now," Hubbard responded still unwilling to bend. Bishop Capers realised now that there was no rushing the man who stood in front of him, and smiling at Hubbard said, "Well, take your time, Brother Kavanaugh". Hubbard smiled back at the bishop and said "That is what I was doing, but you have taken so much of it that I do not know where I left off, so I must commence again at the beginning."

At the general conference held in Columbus, Georgia in 1854 representatives of the Kentucky conference approached

---

[21] Life and Times of H. H. Kavanaugh, D.D, Redford, A. H. (P.380)

Hubbard and stated that it was their intention to nominate him to the office of Bishop. Though visibly pleased at the honour he responded firmly that he could not allow his name to be put forward, arguing that he knew himself better than any man and that he felt he was ill qualified to be elevated to such high office. However the more he resisted the more convinced the others became of his suitability. Hubbard was nominated on May 19th alongside George Foster Pierce and John Early and on May 25th 1854, now aged 52 he was elected Bishop of the Methodist Episcopal Church, South.

Hubbard returned home to Kentucky where he received the congratulations and good wishes of all the states citizens regardless of their denomination. The Western Recorder noted that "If such an office can be filled with divine acceptance, and for the advancement of vital godliness, we confidently predict it will be so filled by Bishop Kavanaugh" and went on to suggest that "He will elevate and adorn his new office."[22] As a bishop of the church Hubbard's horizons expanded significantly for having grown to know every inch of his beloved Kentucky he was now free to wander a large piece of the continental United States from Florida on the east coast to San Francisco on the west. Although still free to preach his responsibilities now included more administrative roles and one of these was to preside over the Annual Conference of various circuits. His first conference was in Brunswick, Missouri in October and while unused to the procedures and etiquette of his new role he nevertheless acquitted himself well. Hubbard learned quickly and at the Memphis conference of 1855 the Memphis Advocate reported that "The impression produced by Bishop Kavanaugh on the conference, the church and the community will tell for the interests of Methodism for a long time to come."[23] Hubbard spent the next couple years presiding over the circuit conferences and while he never completely mastered the role of presiding officer, his natural warmth, kindness and good

---

[22] P.397
[23] P.399

humour always carried him through any difficulties he encountered.

In 1862 a dark shadow hung over the United States as the country faced its greatest trial since its foundation. The civil war which had begun the previous year at Forth Sumter, South Carolina was continuing to grow in ferocity and savagery. The growing confusion throughout the country confined Hubbard to his home state of Kentucky and the annual conference that took place in October was a heated event as delegates envisioned the prospect of a division between north and south. Though he personally favoured the Southern cause Hubbard did not actively canvas on its behalf. The Louisville conference which followed some weeks later was a potentially more precarious event and Hubbard needed all of his powers of persuasion to prevent it from exploding into open hostility. It required a great deal of personal courage to ensure equal time and treatment for the supporters of both sides, regardless of the influences which tried to guide his hand one way or the other. The following year in the midst of a war that continued to divide friends and family alike, Hubbard suffered a terrible personal tragedy when his wife Margaret took ill and died on October 7th. For over thirty years Margaret had witnessed his triumphs, consoled him in times of sadness and spurred him on through his moments of doubt. She had contributed greatly to both his private and public life and her loss was heartbreaking. The months following her death were lonely ones and Hubbard remained at home until the following spring when the pain of his loss had subsided.

Hubbard was again leading the life of an itinerant preacher and his travels eventually took him to California where he delivered another powerful series of sermons. However during his stay he was involved in a most unsettling incident. Attending a camp meeting at Calaveras on July 19th 1884 Hubbard was about to delivery his address when he was approached by a Captain Jackson, a provost marshal of the Union army. The captain discreetly made it known that he was under orders to arrest Hubbard and escort him to San

Francisco where he was to face charges. On hearing that Hubbard had an appointment to preach before the assembled audience the captain allowed him to fulfil his obligation. When the sermon had finished Hubbard and the Captain agreed to meet the following day at the boat where they would travel to the Captains office in San Francisco. When Hubbard arrived at the office his bags were searched and his correspondence carefully examined. He was then escorted to the assistant provost general where charges were put to him. The general stated that an unnamed person had alleged that Hubbard was a citizen of the state of Georgia, that he was travelling on a Confederate pass and that he was in California with no visible purpose. Though not alleged directly it was the clear that the thrust of the charge was one of spying on behalf of the south.

In response Hubbard outlined that he was in fact a citizen of Kentucky, a state in which he had lived all his life except when his church commanded he go elsewhere for a short period. He then declared that he had never crossed a military line and that on only one occasion had he entered a rebellious state and even then under a Federal escort. He also stated that he never interfered in political matters and finished by outlining the purpose of his visit to California. In evidence he produced correspondence from the Pacific Conference requesting a Bishop to preside over their annual assembly and to ordain new preachers for they had been without a bishop for the previous four years. When Hubbard had finished there was obvious relief on the part of the general and it was clear that he was just following formality in completing the investigation. Nevertheless the incident caused much excitement in California with many, including the newspaper columnist Mark Twain taking particular exception to the secrecy surrounding the identify of the accuser and the nature of the charges. On the 2nd of August a Democratic meeting at Hayes Park passed a resolution which stated in part "Resolved, That the spotless reputation of Bishop Kavanaugh and the well-known patriotism and devotion of Charles L. Weller, to the Constitution and the Union, justify the belief that the arrest of these Gentlemen was procured by the perjury of mercenary spies and informers, or by persons actuated solely by personal malice, and we can but express the sentiments of all honorable men in denouncing the employment of those degraded wretches, an offence to civilization, and a disgrace to humanity."[24] In the San Francisco Daily Morning Call of July 22nd Samuel Langhorne Clemens, more commonly known as Mark Twain, wrote about his frustration in attempting to determine the exact nature of the charges levelled at Bishop Kavanaugh.

Following a return to Kentucky Hubbard devoted much of his time and effort in maintaining unity within the Methodist church. His time was not spent exclusively on the interests of the church however and on March 7th the following year he was delighted to marry Mrs. Martha Lewis. The first General Conference for eight years was held in New Orleans in 1866 and during its deliberations many matters that had been placed on hold because of the war were resolved. Four new bishops were also appointed to reinforce the existing number and Hubbard was assigned to the Pacific and Columbia conferences. As soon as the Conference had drawn to a close Hubbard was taken seriously ill and he was forced to spend the next few weeks recuperating before he was in a fit state to travel to California and assume his duties. From California he travelled north to Portland, Oregon and from there on to Lafayette via Albany, Dallas and Salem before finally returning to San Francisco. At every point on his journey he preached to his usual high standards and many converts were won to his church. In 1867 he was working as hard as ever and shortly before he left California the Spectator carried an article on his labours: "Of Bishop Kavanaugh it may be said that he is emphatically a working bishop. If we had at hand the statistics showing the number of miles he has travelled and the number of sermons he has preached during the past year, an aggregate would be presented that would perhaps astonish some of our readers." It concluded, "Bishop Kavanaugh has fully won the affection of our people. They will accompany him in his homeward-bound voyage by their

---

[24] The San Francisco Daily Morning Call, July 22, 1864

prayers, and should he return to us he will be welcomed joyfully by all."

Alas, though Hubbard still possessed the keen intellect and spiritual power of his youth it was constrained by the body of a man aged sixty-five. His punishing schedule exacted a heavy price on his health after his return to Kentucky. The exertions had sapped him of his strength and though he hated being idle he was forced to abandon preaching completely for some weeks. He recovered in time for the General Conference held in Louisville during May where he was assigned to the Missouri, St. Louis, Mississippi, East Texas and Louisiana conferences. He embarked on the campaign with renewed vigour and a member of one of his audiences was moved to say: "There was power and unction in discourse which so overwhelmed the hearers that, convulsed and transfixed, many of us did not know, for the time, whether we were in the body or out of the body." In 1870 he was touring Alabama, Georgia and Florida in addition to attending many meetings in Kentucky and the following years his schedule seems to have increased still further. At the end of the following year Hubbard returned to Louisville to dedicate the new Kavanaugh Chapel.

At the Kentucky Conference of 1873 the church formally recognised and thanked Bishop Kavanaugh for over fifty years of dedicated service to Methodism: "It is eminently proper that the Kentucky Conference should give expression in a suitable manner to their profound sense of divine goodness, in prolonging to so great a length the life and efficient labors of our venerable brother, Bishop H. H. Kavanaugh. We rejoice in the grace of God, which has sustained him in the arduous labours of a ministry which has now reached its fiftieth year. Starting from the humblest place in the Church, he has passed in regular gradation through every efficient station in the Church-exhorter, junior preacher, senior preacher, stationed, presiding elder, agent for educational efforts and bishop. His great intellect and spotless life, ramifying themselves through all these departments of labor, have been seen and felt in the achievements of grand results.

Upon his character career neither blot nor suspicion has ever rested."

Towards the end of the conference Hubbard was to preach a sermon as part of the events to mark his anniversary. For some reason Hubbard elected for the first time in his distinguished career to read from a manuscript he had prepared rather than deliver from memory. His body was now over seventy years of age and was beginning to betray the spirit which still burned within. Hubbard started slowly at first but his true nature could not be contained for long. He broke off from his prepared text and began to speak from the heart. The words flowed easily from his lips and the images he conjured up filled the imaginations of the congregation. All too soon the detour was over and Hubbard attempted to return to the manuscript. The audience watched on in silence as he struggled to identify the relevant passage. Minute after agonising minute passed by and still Hubbard could not establish his position within the text. To the relief of everyone present Hubbard eventually resumed the sermon but before long his mind was again overwhelmed with the desire to share his thoughts with the audience. For a second time he filled the room with his oratory but again he was embarrassed when he attempted to return to his text. It was a painful experience for everyone present to witness such an eloquent and powerful speaker humbled in such a cruel fashion. Hubbard was aware more than anyone of the significance of what had occurred and at a meeting in Russellville some weeks later he insisted that another preacher read the text. Though Hubbard was now showing the physical signs of ageing he was still fluent and persuasive when speaking directly from the heart. At a conference in Waco towards the end of the year the Rev. Bennett reflected "My verdict at that time was that in wondrous flights of eloquence he could soar higher and remain up longer, and descend more gracefully than any man I have heard."

May 1874 took Hubbard to the General Conference at Louisville where he was allocated to White River, Little Rock and Arkansas conferences. In July the following year

Hubbard prepared the groundwork for a project that had been close to his heart for some time. He sent a letter to the leaders of the Kentucky and Louisville conferences outlining his desire to build a permanent camp in Kentucky that would acknowledge the successes enjoyed by the church in thousands of camp meetings throughout the South. A meeting was convened outside Louisville in August and there it was agreed to construct a permanent campground in Oldham County, Kentucky. Hubbard purchased fifty acres and a Mr. T. J. McCoy later purchased another fifty and he also financed the construction of a chapel, hotel and dormitory. The camp has proved to be a great success and is still in existence today.

The following years saw the workload continue at an unrelenting pace. In 1877 he attended the conferences in Illinois, Arkansas, Louisville and Little Rock In. Later he was at the General Conference in Atlanta, the district conferences of Illinois, Tennessee and Alabama before moving on to Tennessee and Kentucky. In 1880 the church took him to Indiana, Tennessee and Kentucky. The death of a colleague left Hubbard once more with responsibility for the Pacific Coast and during his time there he called to Oregon for the Columbia Conference. In September Hubbard was on the road again taking in Montana, Colorado and Texas before returning home to Kentucky. In May 1882 he opened the General Conference in Nashville where the District Conferences of South Georgia and Florida were entrusted to his care. The miles were exacting a heavy toll on his physical health but he would not yield to any thoughts of easing into retirement even though now he had reached his eightieth year. It was through preaching that Hubbard was able to give expression to his love of God and travel was necessary in order to spread the word of God to as many as possible. 1883 found him at conferences in Richmond, Virginia and Augusta, Natchez, Vicksburg and finally in New Orleans for the Louisiana Conference.

Hubbard remained in New Orleans until February 12th before embarking on the journey home to Kentucky. He paused en route in Ocean Springs with the intention of preaching a sermon on Sunday 17th and lodged with a good friend by the name of W.R. Short. The night before the sermon Hubbard was uncomfortable with severe bouts of pain and got little or no sleep. His wife advised him not to attend the sermon but Hubbard was determined to keep the appointment. Hubbard appeared exhausted and during the second reading of his text was forced to stop and request a glass of water. Taking a small sip he attempted to continue the reading but once more found it too much and requested a colleague to close the meeting. Hubbard was then taken back the home of Mr. Short where he was under the constant supervision of a doctor, his friends and family. When they had judged him well enough to travel they set him on the road for home but he insisted on making a stop on the way in Columbus where he had accepted the invitation of another good friend.

On his arrival in Columbus on the morning of the 27th of February it was soon apparent that Hubbard was extremely ill and in great pain. For the next twenty-four hours Hubbard's body was wracked by intense bouts of pain occurring approximately every half hour. A doctor was sent for and a treatment commenced immediately but there was no positive response from the frail body. The doctor diagnosed cystitis which had lead to blood poisoning. In fact the condition was now so advanced that Hubbard had at best six months to live. Plans were made to return him home to Kentucky but they were quickly abandoned when it became clear that he was too ill to travel. Pain surged through Hubbard's body in waves leaving him doubled up in agony and eventually morphine was administered to relieve the suffering.

For a few days from Monday to Thursday the 13th it appeared that Hubbard's spirit was returning, only for it to sink once more under the weight of his illness. His condition deteriorated rapidly until at 3 o'clock on Wednesday the 19th of March 1884 Hubbard Hinde Kavanaugh departed the earthly life. On the 21st his wife, Martha escorted her husband's remains to Louisville and the following day a service was held in Bradbury Methodist Church. Reflecting Hubbard's upbringing and education the congregation was composed of many denominations including Presbyterian and Baptist. At the conclusion of the service the presiding Bishop said, "We have now done all that Christian hands can do. This body is sown in corruption; it shall be raised in glory. We hasten to that day." A memorial service was held in Nashville on the 30th and at other cities throughout the South as the church sought to acknowledge its debt to Hubbard and to give testimony to his character and spirit.

The loss of Hubbard was acutely felt at all levels of the church for although elected to serve at the highest level he always had time and energy for the humblest sinner. He had helped to build the Methodist church in the United States and was one of the foundation stones on which the Southern Church had built so fruitfully following its split from the General Conference. His passion was to preach and it was in the pulpit that his heart was at its most joyous. In the weeks following his passing the Christian papers were fulsome in their praise for his work and his life. The Christian Advocate stated "The Church sorrows and rejoices for him – sorrows that his face shall be seen no more among us, rejoices that his life was, by the grace of God, so pure, so truly grand, so fruitful, so completely rounded." The New Orleans Christian Advocate – "Thus passes to his reward one of the purest and noblest of God's heroes, Guileless, transparent, generous, gentle, large hearted, and saintly, he illustrated the graces of our holy religion, going in and out among us his brethren for over four score years without a blur on his name or a stain on his shield, and at last has gone up to a rich reward of a dauntless, tireless chieftain." The Wesleyan Christian Advocate – "He was a bishop, not merely in the ecclesiastical sense for the exercise of peculiar functions, but in the evangelical sense, he cared for souls."

Generous to all men and women regardless of their faith Hubbard possessed close friends from many denominations. He once remarked, "I could not be a bigot; my father was a Protestant Episcopal clergyman, mother a Methodist, I was awakened under a sermon preached by a Baptist preacher, and converted while travelling with a Presbyterian preacher. So I owe something to all the Churches, and could not be a bigot, if I were to try." It was appropriate that, as perhaps the greatest itinerant preacher the Southern Church had known, Hubbard should have died on the road.

Williams Marmaduke Kavanaugh
(1866 – 1915)

Williams was born on the 3rd of March 1866 in Eutaw, Greene County, Alabama to the Rev. Hubbard Hinde Kavanagh and his wife Anna Kimbrough. The Rev. Kavanaugh had served as a minister to the "Orphans", the only confederate brigade to represent the state of Kentucky in the civil war, and his father had served as bishop of Kentucky. While still a boy Williams and his family moved to Frankfort, Kentucky and there he was educated at the Kentucky Military Institute. When he graduated in 1885 he was the ranking cadet officer, the highest rank a student could hope to attain, and received a Master of Arts. His roommate, F.B.T. Hollenberg, remembered him thus:

> "At school, as elsewhere, he was a leader, well loved and popular. Even as a boy his judgement and fairness were preeminent" [25]

Following graduation Williams moved to Clarksville, Arkansas a state to which he was to give great service. He found employment in a bank under the guidance of John C. Hill and met and subsequently married a Miss Ida Floyd. Miss Floyd came from a prominent family; her father, W.W. Floyd, had served as a judge and her brother would eventually become postmaster for Little Rock. In 1886 Williams took his wife to live in Little Rock and there he was reunited with his school friend Hollenberg who employed him as a bookkeeper with the Hollenberg Music Company. Shortly after he left Hollenberg to join the reporting staff of the Arkansas Gazette and within three years was the managing editor.

Following the resignation of W. H. Booker in 1896 Williams was appointed as county sheriff for Pulaski by Governor James P. Clarke. He served for two consecutive terms and in 1900 was elevated to the position of county

---

[25] The Arkansas Gazette, February. 22nd, 1915

judge which he also served for two terms. During his tenure he improved the infrastructure of the area with the construction of roads and the purchase of land for county buildings. In 1901 Williams took an interest in baseball and became a director of his local club the "Little Rock Travellers". Terms as vice president and president of the league followed and in 1903 he was elected to the Board of the National Association of Professional Baseball Clubs to represent the Southern and Western regions. He served on the board until 1915 and his organisational skills were a great asset to both the board and to his local club. Charles Frank a fellow official from the baseball league described Williams as *"The finest man in the world – a born leader"*

In 1905 Williams formed the Southern Trust Company which was followed in 1906 by the Southern Construction Company. Through the later he constructed the first modern office block seen in the state of Arkansas, the Southern Trust building. 1906 was also the year in which he entered the political arena when he joined the Democratic Party serving for six years on the County Central Democratic Committee. At the state convention in 1912 he was elected national state committeeman and represented Arkansas at the national convention that same year. In 1913 the state senator for Arkansas Jeff Davis died and the state legislature elected Williams to succeed him for the remainder of the term. Williams represented Arkansas in the Senate from January 29th to March 3rd 1913.

Despite the shift in focus towards national interests Williams still found time to take care of local matters. He served on and was president of, the School Board for Little Rock and oversaw its modernisation and renewal. Amazingly he also found time to create and manage a myriad of businesses. He was principal owner and treasurer of the Central Heating Company, a director of the American Cities Company, president of the Little Rock Railway and Electric Company, president of the Consumers' Coal Company, and president of the Little Rock Compress Company.

On February 21st 1915 Williams had lunch at his home on Arch Street and shortly after suffered an acute attack of indigestion. After one hour there was no relief and Williams' brother and two doctors were sent for. By the time his brother arrived at his bedside the attack had abated and Williams sat up and said, "Yes, I'm all right now. I can draw a deep breath". Then he drew in a long deep breath and said, "My, that feels good" at which point he immediately fell back on the bed dead. A pulmotor, an early respirator, was fetched but did not revive him. At just 49 years of age Williams was declared dead. The state of Arkansas and Little Rock in particular had been robbed of one of its leading lights.

There was considerable shock among his friends and family. One of them, Charles Frank had meet with Williams the day before and when informed of his death commented, *"His loss is one we cannot comprehend"*. Governor Hays paid the following tribute:

"I consider the death of Judge Kavanaugh one of the greatest calamities which could befall Little Rock and the state of Arkansas." "I feel proud to have considered him one of my closest friends, and I believe he was the most progressive man in the city of Little Rock and one of the foremost men of the nation. Judge Kavanaugh will, in my opinion, be missed more than any other man in Arkansas."[26]

Mayor Taylor was just as complimentary; *"To a greater degree than most men, he had a clear vision of the possibilities of the state, and his death removes one of who would have continued to wield a great influence in bringing about the rapid development of Arkansas"*

Williams's funeral took place on Wednesday the 24th of February 1915. As a mark of respect the state, county and city offices were closed. The offices of all banks in the city closed for the afternoon, as did the Arkansas Gazette. At 2:45 the equipment of the Little Rock Street Railway and Electric

---

[26] The Arkansas Gazette, February. 22nd, 1915

Company was shutdown and the city effectively came to a halt to mark the occasion. Thousands of well-wishers followed the funeral cortège from Williams' house to Oakland cemetery. Floral tributes were everywhere.

There were many citizens of Arkansas who had good reason to give thanks for the life of Williams Marmaduke Kavanaugh and most of them were present at his burial. Officers of the Southern Association of Baseball clubs, representatives of the National Association of Minor League Baseball, Confederate veterans, social clubs and, of course, the many close friends he had made during his years of service to his community. In its report of February 27th, 1915 the Southern Guardian stated *"Few men are followed to the grave by more friends than Judge Kavanaugh"*

In remembrance of the service he gave to their baseball club The Little Rock Travellers played at Kavanaugh Field for many years on what is now the site of Quigley Stadium. The city of Little Rock also honoured Williams's memory in 1936 by naming one of their streets Kavanaugh Boulevard. The Arkansas Democrat carried a tribute to Williams on February 22nd that seemed to capture the mood at the time:

> *"Time in its inexorable turning, brings joy to some and grief to others; yet it seems today the whole state must pause for more that a moment to comprehend the weight of he blow dealt by Fate in the sudden demise of William Marmaduke Kavanaugh, who though at the time of his death held no political office in the gift of the people, nevertheless had earned the sobriquet, Arkansas' Foremost Citizen."*

Frank William Cavanaugh
(1876 – 1938)
The "Iron Major"

The story of Frank Cavanaugh is truly a remarkable one; demonstrating the qualities of dedication, inspiration and bravery. Frank was born on 24th of April 1876 in Worcester, Massachusetts to Patrick Cavanaugh and Anne Cavanaugh. A public school education was followed by attendance at Worcester High School. Those early days were long ones for Frank for in addition to the time spent in class he held down a paper round in the morning and a job lighting street lamps in the evening. In physical appearance Frank was not particularly strong and this may have had some influence on his reluctance to participate in sports. But what Frank lacked in physique he more than made up for in other areas; he was intelligent, streetwise and had a larger than life personality which made an instant impression with people. In his final high school year he eventually tried out for the athletics and football teams and it was in the later that he quickly came to the attention of Ed Hall and Matt Jones on the coaching staff. With encouragement from the staff Frank decided to try for a place in college and Hall persuaded him to apply to Dartmouth. His college education began in 1895 and to help pay for his education Frank waited on tables during college terms and on his summer vacation.

Frank's character was well suited to college life. He was soon a valuable player on the football team and his intelligence, humour, musical ability and personal presence made it easy for him to fit in socially. Frank's emerging leadership qualities and his stunning performances on the football field resulted in his election as Captain of the College football team toward the end of 1897. His academic performance was no less impressive and many of his tutors and peers saw a very bright future ahead for him. After observing that Frank had developed new variations in end-running the coach, Dr. Wurtemburg described him as a "real football genius" But before Frank could complete his studies he decided at the end of his third year to leave Dartmouth College and pursue a career in football. He later confessed: "This is the thing I was born to do."

In 1898 Frank moved to Cincinnati University to coach the college football team and at the end of the season his record showed 5 wins, 1 defeat and 3 draws, which included a 17-12, win over his old Dartmouth team. Though he remained with the Cincinnati Bearcats for only one season it marked the beginning of a remarkable and successful career as a coach. It was his ability to instil unflinching commitment in his players and to extract the best from even the most average player that was to make him such a formidable force in football over the next decade. In his book "Inside Football" Frank wrote:

> *"I have sometimes told a squad at the first meeting: 'If you are not willing to sacrifice an arm or a leg for the good of the cause - not that any one hopes or expects or desires that such a sacrifice be made - the cause is not sufficiently serious to you and you ought not to be on the squad."*

Employing motivational techniques and mind games to inspire his players, Frank could probably be described as the first sport psychologist. His techniques and successes were later to lead to accusations that he would go to any lengths to achieve his goals. Though he encouraged his players to push right up to the very limit of the laws he never once asked a player to step outside them. His teams may have been founded on physical strength but they could never be accused of playing dirty. During his introductory speech to a new squad he would say "There is only one way to play this game, and that is to the uttermost limits of respectability." And in his book he wrote of his players "They know that I never taught them one un-sportsman-like trick. They are my jury and I'm sure of their verdict."

After Cincinnati Frank spent the three years in charge of the Denver Athletic Club where he also played a number of positions including end, quarter, half and full back. In 1902 he returned briefly to his hometown to study law at Boston University and during his spare time to coach Worcester High School. Frank graduated from law school on June 3rd 1903 and was admitted to the Bar while his football team recorded a 100% record. In the middle of planning a legal career he was approached by Holy Cross who offered him a position as coach and it did not take too much persuasion to convince him to join. He remained for three years posting seasons of 8-20, 2-52 and 6-3-0. A two-year break from football followed when Frank concentrated on his law practice. In 1908 he married Florence E. Ayers and that same year took the team of Worcester Academy under his wing dividing his time between law and football.

The years at Holy Cross and Worcester allowed Frank time and space to refine his coaching skills and to develop the tactical side of football. It had also allowed him to appreciate that football was his true calling and that given the choice of a career in law or a career in football he would unhesitatingly choose the latter. In 1911 the time for making that choice arrived. Dartmouth College on whose fields and in whose classrooms he had shown so much promise offered him a position as their full time coach and it was no surprise to anyone that he promptly accepted. His self-belief and the experience he had gained elsewhere now gave him the confidence to take his game philosophy to the next level. He instituted a program of intense physical workouts and rigorous mental preparation for games. The results were immediate and dramatic; in his first season he delivered eight wins out of ten matches. The only defeats came at the hands of the distinguished colleges of Harvard and Princeton, the latter the result of a freak field goal. Five years of increasing success and fame for Dartmouth followed as the college joined the ranks of top-flight football. 1913 saw victory over Princeton by a margin of 6-0 and Pennsylvania was defeated on three occasions. The year 1916 saw a first in football when on Saturday, September 16th Frank introduced the numbered jerseys for the match against the Carlisle Indians in New York. By the time Frank resigned in 1916 Dartmouth he enjoyed an enviable reputation and was widely considered one of the most talented coaches in the country, with statistics showing 49 wins, 3 draws and 9 loses.

The following year Frank discussed contracts with Holy Cross but before he could sign on the dotted line war intervened. America had entered World War I in April 1917 and Frank had decided to play his part in the Great War for freedom. There were many reasons why Frank should not have signed up; he had a wife, six children and he was now forty-two years of age. He discussed his desire to join the army with Florence and she, perhaps realising it was futile to argue agreed. Too old to gain a place at officers' training school Frank signed up as a private on April 28th 1917 and joined Battery B, 1st Massachusetts Field Artillery. It was soon apparent to his superiors that Frank's ability to lead with confidence and mental strength marked him out as officer material. He quickly rose to the rank of First Lieutenant on May 28th and later to Executive Officer.

When the unit was transferred to the US Army its designation changed to the 102nd Field Artillery. On September 22nd 1917 Frank and his comrades sailed for Europe and toward an uncertain and dangerous future. In November Frank wrote a letter home to his oldest child David who was then Seven years old:

November 7th 1918.
Somewhere in France

Dear Dave Boy:

Your good mother writes me that you have a chum, and she says that he is a fine boy and lives next door. Isn't that fine? I wish I had a chum. You and your mother used to be my chums, and sometimes Joe and Billie and even dear little Rosemary, and Phil, too, when he was home.

But, now, that is all changed and I have no chum at all in the world. I think it's rather sad sometimes, don't you? But I have your pictures, which I take out and talk to when I am lonesome.

I'm happy to know you like our new school and home and I'm sure you'll only play with the clean boys who don't do anything very bad, and who also like to go to school.

Didn't we have the good times together, and wasn't it great fun when you'd come up to the car to meet me; then, when you saw me getting off, do you remember how you'd come and hide behind a tree and run up behind me and scare me after I had passed?

And do you remember how sometimes you and I would race, and you were getting so you could run pretty fast, because you were growing up to be a big boy. And then we'd all go down to see the circus and the parade and hold hands so we wouldn't get separated or lost. And then, Christmas! Oh, wasn't that a wonderful day! Early in the morning how you'd all rush downstairs to see your presents...And then poor tired mother would work and work to give all her boys and girls a big Xmas dinner – turkey, cranberry sauce, and dressing and plum pudding and candy, nuts and "evathin." Oh, Dave, did any little boy ever have such a good mother as you, I wonder.

And now, you are soon to have another Xmas, and old Cav won't be home; but I want you to have the finest time you ever had on that day, so that I may be happy over here thinking of you.

I wish I knew some little boys and girls over here, so that I might talk to them and hold their hands, and then I would call them by my little boys' and girls' names and pretend I was home.

The other night I had a lovely dream, and I was so disappointed when I awoke. I dreamed I was sitting in our kitchen with mother and Dave and all the children, and my chair, which was tilted back against the wall, slipped and I fell gently and without hurting me to the floor. And then mother and you and all the children laughed and laughed like good naughty folks, and you came over and took my hand in yours and lifted me right up easily.

Isn't that funny, Dave? Think of any boy lifting a big, fat father like me from the floor with one hand. Then we laughed some more and suddenly I remembered it was nine o'clock and I said: "Why, kids, what are you doing out bed at this hour of the night?" And you said "Well, it isn't very often our father goes away to war, so we thought we ought to stay up and say 'good bye.' And then I was so surprised to learn that I hadn't gone away to war yet, that I suddenly awoke only to find myself in my lonely barracks, and the rain was coming down hard outside and I was lonesome for my family, my dear family.

And now Dave "old Hoss" everyone is in bed but me, trying to get lots of strength and health for the big fights that we will soon be in, so I must do likewise and end this letter to you.

You must always remember that your father came into the great war for the sake of all the little children, and I know that you will, while I am gone, take good care of mother and all the children.

I can see you now growing up, tall and straight, with shoulders back and head up, 'cause that's what old Cav wants and you love Cav, I guess, don't you Davie boy?

Davie, will you do something for me? I know you would. Well, then, kiss mother and Ann, and Billie, Rosemary and John for Cav, and send one to Phillip in Maine.

> *Excuse me, Dave for writing in pencil instead of ink, but ink is hard to get. The lights are going out in a few moments so Good-night, Good-bye, Dave, and God bless you.*
>
> *Your old man,*
> *Cav.*

A friend visiting the Cavanaugh home spotted the letter and asked Florence for permission to show it to a newspaper. It was duly reproduced in full in the Boston Herald. The response from the public was overwhelming and the Herald's switchboard was inundated with requests for copies. The Evening Sun newspaper was preparing a piece on Frank and the letter was reprinted as part of that article. It too was flooded with messages of good will and requests for copies. Frank's letter had touched a nerve with many families who had fathers, mothers, brothers and sisters serving thousands of miles from home. His words had captured the sense of loss felt by many soldiers who would miss the early formative years of a child growing up and the isolation experienced when you step outside the security of a loving family. It also echoed America's attitude to the war – reluctant to enter, but once in determination to see it through to a successful conclusion. This simple communication from a father to his son became one of the most widely read war letters.

Franks conduct brought promotion to the rank of Captain on May 27th 1918 and in July he was cited for "meritorious service" at Gael, France. Two troop trains had collided and left a tangled mess of twisted metal and wounded soldiers one of whom was found pinned under a truck wheel and three cars. To free the unfortunate man the cars had to be raised and someone would then have to crawl under and work underneath tonnes of metal that might collapse at any moment. The natural fearlessness that Frank had tried to instill into his football teams now showed itself when he volunteered to try and free the trapped soldier. Alongside two fellow officers and a private, Frank laboured for over three hours and eventually they managed to disentangle their comrade.

On August 31st 1928 a second citation for "marked gallantry and meritorious service," for his part in taking fortified enemy positions was recorded in Frank's service record. Frank had coordinated a heavy barrage that helped to save an infantry company from being overwhelmed by superior numbers of enemy troops. For both citations Frank was fully entitled to apply for a military decoration – The Purple Heart and the Silver Star.

Franks division was the most widely travelled of the US Army in France and it soon earned the nickname the "Gypsy Division." Many times Frank was forced to drive young men to the very limits of human endurance and it was on those occasions that his instinctive ability to unite and drive a team of men forward stood out. On one occasion he took command of a unit that had been engaging the enemy for days without rest. Bogged down in mud holes and a miserable rain the men were looking forward to rest, when instead they were given the order to continue fighting. When Frank arrived he found the morale of the men about as low as it could get. He addressed the men:

> *"Listen, you soandsos came over here to die. I'm going to make sure that you get the chance. I don't want to hear anymore of your bellyaching. What do you think you rate? The Waldorf Astoria? You're going to dig up those guns and you're going to move 'em to the top of that hill. And you're going to hold that hill come hell or high water. And if it's a little too muddy or a little too tough for some of you sissies up there step over into my dugout and maybe I can fix you up a cup of tea."*

He then allocated the most dangerous dugout to himself. Inside Frank was choking for he knew what the young men who stood in front of him had gone through and he knew it wasn't fair that they should be asked to go through it all over again. But war is not about what is right or fair and he knew that they had to keep on fighting. To take their minds of the misery of their situation Frank channelled all of their hatred on himself. Too busy hating him the soldiers has less time to focus on their own misery. At a reunion years later Frank had the opportunity to address them same unit:

> "The hardest thing I ever had to do was to try to pay the bully to great soldiers, and great Americans such as you were in France. The words burned in my throat. I didn't dare look you in the eyes for fear you'd see that I was lying. But when I joined you, your nerves were raw, your fighting spirit had lost direction. You'd been left in there too long. You'd taken more than any human beings should be asked to take. You hated the job. You hated the war. You hated everything in general and nothing in particular. I gambled on the chance that if I could concentrate your hatred upon me, could give you something definite and personal to hate, that you'd hate the job less and would proceed to do it better. It almost killed me, and I've been waiting all these years to tell you that I didn't mean it, that I couldn't have meant it, that you were really great soldiers and that it was an honor to serve with you, even if I couldn't tell you at the time."

Before Frank could finish the audience stood in ovation and he was soon overwhelmed with embraces and heartfelt thanks from the men whom he had helped to endure the unendurable. On October 23rd 1918 Frank's war ended abruptly just weeks before the armistice was signed. Fighting near Argonne, Frank had positioned his unit in a small building when the Germans artillery quickly began to find its range. Two shells landed close behind the building, a third just in front and then the fourth found its target. The shell exploded at the door and the room was immediately filled with flying metal, masonry and splinters of wood. Sitting near the door Frank was hit by the backwash of the explosion and shrapnel struck him on the head and in the face. The result was a fractured skull, jaw and cheekbone, a broken nose, damage to his right ear and pieces of metal embedded in his head and face. When his condition had been evaluated the medical staff gave him little or no hope of survival.

After transfer to hospital the surgeons immediately set to work on Frank's injuries and thanks to the combination of their skill and his determination to win every fight, he slowly recovered. Frank was promoted to the rank of Major on November 7th and for his courage and resilience he quickly earned the nickname "The Iron Major". Frank spent the next couple of months in one hospital or another until he was fit to travel home in April 1917, where he completed his recuperation at Camp Devens. In March 1919 the trustees of Dartmouth College awarded Frank an honorary degree which he received in June. Later that year on September 6th he received an honourable discharge from the army. By now, thanks to skin grafts and bridgework the visible signs of his injuries were all but gone.

At home Frank turned his attention to the future. Like tens of thousands of other men home from Europe he was unemployed and looking for work. He accepted an offer to join the coaching staff at Boston College where he was also appointed professor of Jurisprudence. The squad at Boston was not one likely to draw much attention for its potential but the "Cavanaugh system" was quickly in place and began to show dividends. 1919 saw five victories and three defeats, they following year saw the team undefeated with eight victories and in both years the mighty Yale was humbled. Frank spent another four years at Boston wining national recognition for the team and the respect and admiration of his fellow coaches. At one point his football team was acknowledged as the national championship eleven and Frank was considered the number one coach in America.

In 1926 Frank resigned from Boston College to join Fordham University. The first two years at Fordham were painful for Frank; 1927 brought just three victories and five defeats while 1928 yielded four victories and five defeats. There was mounting criticism of his tactics and Frank began to doubt his own ability to field a winning team against the emerging younger coaches. But he persevered and the 1929 season saw a dramatic turnaround in fortunes when Fordham recorded seven wins, two draws and no defeats; the first team in the universities history to post an undefeated season. 1930 brought more success when the team won all but one of its games. The university began to gain a reputation for football and now enjoyed a high profile across the country. But the success on the field was mirrored by personal difficulties off it. Due to the extensive injuries suffered during the war Franks had never enjoyed full health since his return home and with each year that passed he weakened a little more. Especially debilitating was the rapid loss of his eyesight. Frank remained with Fordham for two more years before he was finally forced to retire due to ill health.

By now Frank's wife Florence and the rest of the family were seriously concerned about his physical and mental condition so they purchased a farm at Marshfield where they hoped he might improve in the tranquillity of the countryside and far from the pressures of coaching. Sadly it was too late. Frank began to loose track of time and place for long periods. Following an operation in July 1938 Frank returned to Marshfield in early August where the initial signs of recovery looked promising. However towards the end of August he suffered a cerebral haemorrhage and his family began to assemble by his bedside waiting for the inevitable. Florence, his nine children and his brother George were all present to see him finally pass away the following day. Frank Cavanaugh, the Iron Major had lost his last fight.

The funeral services drew many of Boston's dignitaries including the mayor, members of the church and officials from the institutions with whom he had coached. Also present were his classmates from Dartmouth as well as many of the ordinary folk with whom he had left a lasting impression. He was buried with his mother, father and brother in his hometown of Worcester. He was missed most of all by his devoted wife Florence and their children; David 24; twins Anne and Phillip 22, William 21; Rosemary 18; John 17; Francis 12 and a second set of twins Paul and Sarah aged 11.

In 1943 Franks story was presented on the silver screen when Pat O'Brien starred in the Film "The Iron Major". In 1954 Frank was inducted into the National Football Foundation & College Hall of Fame. Today Fordham University honours his memory with the annual "Iron Major" award for coach of the year as selected by their fellow coaches.

Clann Gathering Journal 2002

The following account is taken from a diary I kept of my very first Clann Gathering. I hope it will give a flavour of what it is like to attend one of these wonderful occasions.

This year's journey to the Clann Gathering began on Thursday the 19th of September. In order to break up the trip I had decided to stay overnight with my brother Michael and his family in Wicklow. It may seem ludicrous to those cousins from the southern hemisphere who endured over twenty hours cramped in economy class and god knows how many time zone changes that I saw it necessary to break a total journey of two hours into more manageable one hour stints. The evening went well but at one point, in a moment of madness or forgetfulness, my sister in-law Sarah enquired what kind of activities would be taking place over the coming weekend. There was a collective intake of breath and murderous looks were thrown in her direction for having given me this opportunity to bore the pants of everyone.

Caitlin, the baby of the family who can only manage half a dozen words and is still mastering the art of walking, made a dash for freedom. Grabbing her feeding bottle and a spare diaper she said "Bye bye" and sped out of the room at something approaching world record pace for the fifty-metre sprint. The eldest child Liam had no escape route for I had been holding him in a big hug when his mother had posed the fateful question. Unable to escape my grip he promptly stuck his fingers in his ears and began to hum to himself. Michael and Sarah were of course bound by etiquette to feign interest in the subject and smiled as I began to relate the timetable of events. As I spoke my enthusiasm slowly took over and I lost the run of myself. When I had finished I noticed that both Michael and Sarah had that glazed far away look that sets in when you are in the middle of a meeting that is going nowhere slowly and has already taken up half of your precious one hour lunch break. Thinking I had rambled on for hours I glanced at my watch to find that I had only been speaking for two minutes. Crestfallen, my grip on Liam relaxed a little and he ran out of the room shouting: "Time for bed, I have playschool in the morning"

I know that a lot of us encounter this kind of reaction when we speak to friends and family about our family history. It seems to require a significant event such as the loss of a loved one, the discovery of a family heirloom or a skeleton in the closet to spark an interest in the past. So, realising I had put my gracious hosts through enough mental cruelty I left the subject of the Gathering to one side and proceeded to enjoy a very pleasant evening. I awoke the following morning to clear blue skies and warm sunshine; the gods were smiling. As I set the car in motion towards Ferns I noticed that the smiles of those stood in the doorway were unusually brilliant, and that their waves of goodbye were particularly energetic.

Driving south I reflected on the fact that I was heading to my second Gathering and that as a member of the Executive Committee, people would now be coming to me with questions and requests for help. How quickly things had changed since my first gathering two years earlier. When I reached the town of Gorey I took a small detour to see some of the scenery and was pleasantly surprised to find a small cottage having its thatched roof redone before the onset of winter. Although still numerous in many parts of Ireland they are increasingly difficult to find along the primary routes of the east coast so I stopped to stretch my legs and take a photograph.

I arrived in Ferns around midday and parked opposite the Courtyard pub. Those of you who have attended previous gatherings will remember this establishment well, as it is the focal point for most of the activities. Inside I found a number of The Committee huddled in the corner, among them the Terrible Twins, James J. Kavanagh ("German Jim") and James F. Cavanaugh ("Jungle Jim"). The warm rapport that had been established face to face at the gathering in 2000 and built on via email was still evident and I was immediately at ease in their company. We spend the next hour or two going over the arrangements and getting to know the new members of the Committee.

Later in the afternoon I decided it was time to check-in to the accommodation that would serve as my home for the weekend and headed to Clone House, a guesthouse five minutes outside of town. Before I had even parked the car in the farmyard the proprietor, Mrs. Betty Breen was striding forward enthusiastically to greet me. In addition to myself Betty was also responsible for housing German Jim, Jungle Jim and his daughter Melissa. Betty did a fine job; every morning she ensured that we were all well fed on a hearty breakfast and saw to it that Melissa had the four gallons of coffee she required to start the day. For some reason German Jim proved to be her favourite as a chair at the head of the breakfast table was always reserved in his honour. I had to content myself with a compliment on one of my jumpers. Betty was wonderful and I have no hesitation in recommending her establishment to anyone considering a stay around Ferns area.

After carefully unpacking and arranging my clothes into a neat mess, I changed into a little black number and headed back into the town centre to take a look at the Clann archives. At each gathering a room is reserved to hold the vast amount of journals, newspaper clippings, photographs and other paper records that have been uncovered and extracted by cousins around the world. German Jim serves as the guardian for some of this material and he also maintains one of our more valuable resources – the Clann databank. The last time I checked the databank it contained the records of over eight thousand individuals and these have proven to be of immense value to many of our members hoping to locate a long lost ancestor. As a rule of thumb you can expect to find Jim in close proximity to the archives and as I entered the room I was not disappointed. There he was in familiar pose; hunched over his laptop, a four-foot pile of CD ROMs and diskettes to one side, a two-foot stack of paper and manuals to the other side, and the usual vipers nest of cables at his feet. We chatted a while and then I left him to answer data bank enquiries.

Outside I noticed the car in which Jim had transported all of his material across Europe. It had a huge boot and I made a mental note that should I consume a little too much alcohol and be unable to make it back to Clone House that it was spacious enough to sleep three adults, two kids and a cat in comfort.

The first event of the Gathering took place at 7.30 on Friday evening when we assembled in the function room of the Courtyard for the official welcome. I imagine the locals are accustomed to seeing a procession of weirdo's file through their pub every two years in September, each helpfully labelled with a large friendly name tag, but we did get the odd look here and there. Jungle Jim and Bridget Kavanagh Dalton were our MCs for the evening and Jim began by thanking our cousins one by one for their attendance and then gave a short talk on the origin of the Celts. After that Bridget oversaw the presentation of awards to those individuals who had worked tirelessly on behalf of the Clann. This year recipients included Michael Kavanagh from England who had managed to uncover important family records from Barbados and Judi King from Little Rock, Arkansas who had helped track down documents on various people in the US. There was also a presentation of a birthday cake to Jim Gethings, a stalwart of the Clann and a regular sight at our Gatherings.

Following the award ceremony we all sat down to a buffet dinner. A tour of the tables revealed some faces from the last time I had been in Ferns in 2000 but most of the attendees were new to me. One of the new faces I was delighted to meet was Michael Cavanaugh from Cincinnati, Ohio. Michael's ancestors originally hailed from Wexford but he had no information as to which parish they had left when they embarked on the long and dangerous journey to America. The family established farming roots in Indiana and he has spent many hours on the road and going through local records to determine the exact location and extent of their homestead. I enjoyed the time I spent with Michael; I found him to be warm and easygoing and I do hope that he makes a breakthrough soon. Around midnight I was flagging a little and decided to call it a day, luckily I had managed to avoid the alcohol so there was no need to stowaway in German Jim's car boot.

I awoke around seven thirty on Saturday morning to the sound of cows in the field outside my window. It brought back pleasant memories of summers spent on my grandmother's farm in Wicklow. A peek through the curtains revealed another splendid morning as the sun rose steadily above the horizon. A light mist was draped across the ground and a herd of cows moved lazily towards some favourite corner of the field or perhaps to the gate ready for milking. I closed my eyes and tried to get back to sleep but the thought of the countryside springing into life just behind my head was too much to resist. I had a quick shower, dressed in some warm clothes and went for a walk. It was truly magical to be back on a farm again at daybreak. Well, I say daybreak but any self-respecting farmer would have already been up two or three hours by the time I had raised my head from the pillow. Breakfast was a mighty instalment of sausages, bacon, eggs, tomatoes and brown bread. To ensure I didn't go too far overboard I took great care to balance all of that with a healthy glass of orange juice.

At 9.30 we rendezvoused at the top of the town outside Ferns castle for a field trip to Kilkenny. I was beginning to regret the warm clothes I had put on earlier, for with each minute that passed the day grew brighter and the temperature climbed higher. We set off and before long took to the winding and rolling back roads so that we could see for ourselves the land once known to the English crown as "Kavanagh Country." Bridget Kavanagh Dalton was our guide for she is a local lass and knows intimately the nooks and crannies of Wexford and Carlow. She brought the countryside to life with local stories, folklore and gossip that cannot be found in textbooks. But she didn't have it all her own way for throughout the trip she was constantly heckled by the Terrible Twins who brought their own colourful interpretations of Irish history to the tour. An enjoyable dialogue ensued between all three of them until they were more like the Three Stooges rather than three historians. Many jokes and insults were thrown from one side to another and this alone made the trip worthwhile.

Once in Kilkenny we took a 15-minute break for refreshments in the café at Kilkenny Castle where I had a nice chat with the brightly dressed Robert Cavanaugh from Peabody, Massachusetts. Robert has been with the Clann since its inception, is a regular face at the gatherings and has already booked his accommodation for the 2004 event! After the tea break we proceeded on a guided tour of the magnificent castle itself. Although it was never a MacMurrough or Kavanagh home it does hold links to our Clann as some of our womenfolk married into the powerful Butler family who had built it. The purpose of the visit was to get an idea of how the "other half" lived in bygone days and it appears that the "other half" lived very well indeed. For a number of years a government and EU program has been restoring the castle to its former splendour. Each room is lavishly decorated with enormous carpets, unique wallpaper and valuable paintings. When the official guided tour has finished we were free to wander through the grounds. After Kilkenny Castle we took an hour out for lunch and a visit to the craft shops before moving on to Rothe House located on one of the busy shopping streets. John Rothe, a prosperous merchant of the city constructed the house in 1594 and today it provides a glimpse of what life was like in the sixteenth century.

At five o' clock we clambered back onto the bus for the journey back to Ferns with Bridget again acting as our guide. It wasn't too long before we were in giggles as the Three Stooges kicked off their evening road show at the front of the bus. Bridget did manage to bring some gravitas to the affair however by introducing a crash course in the Gaelic language. As we drove back through the Blackstairs Mountains the hedgerows began to draw closer and closer, the bends grew more and more acute and the gradient grew steeper and steeper. It was great fun for us but I imagine that John Murphy the poor driver, struggling to manoeuvre a 50-seat coach over such terrain must have been a nervous wreck despite his outward appearance of calm. At one stage we had to yield to a flock of sheep that steadily advanced towards us, but just as we anticipated a sea of white fluff enveloping the coach they swung right into a field.

A short stop near the summit of Mount Leinster, the highest mountain in the region proved the perfect vantage point from which to take in the countryside. It was a memorable sight, with unobstructed views for miles in nearly every direction. As our intrepid band of travellers absorbed the landscape many of us felt deeply moved by the experience. It was both humbling and inspiring to know that from horizon to horizon, every field, hill and valley, river and wood that we could see once belonged to our Clann. It was difficult to imagine how it might have looked at the height of our power, for today only small clusters of trees dot the land where once dark luxurious woods gave protection to our ancestors. What a glorious sight they must have been, but alas the English cleared the woods and then used the timber for shipbuilding and the production of charcoal. Returning to the bus we embarked on the last leg of the trip, arriving in Ferns around 6.30. There was just enough time for a wipe with a damp facecloth and a change of clothes before the evening entertainment began at 7.30. I took great pleasure in removing my shoes, which had been slowly and painfully performing surgery on my heels all day. Is there anything a man will not put himself through for fashion?

In the bar of the Courtyard pub I met up with Pat O'Shea from New Zealand. Over a quick bite to eat and a pint of beer we had an interesting chat on many topics ranging from aboriginal land rights, the transportation of nuclear material on the high seas and the 1985 bombing of the Rainbow Warrior in Auckland by French secret service agents. It sounds very serious now but we managed to keep the conversation light with humour and a good old moan about our respective governments. We got on well and sat together in the function room for the evening of song and dance. It all began with a handful of songs by the John Furlong Group, who I seem to remember also played at the previous gathering. Later a troupe of young Irish dancers from the Furlong Dance School quite literally kicked things into life with an energetic and well choreographed display of traditional Irish dancing. The dance floor was a blur of colour and movement as the brightly dressed young things danced feverishly to the music. The audience loved every minute of it and showed their appreciation with a loud round of applause.

The band then proceeded to play a set of traditional Irish tunes and emigrant songs, which was appropriate considering the large number of cousins from overseas. As the evening wore on I began to realise that Pat O' Shea knew the words to nearly all of the songs whereas my ignorance of them was almost totally complete. Pat informed me that she played in a band back home in New Zealand and that her children were also involved in music. With each song she became a little more animated and vocal. Then I took leave of my senses and did something I would never normally contemplate; I went up to the bandleader and told him about Pat. Three minutes later her name was called out and my heart sank - I had put her on the spot and I felt horribly responsible for what might happen in the next thirty seconds. Pat had a quick word with the musicians and I considered doing a runner while her back was turned. I decided to stay and thank god I did, for as soon as the first pure, clear note left her I knew everything was going to be okay. With each successive note Pat grew in confidence and the band, recognising her obvious talent contented themselves with a gentle supporting role. Pat sang two songs; "Spinning Wheel" and "You Will Be The Light" and the audience were vocal in their approval. When she returned to her seat I explained that, having heard her voice I no longer felt the slightest tinge of guilt at putting her name forward. I would urge any of you in New Zealand to find out where Pat plays for you will not be disappointed. Later in the evening Martin Slater from Southampton, England gave us a beautiful demonstration of classical guitar. The evening finished around midnight and I headed back to Clone House. As usual a few diehards stayed behind running the risk of having their coach's turn back into pumpkins.

On Sunday morning I was able to relax a little as the first scheduled event; a walking tour of Ferns was not due to kick off until midday. I took a nice bath, lounged a little in my room and then headed downstairs for breakfast where I discussed the previous evening's gossip with Jungle Jim, German Jim and Melissa. Suitably nourished for the day ahead, I returned to my room to change into something respectable. The day ahead was very important for two reasons; the Clann AGM was due to start at 2 o'clock and the inauguration of the new Chief at 4 o'clock. I headed into Ferns and promptly spent the next few hours in a Committee meeting, which unfortunately meant that I missed the walking tour around the town. In fact the meeting was still going on as people began to file in for the AGM. But the overrun did have one positive side effect – it took my mind off the fact that I would have to stand up and present a report on the website to the AGM!

You must understand that I prefer to stand in the shadows and observe events rather than take part in them. The next forty minutes were absolute hell; I began to suffer from sweaty palms, extensive forehead wrinkling and fidgety fingers. In honour of my mother I double-checked that I was wearing clean underwear in the event of my fainting and being carted away to hospital by strangers. My appointed time duly arrived and I forced myself to speak sl-o-w-ly, to keep my hands out of my pockets and not to run from the room screaming "the Normans are coming! The Normans are coming!!" In the end I managed to drag things out for three to four minutes and make it appear as if I had something interesting to say. For the rest of the AGM I tried not catch anyone's eye for fear of provoking someone into asking a question.

With the AGM out of the way there was just enough time for those involved in the inauguration of the new chief to change into costume. The Clann likes to conduct the inauguration ceremony in a style similar to how it would have looked centuries ago. Although medieval costume is not compulsory many of the people involved to date have enjoyed dressing up and getting into character for the occasion. The philosophy is to have fun - do it only if you enjoy it. The inauguration was to take place in St. Aidans church at the lower end of Ferns so I made my way from the Courtyard pub down to the church and waited on the road outside the cemetery for the principal characters to arrive. After a short wait Fergus Kavanagh from Dublin, one of the honour guards pulled in and parked his car. Within seconds he had the boot of his car open and began to change into his costume. Thanks to a uniform provided by his daughter his transformation was immediate and dramatic. Where once stood a mild mannered man from Dublin, there now stood a man straight out the pages of a history book. Minutes later the Clann Herald James F. Cavanaugh arrived in a fantastic costume designed by Cathi Taylor of California. Jim's long flowing hair, and mighty white beard combined with his colourful attire to create a very impressive figure. Passing motorists could not resist slowing down and craning their necks out the window to see what was going on.

Finally the star of the day, Celia Kavanagh Boylan arrived in a flowing emerald green velvet dress and white headscarf. She was accompanied by her ladies in waiting; Joan Kavanagh Slevin, Alice Kavanagh and Melissa Cavanaugh. Celia's partner John Marshall, constantly at her side throughout the weekend was also in attendance ready to pounce should there be the slightest hint of something going wrong. With the cast assembled a procession was formed, lead by Fergus and we all headed into the grounds of the church. For the first time all weekend the skies were grey and brooding as we made our way through the entrance gate. The rain held off but a slight wind began to build; this only added to the drama as it caught Celia's robes and gave them a life of their own. Dr. Gary Cavanaugh from California conducted the ritual with the crowd playing a supporting role where required. The chief of the Clann Nolan, Judith Nolan who had travelled over from England especially for the ceremony conferred the title upon Celia. It was obvious that her confirmation had touched Celia deeply and she knows it is a great honour to be elected by cousins from all over the world.

It was a colourful spectacle and great fun to be part of it. A bit like a wedding really – enjoyable if you are on the sidelines but nerve-wracking if you are the centrepiece.

We formed another procession and followed the new chief to the nearby grave of Diamuid mac Murchada and Domhnal Caomhánach. There the Clann Herald laid an evergreen wreath in honour of these ancestors who were once Kings of Leinster and from whom all our families descend. Then it was time to take some pictures for the scrapbook. We assembled into a large group and people took it in turns to dart in and out with their cameras for a photograph. When everyone had a memento to take home we broke into small groups and headed to the pub for, what else, but a celebratory drink. Some drifted off to change for the banquet to come later while others, myself included stayed in the pub for a chat and drink or three. I found Bridget Kavanagh Dalton and Melissa Cavanaugh in a quiet corner and spend a pleasant hour or so in their company.

At 7.30 we were all together again preparing to enter the function room of The Courtyard for a candlelit banquet. As we entered each of us received a glass of mead and a piece of bread. We were then presented one by one to our new chief Celia, who bade us welcome, thanked us for our attendance and accepted our best wishes. A number of chiefs from fraternal Clanns were also present; Mrs. Judith Nolan (Chief of Clann Nolan), Mr. and Mrs. Eddie Kinsella (Chief of Clann Kinsella) and Mr. and Mrs. Kevin O' Toole (Chief of Clann O'Toole). All of the visiting chiefs were seated at the top table as guests of honour. Each of these Clanns has close historic ties to our own Clann Chaomhánach.

When everyone had been received and seated the music began. The Kennedy Sisters who hail from Gorey provided a delicate and delightful background for the evening with a combination of harp and violin and the occasional ballad. For the meal I was seated beside German Jim who, I quickly discovered had an insatiable appetite for mead. I had never tried this golden liquid before and found it to be a potent combination of honey and alcohol all the more dangerous because of its wonderful taste. As the evening wore on people began the usual migration between tables to share their experiences of the day's events. For once I remained stationary to enjoy the company of German Jim, Fergus Kavanagh and Michael Kavanagh from Hove, England. At 1 o'clock I made by farewells and returned to Clone House.

And here gentle reader my story must end for on Monday morning I left the bosom of Clann Chaomhánach to return home to Dublin. In store for those I left behind was a wonderful field trip to Clann castles conducted by Jungle Jim. If anyone would like to send me a report of the trip I would be delighted to include in here.

I take away wonderful memories, funny stories and new friendships from the 2002 gathering. I hope those lucky enough to make this year's event found it as enjoyable as I did and that we will meet again in two years time. For those of you who could not make it on this occasion remember - there is always Ferns 2004.

Clann Gathering 2004, Borris, Co. Carlow

Notable People Index

Caomhánach
Domhnall "Spáinneach" 35

Cavaignac
Eléonore Louis Godefroy 35
Jacques-Marie 35
Jean Baptiste 35
Louis Eugene 35

Cavanagh
Aileen 36
Archdeacon Bartholomew Aloysius 37
Bernard (c1813 - 1845) 38
Christian "Kit" 38
Dan J. 38
Donald J. 39
Eduardo 38
Edward 38
Edward F. 39
Ernest William 39
George 39
James (Major) 40
James Luke 40
James P. 40
Jerome Patrick 40
John 41
John Albert 41
John Bryan 41
John Joseph 42
Joseph A. 42
Maeve 43
Michael 43
Michael F. 44
Moyra 44
Patrick 44
Paul 44

Peter 45
Roberto 45
Sarah 45
Terence James 45
Thomas "Tommy" 45
Thomas J. Jr. 46
Tony 46
Victor George Jnr. 46
Victor George Snr. 47
Walter Frederick 47
William J. 48

Cavanah
Charles Cheatham 48
Frances 49

Cavanaugh
Bartley W. 49
Carey Edward 49
Christine 50
Christopher 50
Daniel J. 50
Frank William 50
G. J. 51
Gary (Dr.) 51
Hobart 51
Inez Maude 51
James 52
James Francis 52
James H. 53
James Michael 53
John B. 54
John William (Rev.) 54
Larry 54
Lawrence James 54
Martin J. 55
Matt 55
Matthew P. 55
Page 57
Peter 55

    Peter C. 56
    Thomas 57
    Thomas Horne 57
    Thos 57
    Walter Page 57
    William H. 58

Cavanaugh Crum
    Bartley 58

Cavanna
    Betty 59
    Elise 58
    Elizabeth Allen 59

Cavanough
    Owen 59

Cavenagh
    Francis Alexander (Prof.) 60
    Orfeur (Sir) 60
    Wentworth 60
    Wentworth Odiarne (Lt. Col.) 60

Cavenagh Leveson
    Arthur (Sir) 61

Cavenagh-Mainwaring
    Maurice Kildare (Captain) 61

de Boulger Kavanagh
    Demetrius Charles 62

Dillon-Kavanagh
    Georges A. 62

Kavanagh
    Arthur MacMurrough 62
    Blatchford 62
    Brian "na Stroaké" 63
    Corina 63

Denis 64
Dermot MacMurrough (Sir) 64
Dudley 64
Edward 65
Fergus 65
Giles 65
Graham 66
Henry Edward 66
Jack 67
James 68, 69
James (Bishop) 68
James (of Ballyane) 67
James Joseph 69
John Baptist 70
John Patrick 70
Joseph 71
Joseph Malachy 71
Julia 71
Ken 81
Lawrence 72
Lawrence II 72
Lawrence III 72
Lawrence IV 72
Leneen 74
Liam 73
Lionel B. 74
Marcus A. (Judge) 74
Martin Joseph 74
Michael 75
Morgan Peter 75
Muiris "Kruger" 76
Niamh 76
Patrick 76, 77
Patrick Alexander 77
Patrick J. 77
Peter 78
Rose 78
Simon Henry (of Ballyane) 79
Stan 79
Ted 66

Terrence...79
Terry..79
Thomas Christian.. 82
Thomas Giles (Justice)...79
Thomas Henry... 80
Thomas Kenrick 81
Thomas MacMurrough (MP)..................................... 81
Thomas S. J. (Captain)... 83
Trevor 83

Kavanagh Abdullah
Mikaail (Dr.).. 83

Kavanagh Boylan
Celia... 83

Kavanagh Dalton
Bridget... 84

Kavanagh Wachtel
Marion 84

Kavanaugh
Benjamin Taylor.. 84
Daniel 85
Delaney C. (Major).. 85
Ethel 85
Frances 85
Frank Kimbrough.. 85
Harry C.. 86
Hubbard Hinde (Bishop) 86
James.. 86
Kenneth William 87
Mags 87
Margaret "Mags" 87
Rhoda 88
Walter J.. 88
Williams Marmaduke... 88

Kavanaugh Oldham

William 89

Mac Murchada
Diarmuid 90

Moling
Saint 90

Ross
Mother 38

Saint
Moling 90

Place Index

Cavaignac
Rue Godefroy - France 122

Cavanagh
Brook - NS, CA 116
Cave - Anguilla 121
Cemetery - IL, USA 102
Creek - BC, CA 115
Dam - SA, AUS 120
E.J. Park - NY, USA 109
Early Childhood Center – MN, USA 106
Ernest Street - ACT, AUS 119
House - IA, USA 101
House - MI, USA 106
Inn - CA, USA 98
John Road - ON, CA 117
Lake - NS, CA 116
Locality - Argentina.. 121
Oaks – MN, USA 107
Park - CA, USA 98
Park - MN, USA 107
Reef - QA, AUS 120
Road - CA, USA 98
Road – Dover, England 122
Run - NS, CA 116
Stadium - MA, USA 105

Cavanah
Barney Ridge - CA, USA 98
House - ID, USA 101
Lake - IL, USA 102

Cavanaugh
Bartley W. Golf Course - CA, USA 98
Bay - ID, USA 101
Bluff - IL, USA 102

Bottom - IA, USA 101
Brook - CT, USA 100
Canyon - CA, USA 99
Cemetery - VT, USA 111
Charles J. Hall - LA, USA 103
Creek - AK, USA 97
Creek - KY, USA 103
Creek - OR, USA 110
Creek - WA, USA 113
Ct - MN, USA 107
Dr - MN, USA 107
Drive - NY, USA 108
Grade - CA, USA 99
Gulch - CA, USA 99
Hall - IN, USA 102, 103
Jacob Cemetery - NC, USA 110
James Memorial Park – NY, USA 109
Lake - MI, USA 106
Lake - MN, USA 107
Lake - ND, USA 108
Lake - WA, USA 112
Locality - AK, USA 97
Mount - WA, USA 112
Park - OH, USA 110
Peak - WY, USA 113
Pond - CT, USA 100
Pond - WA, USA 112
Road - MI, USA 106
Road - MN, USA 107
Road - NY, USA 108, 109
Sally Mine - SD, USA 111
Siding - ID, USA 101
Spring - NV, USA 108
St. - CT, USA 100
Street - MN, USA 107
Street - TX, USA 111
Wash - ND, USA 108

Cavanaughtown Rd. - NC, USA 110

Cavanough
Street - ACT, AUS 119

Cavenagh
(Hundreth of) - NT, AUS 119
Bridge - Singapore..123
Gardens - Singapore...123
Locality - SA, AUS 120
Mt. - NT, AUS 119
Range - NT, AUS 119
Range - WA, AUS 120
Street - NT, AUS 119
Street - Singapore..123

Cavenaghi
Palacia de - Italy..122

Kavanagh
Avenue –Dublin, Ireland 122
Bay - WI, USA 113
College - New Zealand...123
Corina Passage - Argentina 121
Creek - NS, CA... 116
Creek - NSW, AUS... 119
Creek - QLD, AUS 120
Edificio - Argentina 121
Field - NH, USA...108
Hollow - PA, USA 110
Homestead Ruins - NS, CA 117
House - KY, USA 103
Lake - ON, CA..117
Lake - SK, CA... 118
Lane - NF, CA... 116
Lawrence Monument - NS, CA 117
Ln. - AZ, USA...97
Locality - AB, CA 115
Mansion - ME, USA 105
Park - CO, USA 99
Park - MB, USA 116
Point - NS, CA 116

Road - MD, USA 104
Road - New Zealand 123
School (site of) - ME, USA 105
Street - England 122
Street - MB, CA 115
Street - ME, USA 105
Street - NS, CA 117
Street - VIC, AUS 120
Thomas Stadium - IL, USA 102
Way - AZ, USA 98

Kavanaugh
and Shea Building - OK, USA 110
Ave. - NY, USA 109
Boulevard - AK, USA 97
Branch - PA, USA 111
Camp - KY, USA 103
Cemetery - IL, USA 102
Cemetery - KY, USA 103
Cemetery - NY, USA 109
Creek - CA, USA 99
Creek - ID, USA 102
Creek - MT, USA 108
Dr - MN, USA 107
Drive - AL, USA 97
Hill - CT, USA 100
Hills, MT - USA 108
House - AK, USA 97
Park - GA, USA 100
Place - WI, USA 113
Ridge - CA, USA 99
Road - KY, USA 103
Road - LA, USA 104
Road - NY, USA 109
Street - MD, USA 104
United Methodist Church - TX, USA 111

Mali Tabor
Castle - Croatia 121

McCavanaugh
Pond - NY, USA 109

Whitemore
Hall - Staffordshire , England 122

About The Author

Born on March 17th, 1966 to James and Kathleen (Ronan) Kavanagh. Mars was rising, Jupiter was on the cusp and the wheels on his fathers car were in complete alignment; conditions like this would not occur for another thousand years. In keeping with tradition he arrived naked and a little cranky. The 17th is St. Patrick's Day, a day that is very special to the Irish, so naturally his parents named the new arrival James.

James was raised and educated in Wicklow, a small coastal town 32 miles south of Dublin. School was very easy; in fact he waltzed through it without any difficulty. Alas, there's not much call for people who can waltz through schools in the business world. Or the dance world for that matter.

Many of his early summers were spent on his grandmothers' farm just outside the town. The term "summer" is used here in its loosest sense, as any of you who have visited Ireland will understand. On the farm he learnt how to talk to animals and capture and skin wild potatoes. Of course the conversations with animals never led to any great insights, but he soon found that skinned potatoes made a plain meal when allowed to sit undisturbed in boiling water for around 12 minutes.

With just days left before graduation from school James still had no clear idea of what he wanted to do. He felt confident in his waltzing abilities but not much else. Then a friend showed him one of the latest home computers, a Sinclair ZX-81. From that moment on, nothing was ever the same. He quickly learned that he had a knack for not making computers crash; a knack which he painstakingly developed into a career.

www.ingramcontent.com/pod-product-compliance
Ingram Content Group UK Ltd.
Pitfield, Milton Keynes, MK11 3LW, UK
UKHW041450180426
11946UKWH00013B/145/J